Lasting Prayers

بسم الله الرحمن الرحيم

وَقَالَ رَبُّكُمُ ادْعُونِي أَسْتَجِبْ لَكُمْ

And your Lord said,
"Call upon Me;
I shall answer you."

— The Quran, 40:60

Lasting Prayers

of The Quran & The Prophet Muḥammad

صلى الله عليه وسلم

Ahmad Zaki Hammad

Printed in the United States of America

Published by: *Quranic Literacy Institute (QLI)*
P.O. Box 1467 • Bridgeview, Illinois 60455

Cover design by A. Whiteman. Cover photography by A. Sanders. Both under commission of the Quranic Literacy Institute.

FRONT COVER PHOTOGRAPH: The Kaʿba, the first House of God on earth, the foundation of which was raised by Prophet Abraham عليه السلام and his son, Ishmael عليه السلام. At the center of the surrounding Sacred Mosque in Makkah, the Kaʿba is visited each year by millions for pilgrimage and spiritual retreat, circumambulating the Ancient House, praying and drawing nearer to God.
BACK COVER PHOTOGRAPH: The *miḥrâb* (prayer niche) in the Prophet's ﷺ Mosque in Madinah.

ISBN (cloth): 0-9650746-1-7

Lasting Prayers of the Quran & the Prophet Muḥammad ﷺ is printed on premium acid-free paper that is in compliance with standards set for alkaline papers by the American National Standards Institute, Inc. The paper's permanence is estimated at more than 300 years. The binding materials were chosen for strength, durability, longevity, and ecological concerns. The text is set in Palatino Diacritic, a special type to facilitate Arabic transliteration and the use of features special to Islamic literature, such as " ﷺ " and " عليه السلام ".

A LASTING PRAYER

in memory of my parents,
my grandfather, MANSOUR,
and my grandmother, ḤIJÂZIYYA,
from whom I learned firsthand
the power of prayer

And a special prayer of healing for
two distinguished worlds of friendship,
YASSIN & KAMAL

TRANSLITERATION NOTE

The transliteration of Arabic names and terms into English follows a well-established scheme shown below.

Also, nearly every mention of the Prophet Muḥammad's ﷺ name is followed by the Arabic "ﷺ" which may be translated as "God bless him and give him peace," a prayer of endearment reflecting Muslim veneration for the Prophet ﷺ. Likewise, out of veneration "عليه السلام" appears after the names of other prophets mentioned (as well as Angel Gabriel عليه السلام), and it means "peace be upon him."

ء	’	ر	r	ف	f
ا	â *or* a	ز	z	ق	q
ب	b	س	s	ك	k
ت	t	ش	sh	ل	l
ث	th	ص	ṣ	م	m
ج	j	ض	ḍ	ن	n
ح	ḥ	ط	ṭ	ه	h
خ	kh	ظ	ẓ	و	û *or* u w (consonant)
د	d	ع	ʿ	ى	î *or* i *or* iyy y (consonant)
ذ	dh	غ	gh		

QURANIC CITATION NOTE

Nearly each of the hundreds of references made to the Quran's verses is cited following an established numerical system. For example, the third verse of the Quran's first sura is cited as *1:3* (the sura number followed by the number of the verse, separated by a colon).

BRACKETS NOTE

Within several translated texts are half brackets ⌜ ⌝ that contain clarifying text that should be read as if it were part of the text. For example: *It is He who sends prayers ⌜of blessings⌝ down upon you…* (33:43). The full brackets [ ] present information that is only explanatory and is not meant to be read as part of the text. For example: *The Prophet ﷺ said, "Supplication between the* Adhân *[the Call to Prayer] and the* Iqâma *[the Final Call to Prayer] will not be rejected."*

CONTENTS

II. Prayers for All Times and Occasions

Appendix: Form & Substance

Notes, Bibliography, and Indices

Preface

THE EARLIEST MEMORIES I have are linked to the Quran and my mother, may God have mercy on her. She was eager to see me begin memorizing it in its entirety. So at the age of four or five, with the help of a tutor, I started to commit to memory the verses of the Book of God. She knew my love for sweets and used to reward me with whatever of them I desired whenever I ran to her and recited what I had learned.

Those days went by fast. By the time I reached high school I had acquired a taste for the Quran's own sweetness whenever I read it or heard it recited well, especially during devotional *tarawîḥ* prayers in Ramadan, the month of fasting. For a long time in those middle years I felt as though the Quran was speaking to me alone—about the magnificent Creator and the vastness of His creation in the heavens and the earth; about Believers and disbelievers, the righteous and the wrongdoers; about the rich and the poor, the rulers and the ruled; and about the inevitable destiny of humankind, the end of the world, and the unfolding realities of Paradise and Hellfire.

The Quran's companionship over some forty years has gradually opened my mind to the changeless truths it reveals about existence and has made the most formative impression upon my thinking and sensibilities. Among the principal truths I have learned in the universe of the Quran is that there is no place in existence nor in the heart of a believer for any deity or creator other than God. *And your God is one God. There is no God but Him, the All-Merciful, the Mercy-Giving* (2:163). And, similarly, before humanity became divided into sects and parties, we were one community. *And the people were not but one community, then they disputed* (10:19). Variance in our colors, languages, and ancestry is no justification for prejudice, intolerance, and hatred. Rather, diversity in creation is a remarkable sign for us of the greatness of the Creator.*

I have also observed in the universe of the Quran that the religion which God has sent down to human beings in the course of history is really one religion, as is the message of all the prophets to their communities—including that of Noah, Abraham, Moses, Jesus, and Muḥammad, God's blessings and peace be upon

* For more on the phenomenon of diversity, see my work *Islamic Law: Understanding Juristic Differences* (Indianapolis: ATP, 1992).

them. In essence, all the prophets called to the good life, that is, to uphold a life of high morality, righteous works, and universal brotherhood among human beings based on faith in God and in His revelations and on a certainty that each of us shall stand accountable on the Day of Judgment.

Something equally important has become evident to me as well: The scope of worship in the Quran is far wider than that of prescribed rituals and actions. At the heart of all true worship one finds prayer. Through the portal of the Quran's verses we see how the paragons of humanity—the prophets and the believing men and women—unfailingly turned to God with glorifications and supplications, incessantly beseeching His immediate and ultimate relief, pardon, and forgiveness.

When I took the Prophet Muḥammad, God's blessings and peace be upon him—his words and teachings—as the substance of my studies in the university years, I encountered a new dimension in his model personality when I contemplated the profusion of his prayers and invocations. To come close to the genuineness, the expression, the content of his converses with God—especially in light of the circumstances in which he uttered them—is to feel palpably their harmony with the innate aspirations and fears of not just one man but of all humanity.

The Prophet Muḥammad ﷺ taught his followers that prayer is an arena of life in which human beings have the special opportunity to elevate and purify their souls, to excel spiritually and morally, and to open up their minds to the ever fresh religious experience of drawing near to the Creator. The Prophet ﷺ used to stress to his Companions that prayer is an armament for the believing human being (and more so when one fathoms its secrets with a will to observe its etiquette). With it one repels the devastation of a legion of woes—be it grief, despondency, fear, or restlessness. Thus under its auspices, one is spiritually and physically healed. So if prayer is the seed, then hope is the sturdy tree that brings forth confidence, trust, and optimism.

When human energies are steadily turned toward prayer and invocation, we approach an inner balance that maintains our integrity even under the assault of harm and evil, or when struck with the loss of possessions, well-being, or loved ones, or when we are overcome at those moments when we wrong ourselves. Equally important, we are restrained from growing arrogant and transgressing at times of triumph and achievement.

This and a galaxy of untold other blessings orbit the prayers of the Quran and of the Prophet Muḥammad ﷺ. In the pages of this work, the reader, God willing, shall find how significant is the spiritual idiom of Muslim life, how thoroughly it pervades the individual conscience, and how it establishes itself as the moral compass of personal conduct as well as one's behavior with family, society, and humanity.

The prayers and invocations of the Quran and the Prophet ﷺ evince a spiritual and moral energy that corresponds to an array of major commandments in Islam. Thus, the supplicating voices of the believing men and women that echo in the Quran's verses and resonate in the Prophet's words converge in a chorus that extols the inestimable value of conscious, living faith in God. In other words, these prayers help us to see (and see ourselves through) our role on earth and serve to remind us of our ultimate destiny and of the human soul's need of its Creator—not only for life, which has been granted, but for guidance upon the straight way here and in the Hereafter. These supplications point up the endangered virtues which are indispensable to our humanity and consequently to our individual well-being and civilized existence as a society.

What are these virtues? Certainly there are many in the verses of the Quran and the teachings of its Messenger ﷺ, but some outstanding ones come immediately to mind. Headmost among them is genuine faith in God and a conscious appreciation of the enormous blessing of faith. *Our Lord, indeed we have believed. So forgive us our sins and save us from the torment of the Fire* (3:16). *Our Lord, we have heard a caller calling to faith, "Believe in your Lord!" So we have believed. Our Lord, do forgive us our sins, and absolve us of our misdeeds, and take our souls ˹while being˺ among the virtuous* (3:193). Following upon faith is the excellence of actively seeking out guidance and adhering to it when it is gained. *Guide us to the straight way* (1:6). *Our Lord, let not our hearts swerve after You have guided us, and grant us mercy from Your own ʿbountyˀ. Indeed, it is You who are the All-Granting* (3:8). Ensuing from guidance is a moderation that neither renounces the good life in this world for the sake of the Hereafter, nor permits the world to becloud one's mindfulness of the Afterlife; rather, one hopes for the best in both. *Our Lord, give us good in this world and good in the Hereafter* (2:201).

Then from this rock of faith stream forth virtues which can replenish all the diverse people of the world and restore the Children of Adam to their rightful station of dignity among God's creation. Gratitude is such a quality: *My Lord, dispose me to give thanks for Your grace, with which You have graced me and my parents, and that I do righteous deeds with which You are pleased. And make righteous for me my children. Indeed, I have repented to You, and surely I am of the Muslims* (46:15). Patience and perseverance in the face of trial is another such characteristic: *Our Lord, pour forth upon us patience, and take our souls as Muslims* (7:126). Sincerity is an additional distinction: *He is the All-Living, there is no God but Him, so call upon Him, making religion sincerely for Him. All praise is for Allah, Lord of the Worlds* (40:65). Being true to God and to oneself is one more honor: *My Lord, let me enter a sincere entry and depart a sincere departing. And grant me, from Your own, supporting authority* (17:80). The capacity of self-rectification—for we are humans and do err—is yet another eminent quality: *My Lord, I have indeed wronged myself; so forgive me* (28:16). Reverence for parents and goodness to family are also of the essence of virtue: *And lower for them the wing of humility out of mercy. And say, "My Lord, have mercy upon both of them just as they have raised me as a small child"* (17:24). *My Lord, forgive me and my parents, and whoever enters my house as a believer, and the believing men and the believing women* (71:28). In addition, cleanliness of heart, harboring no hostility or hatred for the faithful, is indeed an ennobling trait: *Our Lord, forgive us and our brethren who have preceded us in faith, and let not into our hearts malice for those who believe. Our Lord, indeed You are all-kind, mercy-giving* (59:10). Finally, intentional nurture of a longing for wholesomeness and enlightenment is of the most edifying of human attributes: *Our Lord, perfect for us our light, and forgive us, for surely You are powerful over all things* (66:8).

These citations have been chosen to illustrate the intrinsic correlation between the prayers of the Quran and the virtues that the Book seeks to advance—virtues that measure the actual "humanness" of a man or a woman. To those one may add chasteness, fair speech, conservation of resources, open-handedness, kindness, forbearance, and many more. In order to portray the one who embodies these noble characteristics and how he might "look," I append here just one of the Prophet's ﷺ prayers, which presents such an integrated picture of a heart imbued with these virtues as to enable the reader to glimpse his arresting spiritual luminosity, of which most of the human family remains woefully deprived.

> O Allah, I ask You for the best of requests, the best of prayers, the best of success, the best of deeds, the best of rewards, the best in life, and the best in death. And make me steadfast; make my righteous deeds weighty in my balance; make true my faith; exalt my rank; accept my Prayer [*Ṣalât*]; and forgive my misdeeds. And I ask You for the highest stations of the Garden.
>
> O Allah, I ask You for goodness from start to finish, all of it—its beginning, its manifestation, that which is evident of it and that which is hidden of it—and for the highest stations of the Garden.
>
> O Allah, I ask You for the best in whatever I advance, the best of whatever I do, the best of what is hidden, the best of what is disclosed, and the highest stations of the Garden.
>
> O Allah, I ask You to raise my renown, to alleviate my burden, to set aright my affairs, to purify my heart, and to guard my chastity. And illuminate my heart for me and forgive my sins. And I ask You for the highest stations of the Garden.
>
> O Allah, I ask You to bless for me my whole self—my hearing, my sight, my spirit, my physical being, my character, my family, my life, my death, and my deeds. So accept my good deeds. And I ask You for the highest stations of the Garden.

And so, this book is about such prayers and invocations, which have demonstrated, since the first breaths of human history, an undiminished and lasting power to revive the heart and infuse the human soul with renewed spiritual life. For whether in but a fleeting moment, and with almost reflexive phrases, one recalls the womb that bore him or her—"may God have mercy on her"—or in seemingly suspended time one contemplates the inexpressible majesty of God, prayer is as essential to life as the air we breathe. It is no irony that in the times in which we live prayer has very nearly become a lost art when it is so utterly, direfully needed.

O God, enable all believers to respond to Your call of peace and safety: *O you who believe, enter into peace all of you, and do not follow the footsteps of Satan; for indeed, he is to you a clear enemy* (2:208). And bless all those who read this work and who benefit from it. May God bring about in our lives and in our world common goodness, brotherly love, and equanimity.

Introducing Prayer

The Blessing and Favor of Prayer

THE OBJECTS OF our wants and fears far surpass the limits of human genius, energy, and mortal life. The sum of all that we need and desire—spiritual or material, essential or superfluous—simply exceeds our ability to attain it. What, then, is one to do?

The believer turns to his or her Creator in prayer (*duʿâ’*, in Arabic). The response is natural. Whether moved by need or hope, or faced with misfortune or danger, people instinctively call upon God. We remember the Lord of the Worlds and implore Him for security, health, and sustenance, and ask for success and fulfillment in this life and in the Hereafter. To echo the wonder voiced by Imam al-

Ghazâlî (d. 505/1111), *how immense is God's mercy upon humanity in endowing us with the refuge and recourse of prayer!*[1]

> *"Indeed, to God do we turn in hope!"*
>
> — The Quran, 9:59

The Homage of Prayer in the Quran

The Quran records supplications from prophets and believers to show people how to find answers and strength in the sanctuary of prayer. In its verses, we meet the parents of humanity, Adam and Eve, seeking forgiveness and mercy from their Lord for their misdeed in the Garden. We learn from the prayers of Noah with regard to his rebelling son, and those of Abraham and his virtuous sons. We live the invocations of Moses, Solomon, Jesus, and Muḥammad, God's peace and blessings be upon them. Alongside the prophets, the believers voice their yearnings, great and small, for this life and the next.

The Quran presents as heroes of prayer men and women who kept profound remembrance of the Creator. They adjured Him in myriad contexts and moods: Lot for help against a corrupt people; Joseph for enduring faith and the companionship of the righteous in Paradise; David for patience and firmness in battle; the elderly Zechariah for a righteous child; and unnamed believers in the sundry circumstances and conditions of life for

The Prophet ﷺ said to his Companions, "Shall I not tell you about the best of your works and the purest of them before your Lord, and the highest of them regarding your ranks, and what is better for you than spending gold and silver, and better for you than facing your enemy in battle, wherein you strike their necks and they strike your necks?" They said, "Yes, indeed!" He said, "It is the remembrance of God, the Exalted."

harming Me so as to harm Me; and you cannot attain benefiting Me so as to benefit Me. O My worshippers, were the first of you and the last of you, the human of you and the jinn[3] of you, to be as God-fearing as the most God-fearing heart of any of you, that would not increase My kingdom in anything. O My worshippers, were the first of you and the last of you, the human of you and the jinn of you, to be as wicked as the most wicked heart of any of you, that would not decrease My kingdom in anything.

O My worshippers, were the human of you and the jinn of you to rise up in one place and ask of Me, and were I to give each one his asking, that would not decrease what I have any more than a needle decreases the sea when dipped into it. O My worshippers, it is but your deeds that I reckon up for you and then recompense you for. So let whoever finds good praise Allah, and let whoever finds other than this blame no one but himself.[4]

The Etiquette of Supplication

Along with exhorting people to seek God's help through prayer, the Quran shows how one ought to call upon God with requests and petitions. We learn that the act of imploring God to answer our appeals itself ranks among the best of prayers, as in one of the supplications of Abraham: "*Our Lord, do accept my prayer*" (14:40). We also learn that in supplicating God, a person should be mindful of the range of human awareness, for which Noah set the standard when he prayed, "*My Lord, I seek refuge in You from asking You of what I have no knowledge*" (11:47). To ensure that the character of one's prayer is appropriate, one should consider the requirements of each supplication as to its scope, occasion, subject matter, and form. This self-examination begins with an understanding of three imperatives of prayer.

The first imperative of prayer is that one turn exclusively to God, seeking in Him alone the fulfillment of one's requests and believing that He alone advances good or withholds harm; for the truth of the matter is that ultimately nothing in creation can benefit or harm itself or others by any measure, except as God Himself has decreed. The second imperative is purity of intention, that is, sincerity of heart, meaning that one must have conscious awareness that he or she is petitioning God. The Quran says, *Then call upon Allah, making religion sincerely His* (40:14). The third imperative is to have certainty in God's answer. The Prophet ﷺ said, "Petition your Lord and be certain of His answer—and know that God does not answer the prayer of a heedless, inattentive heart."[5]

Sound faith, sincerity, and certainty in God's responsiveness comprise an important part of a proper etiquette

And remember your Lord within yourself, humbly and fearfully, without being loud with words, in the mornings and the evenings. And do not be of the heedless.

— The Quran, 7:205

Some Companions asked the Prophet ﷺ, "O Messenger of God, can it be that one of us follows through on his passion [i.e., sexual consummation with a spouse] and there is reward for him in this?" He said, "Have you considered that if one were to fulfill his passion unlawfully he would bear the burden of this? Thus in fulfilling one's passion lawfully does such a person gain reward for it."

of prayer, which stems from the moral principles that ought to govern a person's emotions, thoughts, and actions. These imperatives inform one's approach to prayer and find expression in the attitude and lifestyle that one assumes after supplicating God. Thus one should not become annoyed or disheartened, or nurture ill feelings because of a perceived delay in God's answer to a prayer, for this violates the spirit of worship. Rather, the believer sends forth all that his or her heart desires and leaves the matter to God, trusting His wisdom and mercy.

Closely related to the realm of prayer is a person's cultivation of his or her own moral integrity—especially in relation to the purity of one's earnings and sustenance—for moral laxity subverts the effect of one's prayers. The believer who spends a lifetime seeking lawful and wholesome gain—especially one who works for the good of humankind, lending his energies to God's purposes—is more likely to receive an answer from his or her Lord than one whose earnings come through unlawful means. The Prophet ﷺ said:

> O people, Allah is good and accepts only that which is good. Allah has decreed for the believers what He has decreed for the messengers. He said, *O messengers, eat of what is wholesome and do righteous deeds. Indeed, I am all-knowing of what you do* (23:51). Also, *O you who believe, eat of that which is good from what We have provided you* (2:172).

The Prophet ﷺ then mentioned the example of one who

> bears the mark of much travel, disheveled and dusty, and who raises his hands toward the heavens and cries, "O my Lord! O my Lord!" while his food is unlawful, his drink is unlawful, his clothes are unlawful, and he is nourished by the unlawful. How, then, shall his call be answered?[6]

Like one's sustenance and earnings, prayers in themselves must remain within the boundaries of wholesomeness and revealed moral values. Otherwise they can amount to no more than mockery or absurdity, as, for example, asking God to give one the possessions of all human beings, or the right to deceive without contention, or the power to create life and end it. The Prophet ﷺ said, "A worshipper will be answered as long as he does not pray for something sinful or the severing of kinship and is not hasty." His Companions asked, "O Messenger of Allah, what is haste?" He answered, "It is when one says,

Our Lord, grant us mercy from Your own and furnish us, in our affair, with right guidance.

— The Quran, 16:10

The Prophet ﷺ said, "O God, whoever holds command of an affair of my community and afflicts it with hardship, afflict him with hardship. And whoever holds command of an affair of my community and accords it kindness, accord him kindness."

'I prayed, but without answer,' and then despairs or becomes wearied and ceases to pray."[7] Another report states that the Prophet ﷺ said, "No one calls upon Allah with a prayer but that Allah grants what he has asked for or keeps back from him the like of it in harm, so long as one does not pray for something sinful or the severing of kinship." Upon hearing this, someone said, "Then we shall surely supplicate plentifully." The Prophet ﷺ replied, "Allah is more plentiful in responding."[8]

In addition to the prohibition against praying for misdeeds and breaches within the family, the Prophet ﷺ forbade other abuses of prayer, such as invoking harm against oneself or loved ones or against something for which one cares. He said, "Do not pray against yourselves. Do not pray against your children. Do not pray against your possessions."[9] He further disallowed succumbing to (or even harboring) thoughts of suicide as a means of escaping pressures, for one should not desire death because of the misfortunes, pain, and problems that beset one. "Should anyone be so afflicted," the Prophet ﷺ said, "let him say, 'O Allah, keep me alive as long as life is best for me, and take my soul unto Yourself when death is best for me.' "[10] (The believer may invoke God, however, against those who usurp his or her rights, or the rights of people, or against those who subject them to tyranny. Indeed, no veils come between the prayers of the oppressed and God.) The Prophet ﷺ also discouraged prayers that are said with deliberate distortion or with exaggerated affectation, both of which are unbecoming to a sincere supplicant and betray the true spirit of prayer.

While we may petition God freely, apart from these prohibitions, there are preferred protocols of prayer. It is good to begin a prayer in the name of God and with His praise and then to call upon Him by one or more of His most excellent names (*asmâ' Allâh al-ḥusnâ*), ninety-nine of which He taught to us in the Quran. The more inclusive the prayer the better. ʿÂ'isha, the Mother of the Believers, said, "The Prophet ﷺ used to favor comprehensive prayers and refrain from other than this."[11] This is consistent with her report of the Prophet ﷺ teaching her the following supplication:

> O Allah, I ask You for every good—imminent and deferred, what I know of it and what I do not know. And I seek refuge in You from every evil—imminent and deferred, what I know of it and what I do not know.
>
> O Allah, I ask You for the best of what Your servant and Prophet has asked You. And I seek refuge in You from the evil from which Your servant and Prophet sought refuge in You.
>
> O Allah, I ask You for the Garden and any utterance or

Abû Hurayra said that the Prophet ﷺ said, "Two phrases are light on the tongue yet heavy in the Balance and beloved by the All-Merciful:
(1) "Glory be to God and all praise is His" [Subḥân'Allâhi wa bi ḥamdihi],
(2) "Glory be to God, the Magnificent" [Subḥân'Allâhi al-ʿAẓîm].

The Prophet ﷺ said, "Supplication between the Adhân *[the Call to Prayer] and the* Iqâma *[the Final Call to Prayer] will not be rejected."*

deed that brings one near to it. And I seek refuge in You from Hellfire and any utterance or deed that brings one near to it. And I ask You to make all the decrees You have decreed for me good.[12]

Also, in times of severity, one may enumerate before God the good deeds he or she has done for His pleasure, in order to emphasize that, despite shortcomings, one has striven faithfully to serve Him.

Naturally, one may express supplications in any language, yet one should strive to learn and invoke the prayers of the Quran and the Prophet ﷺ, since they are peerless in power, impact, beauty, and sheer goodness.

A person may pray in the secret of his or her soul or voice supplications softly or audibly, but one should not pray in a shouting or clamorous manner. The Prophet ﷺ was once traveling with his Companions, and the people around them began shouting out their prayers. "Restrain yourselves," he said to them, "for you do not call upon one who is deaf or absent. He to whom you pray is all-hearing and near, and He is with you."[13]

Prayer should find constant expression in the heart and on the tongue of the believer, whether in moments of prosperity and good health or at times of duress, especially when one is tried with loss of wealth, prestige, valued possessions, or loved ones. Thus, Prophet Muḥam-

from the dead; and You bring forth the dead from the living. And You provide to whom You will without reckoning." (3:26–27)[17]

O Allah, originator of the heavens and the earth, knower of the unseen and the seen, You shall judge between Your servants about what they have been disputing. (39:46)

Indeed, those who believe and do righteous deeds, their Lord shall guide them by their faith. Rivers shall flow beneath them in the Gardens of Delight. Their call therein shall be, "Glory be to You, O Allah." And their salutations shall be, "Peace!" And the last of their prayers shall be, "Indeed, all praise is for Allah, Lord of the Worlds." (10:9–10)

It is a blessing that a person becomes imbued with the tenets of true religion by the very activity that brings about his or her purification. For the supplications of the Quran and those of the Prophet ﷺ reveal to the believer the words that will set one free of trespasses and secure one's pardon for negligence toward family, fellows, and, most importantly, God. Also, from the wellspring of prayer flows strength of character; for prayer steadily diminishes a person's remissness while he or she gains knowledge and seeks protection from moral and physical injury, poverty, sickness, and fear:

Say: I seek refuge in the Lord of the daybreak from the evil of what He created, and from the evil of darkness when it overspreads, and from the evil of those ˹sorceresses˺ who blow upon knots, and from the evil of an envier when he envies. (113:1–5)

وَلَا تَكُونُوا كَالَّذِينَ

And be not like those who had forgotten Allah, so He caused them to forget their ˹own˺ souls.

— The Quran, 59:19

The Prophet ﷺ said, "God extends His Hand at night for those who have done wrong during the day to repent. And He extends His Hand during the day for those who have done wrong at night to repent, until [such a time when] the sun shall rise from where it sets" [meaning the end of time].

Say: I seek refuge in the Lord of all people. King of all people, God of all people, from the evil of the sneaking whisperer—who whispers in the chests of people—from jinn and people. (114:1–6)

We also learn from the Prophet ﷺ about the practical effects of repeating words of entreaty and God's remembrance. Being constant in prayer sharpens a person's understanding of his or her purpose on earth. It opens avenues to a pleasant and reposed inner existence, as the practice of asking of God and praising Him becomes a permanent part of one's life, something renewed daily in varied circumstances. It brings order and definition not only to one's relationship with God, but also to one's relationship with oneself, one's family, past and future generations of believers, and all of humanity. The great value that the Prophet ﷺ—as supplicant and teacher—attached to calling on God impresses upon one the far-reaching influences that it exerts on the worshipful personality. Hence, the Prophet ﷺ frequently appealed to God with the following prayers:

O Allah, I seek refuge in You from detestable characteristics, actions, and longings. [*And he would say,*] O Allah, I seek refuge in You from leprosy, insanity, and malignant illnesses.[18]

O Allah, set aright for me my religion, for it safeguards my affairs. Set aright for me my life, for in it resides my well-being. Set aright for me my end, for to it is my ultimate return. And make life for me ever-increasing in everything good, and make death a comfort for me from every evil.[19]

O Allah, grant us as much reverence for You as will be a deterrent between us and sinning against You, and as much obedience to You as will deliver us to Your Garden, and as much certainty of faith as will ease for us the misfortunes of this world. And let us enjoy our hearing, our sight, and our strength for so long as You extend our lives, and make them endure after us. And set our vengeance against those who have wronged us. And give us victory over those waging animosity against us. And let not our loss be in our religion, nor let this world be the greatest of our concerns, nor the extent of our knowledge, and do not give authority over us to any who will not have mercy on us.[20]

The Messenger of God ﷺ said, "The likeness of one who remembers his Lord and one who does not remember his Lord is the likeness of the living and the dead."

The spiritual elevation that one experiences through the repetition of such prayers is immense. One perhaps reaches the highest refinement, however, with the realization of a special teaching of the Prophet ﷺ : The supplication of a person who prays for another in his or her absence is especially likely to find answer. He added that for every believer God has assigned an angel who says, "Amen! And to you the same," whenever he or she prays for the good of another person.[21]

As forms of intimate communication with God, prayer and remembrance express a believer's total disposition—

The Messenger of God ﷺ said, "When a worshipper says, 'There is no deity but God, alone,' God says, 'My worshipper has spoken the truth. There is no God but Me alone.' And when one says, 'There is no deity but God. There is no associate with Him,' He says, 'My worshipper has spoken the truth. There is no God but Me, and there is no associate with Me.' And when one says, 'There is no deity but God, to Him belongs all the kingdom and all praise,' He says, 'My worshipper has spoken the truth. There is no deity but Me. To Me belongs all the kingdom, and to Me is all praise.' And when one says, 'There is no deity but God, and there is no strength and no power except with God,' He says, 'My worshipper has spoken the truth. There is no deity but Me, and there is no strength and no power except with Me.'"

one's spirituality, aspirations, fears, limitations, and shortcomings—and they manifest one's awareness of the majesty and richness of God. They echo the intuitive human sense that there does indeed exist a perfect Lord of universal mercy, far-reaching power, and ever-unfolding dominion. In the prayers of the Quran, one learns that God's is the most loving patronage, all-answering and limitless, and of abundant reward beyond imagination. And in Muḥammad ﷺ and in the prayers of the prophets and the believers mentioned in the Quran, one discovers the most lucid and dynamic role models of worship, whose communication with God one would be well served to emulate.

The Foundations of Prayer

In a general sense, one's supplications rest on a three-part foundation: (1) Acknowledging God, believing in Him, and remaining truthful and sincere in worshipping Him; (2) understanding the limitations of human nature and, therefore, the human being's profound need for God's help and forgiveness; and (3) realizing the brevity of earthly life and being mindful of the inevitable return to God. Thus, because God's worship is to be the focus of our lives, a special emphasis of supplication is on asking

God to clear away any external or internal obstructions and distractions with regard to our worship of Him, so that our energies can be freely applied to doing good and remaining in harmony with creation through obedience to God. This hope accounts for the oft-repeated supplications of the Prophet ﷺ and the believers for refuge in God against hypocrisy, arrogance, calamity, and delusion. Hence, the Prophet ﷺ used to implore his Lord in the morning and evening to protect him from the ill effects of poverty, disease, ignorance, pride, cowardliness, and injustice, and to save him from the impairments of laziness, selfishness, impatience, and malice.

The expressions the Prophet ﷺ used in some of his supplications restate parts of other prayers that he made regularly but at different occasions. Yet at the heart of his every prayer is the hope for the pleasure of God and Paradise.

The prayers the Prophet ﷺ uttered for a given circumstance also tended to vary in length, in consideration of people's diverse capacities to learn them. A new Muslim, for example, once heard the Prophet ﷺ supplicating in low tones after one of the prescribed Prayers (*Ṣalât*). When he found himself unable to retain all that the Prophet ﷺ had prayed, he went to the Companion

Just as We have sent among you a messenger from yourselves who recites to you Our verses and purifies you and teaches you the Book and the wisdom, and teaches you what you did not know, so remember Me; I shall remember you. And be thankful to Me. And do not be ungrateful to Me. O you who believe, seek help through patience and Prayer. Indeed, Allah is with the patient.

— The Quran, 2:151–53

Al-Ghazâlî said, "The beneficial and effective form of remembrance is remembering ˹God˺ continuously with full presence of the heart. . . . As for remembrance with the tongue while the heart is inattentive, it is surely of little benefit. . . . The presence of the heart at the time of remembrance followed by heedlessness of God, the Exalted, and occupation with this world, is also of little benefit. Rather, the presence of the heart with God, continuously or most of the time, certainly comes before the acts of worship. Indeed, the rest of the realm of worship is sanctified by this ˹conscious remembrance˺, which is itself the ultimate aim of the practical act of worship."

Muʿâdh ibn Jabal, hoping to hear an easier invocation. To his dismay, he heard Muʿâdh repeating a supplication similar to that of the Prophet ﷺ. Somewhat frustrated, he went back to the Prophet ﷺ and said, "I cannot restate your murmuring, nor the murmuring of Muʿâdh; so all that I say is, 'O Allah, admit me into the Garden and save me from Hellfire.'" The Prophet ﷺ then said to him good humoredly, "It is about this that we murmur."[22]

In the perspective of Islam, supplication is much more than rote utterances. It is the marrow of a living, dynamic relationship with God, reflected in the Muslim's remembrance of his or her Lord and consciousness of God's constant presence. (Continual remembrance of God is, after all, an important goal of prayer.) Thus, when someone becomes occupied to a great extent with the remembrance of God and with doing that which pleases Him, God grants such a one—even without that person asking—the best of what others pray for. God says:

> Whoever is deterred from asking Me on account of being occupied with the Quran and My remembrance, I shall give him the best of what I give those who ask. And the excellence of the words of Allah over all other words is as the excellence of Allah over His creation.[23]

This statement underscores the exalted and desirable nature assigned to the contemplation of the Quran and its guidance, which is considered among the highest forms of God's remembrance.

Thâbit ibn Aslam said, "Indeed, I know when my Lord, the Exalted, the Majestic, remembers me." Those who heard him were alarmed by his statement. They said, "And how do you know this?" He said, "When I remember Him, He remembers me!"

God's Favor of Prayer for Humankind

As stated at the outset, prayer is an inestimable favor and limitless source of renewal that gives just a glimpse of the vastness of God's mercy. Indeed, He encourages our communication with and remembrance of Him. *So remember Me; I shall remember you* (2:152). He says also:

> I am at the contemplation of My servants: I am with them when they remember Me. When they remember Me within themselves, I remember them within Myself. And when they remember Me in company, I remember them in better company.[24]

Further, God states that part of His favor upon the believers is that He Himself—the Majestic and the Exalted—bestows His favor of blessings upon us: *It is He who sends prayers ˹of blessings˺ down upon you, as do His angels, to bring you forth from darknesses into light. And indeed, to the believers, He is mercy-giving* (33:43).

About This Book

This book consists of two parts. *Part One,* "Prayers of the Quran," introduces supplications from the Quran that compare in breadth with the subjects the Book itself ad-

Have you not seen that it is Allah to whom all in the heavens and all in the earth bow down—ʿas doʾ the sun and the moon and the stars and the mountains and the trees and the beasts and many of the people? But for many, ʿthose who disbelieveʾ, the torment shall come to pass. And whomever Allah dishonors, none can give him honor. Indeed, Allah does what He wills.

— The Quran, 22:18

dresses: God, reward and punishment, the seen and the unseen, this world and the Hereafter, life and death—and all that these entail. Each of the four chapters of *Part One* highlights the outstanding characteristics of the prayers appearing therein, while introducing those who uttered them. It addresses the common character of these believers, as well as the efficacy of their prayers in general and the often dramatic impact their prayers had on their conditions and on the course of history. In this way, one sees that prayer is the special "essence of worship," as the Prophet ﷺ said, which keeps humankind in balance with the entire worshipping universe.

With each prayer is a commentary that brings its historical circumstances to light and reflects upon the occasion of its revelation to the Prophet ﷺ or some significant moment or statement that he made with respect to it. Although these prayers have specific contexts, they are universal and are meant to be recited as such.

Part Two, "Prayers for All Times and Occasions," records the various daily and common supplications of the Prophet ﷺ to illustrate his perfect reliance upon his Lord and to draw us, through the study of them, closer to his worshipful way of life and to God, Most High. This part contains twelve general categories of life, ranging from personal to social occasions, and from devotional to worldly experiences. Collectively, they guide one's invocation of God throughout daily life. (A companion publication to *Part Two* contains the original Arabic text of the supplications in this part in order to allow for comparison and in the hope that those so inclined shall memorize them.)

An appendix, "Form and Substance: Quranic Calligraphy," briefly discusses the emergence and importance of writing in Islamic civilization and the development of the art of calligraphy as inspired by the veneration of the Quran, for more than 50 calligraphic renderings (most of which are originals and previously unpublished) appear in this volume.

In the end, this book is for all who yearn to taste the beauty of the prayerful consciousness that the Quran shapes and who long to come closer to the worshipful outlook of the model human being, Muḥammad, God's peace and blessings be upon him.

Our Lord, perfect for us our light, and forgive us, for surely You are powerful over all things (66:8). And the last of our prayers is, *All praise is for Allah, Lord of the Worlds* (10:10).

Prayers of the Quran

· 1 ·

The Opening Prayer of the Quran

Sûrat al-Fâtiḥa (Interpreted into English)

1 In the name of Allah,
the All-Merciful, the Mercy-Giving.

2 All praise is for Allah, Lord of the Worlds,

3 the All-Merciful, the Mercy-Giving,

4 Master of the Day of Judgment.

5 It is You we worship, and it is You we ask for help.

6 Guide us to the straight way, the way of those upon
whom You have bestowed grace,

7 not those upon whom there is wrath,
nor those astray.

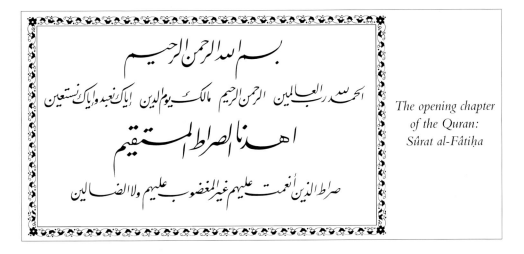

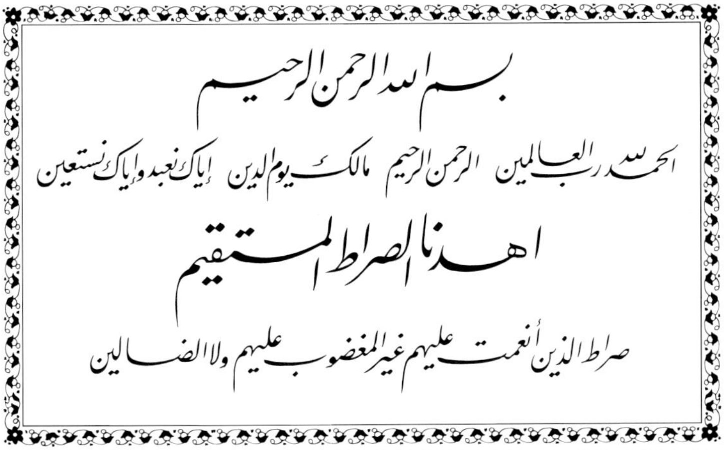

The opening chapter of the Quran: Sûrat al-Fâtiḥa

Themes of al-Fâtiḥa

Of all the verses that God has revealed in the Quran, He chose those of al-Fâtiḥa (the opening sura or chapter) to be repeated in each standing of every ritual Muslim Prayer (*Ṣalât*). Whatever the ultimate wisdom of this may be, perhaps its significance resides in the human need to be constantly reminded of the essential truths of life and that which gives it direction. The truths that al-Fâtiḥa keeps in the forefront of one's mind are no less than the major themes of the Book it opens: Faith in the true and only merciful God; gratitude to the Sustainer of all being; certainty in the Day of Judgment; sincerity in worship and in seeking God's help; a resolve to adhere to the

Truly there has come to you from God a light and a clear book, with which God guides whoever follows His pleasure to the paths of peace. And He brings them out from the darkness into the light by His permission. And He guides them to the straight way.

— The Quran, 5:15–16

straight way of the rightly guided of all ages; and avoidance of the ways of the rebellious, the trespassers, and the lost.

The Meaning of al-Fâtiḥa in Brief

Al-Fâtiḥa begins ***in the name of Allah*** (God) and with two attributes of His benevolence. He is ***the All-Merciful, the Mercy-Giving,*** extending His blessings to one and all. He is the Creator who nurtures His creation and sustains it, encompassing the furthest reaches of every being.

All praise is for Allah. He is the ***Lord of the Worlds,*** who knows all affairs, hears all pleas, responds to all needs. He is ***Master of the Day of Judgment***—the ruler of perfect justice, before whom all people, all beings, all issues shall come. Those who succeed will reside in perpetual delight, and those who fail will dwell in painful regret. But for those who say sincerely to their Lord, ***It is You we worship, and it is You we ask for help,*** a sacred trust is made between the needful human being and God, the Enricher, whose unfailing help provides strength, fulfills every rightful need, and safeguards one from vulnerabilities.

In quest of moral excellence, the fellowship of believers makes a collective appeal to God for lasting guidance upon His path: ***Guide us to the straight way,*** the waymarks of which are not mere material gains or worldly achievements, but rather people blessed with spiritual wellness and moral ascendance, namely, those upon whom You have bestowed grace.

The petition, ***Guide us to the straight way,*** is filled with aspiration and hope, as if one were to implore:

> O God, show us its landmarks, its guidelines, its standards. Inspire us to seek out its signs and traces, to comprehend its truths and realities. Teach us to revere its guiding principles and to look toward its heavenly ends. The straight way is beloved by us, so make its norms dear to us. We have embarked upon it, so grant us the ability to continue our journey, and make our feet firm upon it. Help us overcome any obstacles in its path. Protect us against straying from the moderation and evenness of its way.

The worshipper reaches the peak of human goodness with this plea, seeking guidance not only for him- or herself but for all (guide *us*) who by the same moral contract have bound themselves to God's Way (You *we* worship. You *we* ask for help). There is no greater charity.

The faithful, as much as they are able, remain true to both the letter and the spirit of God's commandments and so are saved from incurring His anger or straying into dogmatic error. They are, in other words, ***not those upon whom there is wrath, nor those astray.*** In essence,

The Prophet ﷺ said, "Learn the Quran and recite it, for the semblance of one who learns and recites the Quran is that of ⌜an open⌝ sack filled with musk, the fragrance of which spreads everywhere. And the semblance of one who learns it and sleeps while it is in his heart is that of a tied sack of musk."

Indeed, We have revealed ˹divine guidance˺ to you, ˹O Muḥammad,˺ as We have revealed to Noah and the prophets after him. And We revealed to Abraham and Ishmael and Isaac and Jacob and the Tribes and Jesus and Job and Jonah and Aaron and Solomon. And We gave David the Zabûr [*the Writ*]; *and there were messengers ˹about whom˺ We related to you from before and other messengers ˹about whom˺ We did not relate to you. And God spoke to Moses by word.*

— The Quran, 4:163–64

al-Fâtiḥa is a personal prayer centering the human spirit on the will of God as expressed in His final Revelation. With its every recitation, the worshipper enters into intimate dialogue with God, as the Prophet ﷺ related:

> Allah, the Almighty and the Majestic, has said, "I have apportioned the Prayer [al-Fâtiḥa] between Myself and My worshipper in two parts—and My worshipper shall have what he has asked for." So when the worshipper says, *"All Praise is for Allah, Lord of the Worlds,"* Allah says, "My worshipper has praised Me." When he says, *"The All-Merciful, the Mercy-Giving,"* Allah says, "My worshipper has extolled Me."
>
> When he says, *"Master of the Day of Judgment,"* Allah says, "My worshipper has magnified Me and entrusted Me with his affairs." When he says, *"It is You we worship, and it is You we ask for help,"* Allah says, "This is between Myself and My worshipper—and My worshipper shall have what he has asked for." When he says, *"Guide us to the straight way, the way of those upon whom You have bestowed grace, not those upon whom there is wrath, nor those astray,"* Allah says, "This is for My worshipper—and My worshipper shall have what he has asked for."[25]

Al-Fâtiḥa* is a beacon to the way of God, warning humanity to avoid wandering down every dark defile made to appear otherwise. To this the believers voice a resonant *Âmîn*, "O God, accept our prayer!"[26]

* See my extended work on Sûrat al-Fâtiḥa, *The Opening to the Quran: Commentary and Vocabulary Reference of al-Fâtiḥa* (Oak Lawn, IL: Quranic Literacy Institute, 1996).

· 2 ·

Prayers of the Prophets

(God’s *blessings and peace be upon them*)

Who Are the Prophets?

ON THE FIRST day that God placed humankind on earth to assume trusteeship and regency over it, He promised to bestow guidance upon all its generations. *He said, “Descend from ˹the Garden˺, all together! So whenever guidance from Me comes to you, then those who follow My guidance, there shall be no fear upon them nor shall they grieve”* (2:38). He sent thousands of prophets to convey His message to all people and revealed through these emissaries His commandments and sacred texts. Thus, God is the

Our Lord, do accept this 'work' from us. Indeed, it is You who are the All-Hearing, the All-Knowing.

— The Quran, 2:127

رَبَّنَا

تَقَبَّلْ مِنَّا إِنَّكَ أَنتَ السَّمِيعُ العَلِيمُ

source of Revelation; angels and prophets are its mediums; people are the recipients or beneficiaries of it; and Revelation itself, in the form of the exact words of God, constitutes His books (or scriptures), which form the criteria by which human beings shall be judged on the Day of Resurrection as to how they lived out their earthly lives.

The Quran stresses that God selected the prophets from among mortal men; they possessed no angelic characteristics and shared no part of God's divinity. On the contrary, they were fully human, model servants of God who dedicated their lives to promulgate a single message: There is but one God, so worship Him. They demonstrated, moreover, the virtues by which God has commanded humanity to live. The Quran says, *And We made them exemplary leaders; they guide by Our command. And We revealed to them the doing of good works, and the establishment of Prayer, and the giving of Charity. And only Us did they worship* (21:73). In diverse languages, lands, and times, the prophets confirmed each other with this highest truth and invited people to believe in their Creator, to do good in this world, and to prepare to meet Him for judgment and recompense in the Hereafter. God says, *And We have not sent before you any messenger but that We revealed to him that there is no God but I, so worship Me* (21:25). He also said:

> *And We do not send the messengers except as bearers of glad tidings and warners. So those who believe and do righteous deeds, there is no fear upon them nor shall they grieve. But those who deny Our signs, the torment shall touch them, for they have been rebellious.* (6:48–49)

According to a statement of Prophet Muḥammad ﷺ the prophets and messengers sent to humanity numbered 124,000 in all.[27] There is an important distinction between the role of a *messenger* and that of a *prophet:* Messengers are those who received a Revelation or scripture that constituted a new message; and prophets are those who, while inspired by God, received no new message but expounded upon the messages previously revealed. Every messenger, therefore, was a prophet, but not every prophet was a messenger.

Belief in all of God's prophets and messengers without exception or differentiation is a cardinal tenet of faith for

The Messenger believes in what has been sent down to him from his Lord, as do the believers. All believe in Allah and His angels and His books and His messengers: "We do not distinguish between any of His messengers."

— The Quran, 2:285

And if you do not bring them a sign, they say, "If only you chose one?" Say, "I follow only what is revealed to me from my Lord. This is an insight from your Lord, and a guidance and mercy to people who believe." And when the Quran is recited, then listen to it and give heed, so that you may be shown mercy.

— The Quran, 7:203–04

the Muslim, as is the acceptance of all of the scriptures they conveyed. This outlook generates a sense of community that transcends time and circumstance.

As recipients of the highest wisdom, these great human beings provided their communities with knowledge about God, the upright life, and the destiny of humanity. In addition, God instructed some prophets, who were also messengers, to alter the course and conduct of their people by challenging the errant assumptions that prevailed among them and by warning them of God's wrath if they persisted with them. To some, God gave scriptures. He revealed such scriptures to Abraham (*ṣuḥuf,* sing. *ṣaḥîfa*) (87:19, 53:36–37) and gave Moses the Torah (*Tawrât*), *in which there is guidance and light* (5:44). To David, He sent down the Writ (*Zabûr*) (4:163), and to Jesus, the Gospel (*Injîl*), *in which there is guidance and light and a confirmation of what preceded it of the Torah, and a guidance and admonition for the God-fearing* (5:46). Lastly, to Muḥammad, blessings and peace be upon him and all the messengers, God revealed His final scripture, the Glorious Quran.

What the Quran Says of the Prophets

The Quran does not seek to detail the biographies of all the prophets; rather, it encapsulates the most relevant and instructive aspects of the stories and struggles of many of them. In this way can believers of every generation learn from their awesome experiences and be inspired to stand for truth against the pressures of disbelief as the prophets themselves did. The Quran mentions twenty-five prophets and messengers by name: Adam, Enoch (Idrîs), Noah (Nuḥ), Ṣâliḥ, Hûd, Abraham (Ibrâhîm), Lot (Lûṭ), Ishmael (Ismâ῾îl), Isaac (Isḥâq), Jacob (Ya῾qûb), Job (Ayyûb), Joseph (Yûsuf), Shu῾ayb, Jonah (Yûnus), Moses (Mûsâ), Aaron (Hârûn), David (Dâwûd), Solomon (Sulaymân), Ezekiel (Dhû'l-Kifl), Elias (Ilyâs), Elisha (al-Yasa῾), Zechariah (Zakariyya), John (Yaḥyâ), Jesus (῾Îsâ), and Muḥammad, God's peace and blessings be upon all of them.

God supported His prophets and messengers with miracles and evident proofs, so that their communities would recognize them as His genuine emissaries, reflect upon the call to which they were invited, and obey the commandments God revealed for them. The miracles and signs that confirmed the veracity of each prophet or messenger varied. God ordered the fire into which Abraham's foes cast him to *be cool and peaceful* for him (21:69). The sea parted for Moses and his followers, and his staff was transformed into a serpent, one sign among many that he presented to Pharaoh and his court magi-

Say, "We believe in Allah and what has been sent down to us and what has been sent down to Abraham, Ishmael, Isaac, Jacob, and the Tribes, and what was given to Moses and Jesus, and what was given to the prophets from their Lord. We do not differentiate between any of them. And to Him do we submit."
So if they believe in the same as you have believed in, then truly they are guided. But if they turn away, they shall then be in schism. Then Allah shall suffice you against them, and He is the All-Hearing, the All-Knowing.

— The Quran, 2:136–37

O Children of Adam, We have indeed sent down to you garments to cover your nakedness, and adornments. Yet the garment of righteousness—that is best. This is of the signs of God so that they may remember.

— The Quran, 7:26

cians (7:132–33; 20:17–23; 27:12). God placed the winds and jinn[28] at Solomon's command (21:81–82). And God established Jesus' truthfulness with numerous striking miracles, including Jesus' miraculous birth and his ability to restore life to the dead, heal lepers, and tell people of the provisions that they had stored up in their homes, all by the permission of his Lord (3:49).

God chose Prophet Muḥammad ﷺ to be the Seal of the Prophets, that is, the final Prophet and Messenger to all people of every generation, locality, and language. He substantiated the Prophet's mission with the glorious Quran, the inimitable word of God that shall endure as a miracle and source of guidance for humanity until the end of time.

In the view of the Quran, the prophets and messengers are the exemplary leaders of humanity. The impact they continue to exert upon the lives and thoughts of people reaches deeper than that of any conqueror, statesman, scientist, philosopher, or poet. Through the intimacy of their supplications, we see their leadership illustrated in a unique manner, by their continual rushing to God, their hearts overflowing with sincere prayers in times of need, affliction, joy, sorrow, deliverance, and calm. Such is the handhold that never breaks.

• *Adam and Eve* •

THE QURAN STATES explicitly that God created Adam and Eve from a single soul and willed, before their physical creation, that they dwell on Earth as an abode for them and their children in this life until the Day of Resurrection (2:30).

The Quran also narrates that when God created Adam and presented him before the angels, they raised a solemn concern saying, "*Will You place therein one who will do corruption therein and shed blood, while we glorify Your praise and hallow You?*" *[Allah] said*, "*I know what you do not know*" (2:30). God then blessed Adam عليه السلام with the gift of knowledge, teaching him *the names, all of them* (2:31).

So the angels bore witness to the eminence of Adam, and God ordered them to honor him by prostrating before him, which they did. Out of arrogance, however, Iblîs (Satan) disobeyed the command, claiming that as a jinn created from fire, he was better and more worthy than a being created from clay. For his rebelliousness and disobedience, Satan was disgraced and expelled from the Garden, but he asked God for respite until the Day of

So they bowed down, except Iblîs, who said, "Am I to bow down to one You have created from mud?" He said, "Do You see this one whom You have honored above me? If You delay me to the Day of Resurrection, I shall bridle his children, except a few." [God] said, "Go! For whoever of them follows you, then Hell shall surely be your recompense, an ample recompense. And incite whomever of them you can with your voice and rally against them with your horsemen and your footmen. And share in their wealth and their children. And promise them—yet Satan never promises them except in deceit. Surely, you have no authority over My servants. And sufficient is your Lord as a guardian."

— The Quran, 17:61–65

Resurrection and vowed to seduce Adam and his progeny away from the straight path and into disbelief. God, the Exalted, granted his request—for a time—and He said, *Whoever of them follows you, I will fill Hell with all of you together* (7:18).

The Quran indicates, as well, that God first settled Adam and Eve in "the Garden," a paradise not intended to be their permanent residence, but a place for them to recognize their capacity as human beings to choose obedience or disobedience, to be responsive or unresponsive to Him. The Garden also served as a setting for them to learn that their Creator would hold each of them accountable for whatever they might do and that they would face the consequences of their actions and be liable to receive reward and punishment.

God provided sustenance for them in the Garden, granted them security and peace, and preserved them from indecency. He also forbade them from coming near a certain tree or eating of its fruit, cautioning them about the avowed enmity that Satan harbored for humankind and about his cunning. God warned them that Satan would try to expel them from the Garden by tempting them to disobey Him. Satan then whispered to Adam and Eve, saying that God had forbidden them from the tree only to prevent them from becoming angels or attaining immortality. Thus Satan deceived them both, and they chose to eat from the tree. After they had done so, Adam and Eve realized the enormity of their action and turned to their Lord, voicing the first human supplication for forgiveness, a prayer which their progeny have not ceased to voice ever since: "*Our Lord, we have wronged ourselves, and if You do not forgive us and have mercy upon us, we shall surely be of the losers*" (7:23).

God, the All-Merciful, the Mercy-Giving, answered their plea. The sin of Adam and Eve ended with God's

Our Lord, we have wronged ourselves, and if You do not forgive us and have mercy upon us, we shall surely be of the losers.

— The Quran, 7:23

The Prophet ﷺ said that when God decreed the existence of creation, He inscribed for Himself in His Book which is kept with Him: "Indeed, My mercy prevails over My wrath."

encompassing forgiveness, and their purity was restored—as shall be the case for all their progeny who believe in the one God and seek His mercy and salvation.

· Noah ·

IN THE QURAN, God distinguishes the prophets Noah, Abraham, Moses, Jesus, and Muḥammad, peace and blessings be upon them, as messengers of the highest resolve (46:35). They steadfastly invited people to believe in God, worship Him, and lead good and moral lives based on His guidance. Of all of them, the quality of long-suffering persistence is most associated with Noah عليه السلام.

The Quran recounts Noah's mission and the story of the great flood that drowned those who denied his message.[29] Noah lived patiently among his people for *a thousand years, less fifty* (29:14), imparting his message to them at every opportunity. He admonished them to shun superstition and the worship of idols and to devote themselves to the religion of God alone. He enjoined them to do righteous deeds that would benefit them on a day when they would stand individually for judgment before the Lord of the Worlds:

> *Indeed, We sent Noah to his people: "Warn your people before a painful torment comes to them." He said, "O my people, I am indeed a clear warner to you, that you should worship Allah and*

Before them the people of Noah denied. Thus they denied Our servant and said, "Possessed!" And he was scorned. And he called upon his Lord, "Surely I am overpowered. So help me." Then We opened the gates of heaven with water overflowing. And We caused the earth to burst forth with springs. Thus the water met upon a matter truly determined. And We carried him upon ⌜a ship⌝ of planks and nails, running under Our Eyes—a reward for he who was disbelieved. And We have left it as a sign. Yet is there anyone who shall remember?

— The Quran, 54:9–15

fear Him, and obey me; He shall forgive you of your sins, and defer you to a stated term. Indeed, Allah's term, when it comes, cannot be deferred, if only you were to know." (71:1–4)

All but a few of Noah's people rejected his call, even his wife who remained behind with the unbelievers. They thought it implausible that God would select a human being from among themselves to convey His religion and commandments. The leaders and notables of his people urged the community to resist Noah's message, attack his person, ridicule his faith, and mock those who believed in him—intimidating the people into remaining loyal to the religion of their forefathers.

> *The noblemen of his people who disbelieved said, "This is only a human being like you. He wishes to attain excellence over you. Had Allah willed, He would have sent down angels. We never heard of this among our forefathers, the ancients. He is but a man in whom there is madness. So wait on him for a time."* (23:24–25)

They persisted in branding him as a deranged liar and threatened his life and well-being. *Thus they denied Our servant and said, "Possessed!" And he was scorned* (54:9). Noah turned to God, repining at his own weakness and humility among his people and entreating God's aid. *He said, "My Lord, support me against their denial of me"* (23:26).

God commanded him to continue his mission in the face of rejection and ridicule. Noah preached to his peo-

رب انصرني بما كذبون

My Lord, support me against their denial of me.

— The Quran, 23:26

ple in seemingly every manner, by night and by day, gently and severely, publicly and privately. He invited them to God's encompassing forgiveness and His blessings of security and abundance in this life and the Hereafter. He reminded them of God's majesty and power as displayed in the cycles and manifestations of nature. He warned them that evildoers earn the wrath of God in this world and eternally in the next. They nevertheless continued in their worship of idols apart from God and accelerated their offense against Noah. They threatened to ruin him, even to stone him, if he did not cease his "heretical" call—if he did not desist from criticizing their idols and the religion of their forefathers. *They said, "Surely, if you do not stop, O Noah, you shall be of those stoned"* (26:116).

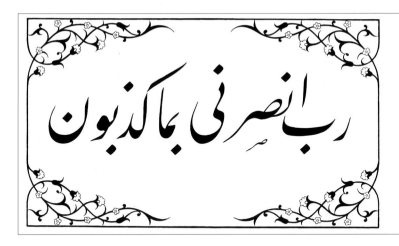

Most of Noah's people, young and old, remained opposed to his message and rejected him. At last, when he lost hope that they would ever respond to his call of faith, he asked God to deliver him, his family, and the few believers with him from the intrigues of his people. He said, "*My Lord, forgive me and my parents, and whomever enters my house as a believer, and the believing men and the believing women. And do not increase the wrongdoers except in ruin*" (71:28).

God comforted Noah and ordered him to prepare for the great flood by building the Ark. He revealed to Noah that the deluge would overtake all the wrongdoers among his people. Noah then began constructing the Ark

My Lord, forgive me and my parents, and whomever enters my house as a believer, and the believing men and the believing women. And do not increase the wrongdoers except in ruin.

— The Quran, 71:28

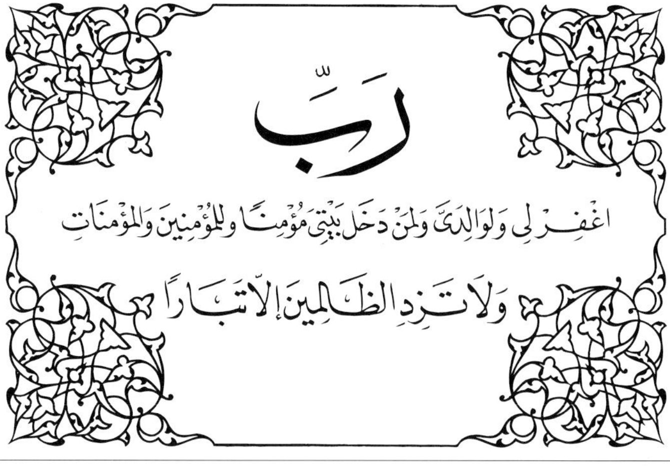

in the vicinity of his people's dwellings. Whenever a group passed by him, they mocked him and called him insane, for there were no great bodies of water near their land. He answered, "*If you mock us, we shall surely mock you as you mock us. Then you shall soon know to whom shall come a torment that will disgrace him and upon whom an enduring torment shall befall*" (11:38–39).

When God's decree came to pass, the gates of the heavens let forth rain in torrents and water gushed from the earth as fountains. God commanded Noah, along with his family and the believers, to board the Ark *in the name of Allah* (11:41). And He bade Noah to take with him a pair of every kind of creature. The wrongdoers, however, imagined that it was possible to seek protection from the water, but God had revealed to Noah that even the summits of the highest mountains would be submerged. One of Noah's sons chose to stay back with the disbelievers. Knowing that all who tarried would come to a tragic end, Noah felt the pangs of a father's love in his heart:

> *And Noah called to his son, who was in a place apart, "O my dear son! Embark with us! And be not with the disbelievers!" He said, "I shall take shelter in a mountain that will preserve me from the water!" He said, "Today there is no preserver from the command of Allah, except those upon whom He has mercy." And the waves came between them, so he was among the drowned. And it was said, "O earth, swallow your waters! And*

*Noah said, "My Lord, surely
they have disobeyed me and
followed those whose wealth
and children have not
increased them except in loss.
And they have plotted a very
great plot. And they have
said, 'Do not leave your gods!
Do not leave Wadd, nor
Suwâᶜa, nor Yaghûtha, or
Yaᶜûqa, or Nasra.'
And truly they have led
astray many. And do not
increase the wrongdoers except
in misguidance."
For their sinful ways, they
were drowned, then made to
enter a fire. So they did not
find for themselves helpers
apart from Allah.
And Noah said, "My Lord,
do not leave upon the earth
from the disbelievers any
dweller. For if You leave
them, they will lead astray
Your servants; and they do
not beget except wicked,
disbelieving ones.*

— The Quran, 71:21–27

رَبِّ
إِنِّي أَعُوذُ بِكَ أَنْ أَسْأَلَكَ مَا لَيْسَ لِي بِهِ عِلْمٌ
وَإِلَّا تَغْفِرْ لِي وَتَرْحَمْنِي أَكُن مِّنَ الْخَاسِرِينَ

Noah said, "My Lord, I seek refuge in You from asking You of what I have no knowledge. And if You do not forgive me and have mercy upon me, I shall be of the losers."

— The Quran, 11:47

O heaven, abate!" And the waters receded, and the matter was determined, and the Ark settled on al-Jûdî. And it was said, "Away with the wrongdoing people!"

And Noah called to his Lord, "O my Lord, my son is of my family, and Your promise is surely the truth. You are the most just of judges." He said, "O Noah, he is not of your family; it is an unrighteous deed. So do not ask Me of that which you have no knowledge. I admonish you so that you shall not be of the ignorant." He said, "My Lord, I seek refuge in You from asking You of what I have no knowledge. And if You do not forgive me and have mercy upon me, I shall be of the losers." (11:42–47)

Thus in the Ark did Noah and his band of believers remain. When Noah saw the heavens clear and the water recede into the earth, he anticipated the Ark's landing and appealed, "*My Lord, settle me in a blessed settlement, for You are the best to provide settlement*" (23:29).

God delivered Noah and those who believed in his message. Of their descendants, some were faithful to the memory of the Ark and the special hope and warning it carried; others were lost, until God sent the great patriarch Abraham عليه السلام, who revived Noah's message and advanced it throughout the known world of his day, establishing believing communities beyond his native Mesopotamia, in fertile Palestine and barren Arabia. It was in Makkah that Abraham raised the foundations of the civilizational center of monotheism for all time.

· Abraham ·

PROPHET ABRAHAM عليه السلام IS known as the Father of the Prophets and is among the most beloved of God (4:125). The Quran introduces him as a great messenger of resolve, an archetype of righteousness, and an exemplary model for believers. His life—a continual demonstration of pure reliance on and trust in God—was marked by genuine and unconditional submission to Him. Abraham always kept before him the promise of inevitably standing before his Lord for judgment in the Hereafter; thus he was in constant preparation for it. In every facet of his life, Abraham translated unwavering faith into profound action.

The Quran records Abraham's resolve to worship only God in the often repeated prayer which he uttered after publicly disparaging the idols that his forefathers and people worshipped.

> *Our Lord, on You do we rely; and to You do we turn; and to You is the ultimate destiny. Our Lord, do not put us to trial by those who disbelieve. And forgive us, our Lord. Indeed, it is You who are the Overpowering, the All-Wise.* (60:4–5)

And when Abraham said, "My Lord, show me how You give life to the dead." He said, "Do you not believe?" He said, "Yes! But it is for my heart to be calm." He said, "Then take four of the birds and draw them to you. Then put on each mountain a part of them. Then call them; they shall come to you rushing. And know that Allah is indeed overpowering, all-wise."

— The Quran, 2:260

God favored Abraham and the believers among his descendants by making them guides for humanity. He bestowed this honor upon Abraham as a reward for his steadfast obedience and for his recurrent migration solely for God's sake and in the hope of earning His pleasure.

After decades of ceaseless devotion to God, Abraham remained without offspring and yearned for righteous children. He prayed, "*My Lord, grant me righteous children*" (37:100). God answered his prayer and granted him Ishmael from his wife Hagar (Hâjar), and Isaac from his wife Sara (Sâra). God then directed Abraham to proceed from Palestine with his wife and infant son Ishmael to western Arabia, known as Hejaz, a rugged, sparsely populated land distant from the centers of culture. There he was to establish the symbolic center of monotheistic civilization that was to remain the locus and sacred sanctuary of all succeeding generations of believers until the end of time.

Abraham, knowing that the wisdom and logic of revelation supersedes that of human thought, heeded the call and established his family in what became Makkah the Blessed, where later he raised the foundations of the first House of God on earth, the sacred Kaʿba. There Abraham purified the surrounding sanctuary for the Prayer (*Ṣalât*) and Pilgrimage (*Ḥajj*) of all who would submit with love to the will of God. Abraham's son, Ishmael, also a prophet, stood by him, a full partner in carrying out the task of raising the foundations of the "Ancient House." As they worked, together they appealed to God:

> *Our Lord, make us obedient to You and, of our children, a community obedient to You. And show us our ⌜religious⌝ rites, and grant us repentance. Indeed, it is You who are the All-Relenting, the Mercy-Giving.* (2:128)

Even as father and son erected the edifice of the noble Kaʿba, stone by stone, this prayer envisioned the solidarity with which the benevolent Muslim family was to be built, cemented together by submission to God's commandments. Abraham and Ishmael dedicated themselves

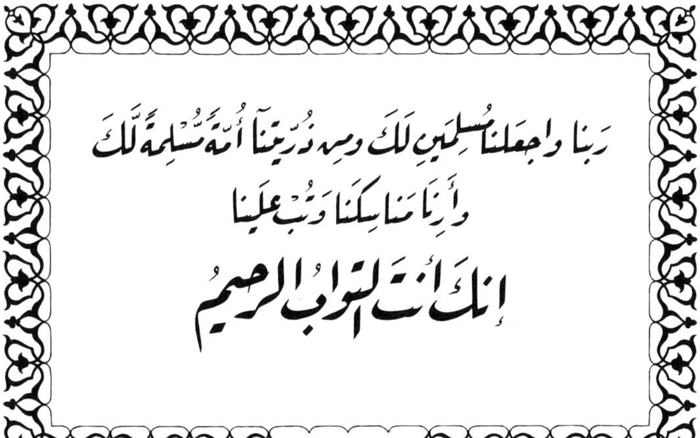
ربنا واجعلنا مسلمين لك ومن ذريتنا أمة مسلمة لك
وأرنا مناسكنا وتب علينا
إنك أنت التواب الرحيم
سورة البقرة الآية رقم ١٢٨

Our Lord, make us obedient to You and, of our children, a community obedient to You. And show us our ⌜religious⌝ rites, and grant us repentance. Indeed, it is You who are the All-Relenting, the Mercy-Giving.

— The Quran, 2:128

رَبِّ اجْعَلْ
هَٰذَا الْبَلَدَ آمِنًا
وَاجْنُبْنِي وَبَنِيَّ
أَن نَّعْبُدَ الْأَصْنَامَ

My Lord, make this land secure and keep me and my children away from worshipping idols.

— The Quran, 14:35

to accomplishing this act of devotion, hoping that their service in constructing this central House for the worship of God would be accepted and rewarded. Their sincerity closed the door on self-indulgence and on the vain whisperings of acclaim and admiration that might follow the completion of such a momentous task. Rather, Abraham venerated and appealed to his Maker, who hears all pleas, "*My Lord, make me steadfast in Prayer—and also my children. Our Lord, do accept my prayer*" (14:40).

We learn from Abraham and Ishmael that being of the community of faith goes well beyond uttering a declaration of belief in God. It manifests itself in one's resolve to dwell in the blessing of faith, to live by the essence of its commandments, and to seek God's help to strengthen and increase faith, so that it does not stagnate in the soul nor lose its warmth and light. It was this that Abraham sought when he prayed, "*Our Lord, make us obedient to You*" (2:128).

He and Ishmael invoked the blessings of faith upon their descendants, for they had tasted its joy and known its meaning; therefore, they asked God to perpetuate this spirit of observance in their offspring: "*And ˹make˺ of our children a community obedient to You*" (2:128). The supplication of the two prophets, moreover, stresses the importance of the natural family as the foundational human institution around which all other social structures revolve. They looked far into the future to secure through prayer and preparation an environment and way of life that would maintain the community of true belief; thus each emerging generation of this community would preserve and persevere in faith, until all would be assembled before the originator of the heavens and the earth.

Since the very essence of worship and submission to God is fulfilling His commandments and performing His bidding, Abraham and Ishmael asked God to teach them—and, through them, succeeding generations—how

Our Lord, on You do we rely; and to You do we turn; and to You is the ultimate destiny. Our Lord, do not put us to trial by those who disbelieve. And forgive us, our Lord. Indeed, it is You who are the Overpowering, the All-Wise.

— The Quran, 60:4–5

And when Abraham and Ishmael raised the foundation of the House: "Our Lord, do accept this from us. Indeed, it is You who are the All-Hearing, the All-Knowing. Our Lord, and make us obedient to You, and, of our children, a community obedient to You. And show us our ⌜religious⌝ rites, and grant us repentance. Indeed, it is You who are the All-Relenting, the Mercy-Giving. Our Lord, and send forth among them a messenger from them who shall recite to them Your verses and teach them the Book and the wisdom and purify them. Indeed, it is You who are the Overpowering, the All-Wise."

— The Quran, 2:127–29

to worship Him in a manner pleasing to Him. "*Our Lord, show us our ⌜religious⌝ rites*" (2:128). They were keenly aware of their need for God to prescribe for them worship that would purify their hearts from the taint of misdeeds that human beings commit knowingly and unknowingly. Thus, in their supplication there is an implicit acknowledgment of human limitations: "*Our Lord, indeed You know what we conceal and what we reveal. And nothing is concealed from Allah—neither in the earth nor in the heaven*" (14:38).

They acknowledged also that it is human to fall short, to falter in piety and virtue. Accordingly, they uttered this supplication for themselves and for their many successors in belief who would not attain their level of commitment and resolution. "*And grant us repentance. Indeed, it is You who are the All-Relenting, the Mercy-Giving*" (2:128). For Abraham often besought God's forgiveness, both for himself and for those whom he loved—especially with regard to the Day of Judgment. "*Our Lord, forgive me and my parents and the believers on the day the reckoning takes place*" (14:41).

Indeed, Abraham's supplications show three clear priorities: Securing personal salvation through obedience and worship; leading his family to God; and praying for the guidance of coming generations among the human family. These concerns are summed up in one of Abraham's most compelling and comprehensive prayers, preserved for all humanity in the Quran:

> *My Lord, grant me wise judgment. And join me with the righteous. And afford me true reverence among the later generations. And let me be of the inheritors of the Garden of Delight. And forgive my father, surely he has become of those astray. And do not disgrace me on the day all are raised up, a day when neither wealth nor sons shall be of benefit—except whoever comes to Allah with a sound heart.* (26:83–89)

Abraham prayed to be remembered for his good deeds and for his example of obeying God to live on long after him. He recognized that reward accrues to those whose good works outlive them and that blessings reach one whom the believers mention with reverence after his or her passing. Abraham aspired to be honored on the Day of the Standing, a day when each person shall come before God for final judgment and shall take his or her place among the ranks of human beings to which one truly belongs.

God more than fulfilled His servant's hope, for there is not a Prayer (*Ṣalât*) performed by a Muslim in which the name of Abraham, the Friend of God, goes unmentioned.

رَبِّ هَبْ لِي حُكْمًا وَأَلْحِقْنِي بِالصَّالِحِينَ ۝
وَاجْعَل لِّي لِسَانَ صِدْقٍ فِي الْآخِرِينَ ۝
وَاجْعَلْنِي مِن وَرَثَةِ جَنَّةِ النَّعِيمِ ۝
وَاغْفِرْ لِأَبِي إِنَّهُ كَانَ مِنَ الضَّالِّينَ ۝
وَلَا تُخْزِنِي يَوْمَ يُبْعَثُونَ ۝
يَوْمَ لَا يَنفَعُ مَالٌ وَلَا بَنُونَ ۝
إِلَّا مَنْ أَتَى اللَّهَ بِقَلْبٍ سَلِيمٍ ۝

My Lord, grant me wise judgment. And join me with the righteous. And afford me true reverence among the later generations. And let me be of the inheritors of the Garden of Delight. And forgive my father, surely he has become of those astray. And do not disgrace me on the day all are raised up, a day when neither wealth nor sons shall be of benefit—except whoever comes to Allah with a sound heart.

— The Quran, 26:83–89

• Lot •

CORRUPTION PREVAILED AMONG the people of Sodom, a city along the Jordan River in ancient Palestine. They committed acts of aggression against the wayfarer and the innocent, accosting them on the open road and robbing them. They made public display of sexual obscenity and flouted divine guidance. They neither honored their guests nor heeded admonition.

So God sent them Prophet Lot عليه السلام. He invited the people of Sodom to believe in their Lord and to recover their innate human sensibilities—and especially to cease the practice of homosexuality, which had become widespread among them. Lot called the people to stand against every manner of indecency. He warned them that moral decay leads to social degeneration and ruin in this life and in the Hereafter.

The Quran says that his people, nevertheless, belied the messengers:

> *Their brother Lot said to them, "Will you not be God-fearing? Indeed, I am a trustworthy messenger to you. So fear Allah and obey me. And I do not ask of you any reward for it. Indeed, my*

reward is only from the Lord of the Worlds. Do you approach only males of all the world and leave what your Lord has created for you in your wives? Rather, you are indeed an offending people." (26:160–66)

Repeatedly, Lot confronted his people about their unlawful sexual practices, which were without precedent, and their practice of highway robbery. He said, *"Indeed, you commit a lewdness with which no one has preceded you in all the worlds. Do you approach men, and cut the roadway, and commit in your gatherings abomination?"* (29:28–29).

His people met his staunch warnings with increased menace and violence. They threatened to exile him and his family members from the land unless he ceased denouncing and censuring of their acts. They rebuked him, saying, *"Surely, if you do not stop, O Lot, you shall be of the outcast"* (26:167). Yet he continued his reproach of them and showed the firmest resolve to persist in standing against their evil deeds. They responded with the call to expel Lot and his family from their home, *"for they are a people who purify themselves"* (7:82), as if clean living itself had become a crime among Sodom's corrupt. Thus, they flagrantly rebelled against God and challenged the authority of His commandments, even in the face of Lot's warning that an impending cataclysmic divine judgment would fall upon them. They mocked Lot, saying, *"Bring*

And Lot, We gave him wisdom and knowledge, and delivered him from the town that had been doing base deeds. Indeed, they were an evil people, unrighteous. And We entered him into Our mercy. He was indeed of the righteous.

— The Quran, 21:74–75

to us the torment of Allah if you are of the truthful" (29:29). At this decisive juncture, Lot turned to his Lord and appealed, "*My Lord, support me against the corrupting people*" (29:30).

God sent His angels to Lot to support him, for God hears the call of every supplicant. Since they appeared in human form, the noble prophet did not know that they were angels but thought them to be travelers and offered them the hospitality of his home. Thereafter, Lot's people surrounded his residence, bent on sexually assaulting the newcomers. Unaware that his guests had come bearing the wrath of God, Lot protested the depraved lusts of the Sodomites, admonishing them that God had created hu-

My Lord, support me against the corrupting people.

— The Quran, 29:30

man beings as males and females so that men and women could enjoy one another as husbands and wives, and warning them that God forbade homosexuality as a deviant inclination. Yet the wicked of Sodom heeded only their passions, aflame with the possibility of sexually assaulting the strangers. Their habituated indulgence in perversion had permeated their very natures to a loathsome extent. At that instant, God's decree to punish them became imminent. The Quran records these desperate moments:

> *And when Our messengers came to Lot, he was troubled over them, and he became helplessly distressed for them, and he said, "This is an intense day!" And his people came rushing toward him, when before they had been doing misdeeds. He said, "O my people, these are my daughters; they are purer for you, so fear Allah and do not dishonor me concerning my guests. Is there not among you a rightly guided man?" They said, "Indeed, you know well that we have no right to your daughters, and indeed you know well what we desire." He said, "If only I had strength over you or that I could take shelter with a mighty defender!"* (11:77–80)

Lot offered the assailants a lawful alternative to their deviant desires, suggesting that they take his daughters in marriage, proclaiming this to be a "purer," righteous option. His statement addressed the imbalance that had stricken the community as a result of men abandoning their wives and the institution of marriage.

And Lot is indeed of the messengers. When We delivered him and his family all together—except an old woman among those who lingered behind, then We demolished the others. And indeed you pass by them by morning and by night. Will you not then understand?

— The Quran, 37:133–38

The Sodomites categorically rejected Lot's final admonition and plea. They had chosen their way and therewith sealed their catastrophic fate. When Lot saw their intransigence, he turned to God, the All-Preserving, and cried out, *"My Lord, deliver me and my family from what they do"* (26:169).

The angels of destruction then revealed to him their identity and mission:

> *They said, "O Lot, indeed we are your Lord's messengers. They shall never reach you. So journey with your family during a portion of the night—and let no one among you look back—except your wife; for indeed, whatever strikes them shall strike her. Indeed, their appointed time is the morning. Is not the morning surely near?"* (11:81)

My Lord, deliver me and my family from what they do.

— The Quran, 26:169

God saved Lot and his family, except his wife, who was destroyed along with her people; for God's angels leveled the city to lowliness and buried it under a shower of marked clay-stones.

> *So when Our command came to pass, We made its uppermost its lowermost. And We rained upon it stones of hardened clay clustered—marked by your Lord. And they are surely not far off from the wrongdoers.* (11:82–83)

The life of this noble prophet is a call for every person to stand in the name of God on the side of faith, morality, and family, and to defend the right of the community to be free from deviant relations and practices that threaten the welfare of society.

And Lot, when he said to his people, "Do you commit such lewdness that no one has preceded you with it in all the worlds? Indeed, you approach men in lust rather than women. Indeed, you are an excessive people."

— The Quran, 7:80–81

· Joseph ·

A GROUP OF Companions of the Prophet Muḥammad ﷺ once asked him, "Who is the noblest of people?" He said, "The noblest before Allah is the most God-fearing of them."

They then said, "It is not of this that we ask." The Prophet ﷺ answered, "The noblest of people, then, is the son of the Prophet of God, son of the Prophet of God, son of the Friend of God."

The story of the noble Prophet Joseph عليه السلام, son of Jacob, son of Isaac, son of Abraham, is the longest biographical narrative of the Quran, comprising the whole of its twelfth chapter, which bears Joseph's name. The *fairest of stories* opens with a youthful Joseph recounting to his father the vision he had seen in a wonderful dream. Joseph said, "*My dear father, I saw eleven stars, and the sun and the moon—I saw them bowing down before me*" (12:4).

Jacob reassured his son, telling him that God would favor him and bless the House of Jacob by selecting him, as He did his forefathers, to invite people to worship the one true Lord and to guide them to His way. The portents of Joseph's vision, however, troubled his loving father, for he well understood human frailty. So he instructed Joseph not to tell it to his brothers for fear that Satan might prompt them to commit some evil against him.

Yet the decree of the All-Knowing, the All-Wise had gone forth, and soon Joseph would be taken from the pastoral environs of Palestine to the center of the ancient world, Egypt. Envy and evil whisperings enticed the brothers of Joseph to conspire to take his life, though he was but a boy. After deliberation, they resolved instead to cast him into the darkness of a well along a caravan route, where he would likely be discovered by merchants and carried off to some faraway land. And indeed a caravan's scout did find young Joseph in the well; later the caravan sold Joseph into slavery for a paltry price to the household of Egypt's high governor, initiating a succession of ordeals through which Joseph—as boy, adolescent, man, and leader—would pass in the crucible of cosmopolitan life.

As a strikingly handsome young man enslaved in a strange land, away from his parents and home, Joseph faced the mighty test of temptation when the wife of the governor tried to seduce him. After literally fleeing from her immoral clutches, he later again resisted her passions

And God prevails in His affairs, but most people do not know.

— The Quran, 12:21

"Joseph, you who are truthful, explain for us the [dream of] seven fat cows being eaten by seven lean ones, and the seven green ears of corn and others withered, that I may return to the people, so they may know." He said, "You shall plant seven years diligently. But what you have harvested leave in the ear, except a little from which you will eat. Then shall come after this seven severe years that will consume what you have reserved for them, except a little from what you will store. Then shall come after this a year in which people are relieved, and in which they will be pressing [grapes]." And the king said, "Bring him to me."

— The Quran, 12:46–50

and those of the ladies of Egyptian high society. For this, Joseph was unjustly threatened by the governor's wife with imprisonment, where, she warned, Joseph would be all but forgotten.

It was at this crucial point—in a room surrounded by the unveiled desires of Egypt's most *elite* ladies—that Joseph took his stand for the godly way of life, an incident that has ever since endured as the epitome of moral resolve. The dignified prayer that Joseph uttered in that room, moreover, proclaimed clearly and eternally that moral rectitude is an integral part (and result) of sincere belief in God, and that immoral behavior of every kind is ignorance in action.

> *[Joseph] said, "My Lord, prison is more beloved to me than what they call me to. For if You do not turn their cunning away from me, I may incline toward them and become of the ignorant." So his Lord answered him. Thus He turned away from him their cunning. Indeed, He is the All-Hearing, the All-Knowing.* (12:33–34)

Had it not been for his remembrance of God and adherence to the godly standards of morality, Joseph would have been a thing forgotten. But God never neglects the reward of those who excel in good. He vindicated Joseph from false charges and established him in the land as keeper of the treasury of all Egypt. From the depths of adversity, trial, and loss, God raised Joseph to the heights of authority and provision. The king of Egypt appointed Joseph as the authority over the granaries of the land, so as to lead Egypt through the severe drought that he prophesied. Facing one of the greatest challenges of his life, Joseph indeed guided Egypt through times of scarcity to days of plenty, which saved, as well, the surrounding lands that depended on harvest of the Nile's fertile soil. His disciplined governance preserved the nation's prosperity and influence.

Through every test, Joseph remained constant in turning to his Lord in prayer and remembrance. He invited people, even in the darkest dungeon of circumstance, to worship the Almighty, the one and only God, and to abandon whatever false deities they feared, called upon, or worshipped.

Joseph's suffering, after being forcibly separated from his homeland and family, did not hinder him. Rather, the noble prophet saw in adversity an opportunity to serve God, thus changing the flow of history, by His leave. Joseph realized great success and authority; his errant brothers repented to him. And upon their reunification in Egypt, they, along with his mother and father, bowed down before him out of love and reverence—the fulfillment of the celestial portents he had seen in his vision

They said, "Our father, what is with you that you do not trust us with Joseph, though truly we mean him well? Send him with us tomorrow, to picnic and play, and certainly we shall safeguard him." He said, "It truly grieves me that you would take him away. And I fear the wolf will eat him while you are heedless of him." They said, "If the wolf should eat him, while we are a band, then surely we are losers!" So when they left with him and resolved to put him in the depths of the well, We revealed to him, "You shall surely tell them of this affair of theirs when they are not aware."

— The Quran, 12:11–15

Originator of the heavens and the earth, You are my patron in this world and the Hereafter. Take my soul as a Muslim, and join me with the righteous.

— The Quran, 12:101

فاطر السموات والأرض

أنت وليّ فى الدنيا والآخرة توفّنى مسلما وألحقنى بالصالحين

years before. Yet even at that culminating moment, Joseph remembered his Lord, the Creator of the heavens and earth, asking Him to complete His great favor upon him when he would finally endure the trial that no soul shall evade:

> *Originator of the heavens and the earth, You are my patron in this world and the Hereafter. Take my soul as a Muslim, and join me with the righteous.* (12:101)

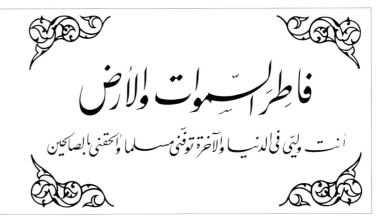

• Job •

THE QURAN CALLS every human being to receive the challenge of life with resolve and to remain dauntless before travails that imperil health, wealth, and beloved persons or possessions. Indeed, it bids one, even in hard times or in desperate moments, to hope in the promise of the future, here and in the Hereafter. *O you who believe, seek help through patience and Prayer. Indeed, Allah is with the patient* (2:153). And then:

> *We shall surely try you with something of fear and hunger and loss of wealth and life and crops. So give glad tidings to those who have patience—those who when an affliction afflicts them, they say, "Indeed, we belong to Allah, and indeed to Him we are returning." Upon them are prayers from their Lord and mercy, and it is they who are the guided.* (2:155–57)

The Quran, in portraying the champions of the godly way of life, repeatedly underlines the virtue of patience. But none personifies this quality like Job عليه السلام, whose mention through the generations has called forth the qualities of endurance among the suffering and hope for deliverance from calamity. Appropriately, Prophet Job's name in Arabic, Ayyûb, literally means "ever penitent." Job was a

And We granted 'Abraham', Isaac and Jacob, all have We guided, and Noah have We guided before, and of his children 'We have guided' David, Solomon, Job, Joseph, Moses, and Aaron. And thus do We recompense those who excel in good.

— The Quran, 6:84

descendant of Abraham and most probably lived before the time of Moses. God blessed Job with vitality, wealth, and many children. His benevolence to family, friends, and the needy was well known among his people, whom he constantly called to heed their covenant with God and to give thanks for His plentiful blessings upon them.

But when God tested Job with a severe protracted illness, Job found no one among those he used to care for or counsel to tend his person or his assets. Although his wife sought to endure alongside him, even she succumbed under the strain of a tremendous trial. Left virtually alone, Job's abundant lands and livestock were lost or destroyed, and his wealth vanished. Riven with an agonizing disease and smitten with poverty, Job endured the yet more painful calamity of abandonment by his own people and loved ones.

Job's illness persisted for a long time. During his suffering, evil whispers stormed his soul, for Satan desired to push this exemplary worshipper over the precipice of despair, to fill him with discontent for his people, himself, and, most of all, his Lord: *And mention Our servant Job when he called upon his Lord: "Indeed, Satan has touched me with weariness and torment"* (38:41).

Yet this prophet of patience, as the Quran characterizes

him, did not waver in his trust of God but remained unshakably hopeful of God's succor and certain of His power to heal all afflictions. As an exhortation to Prophet Muḥammad and to all believers, God said of Job in the Quran, *We found him patient—a commendable servant. Indeed, he was ever penitent* (38:44).

If all in the heavens and earth were to turn aside from Job in his moment of need, Job would not turn away from God, knowing as he did that God is with the steadfast and He is the Restorer, the Faithful.

> *And ˹remember˺ Job, when he called out to his Lord: "Surely harm has touched me, and You are the most merciful of the merciful!" So We answered him, and We removed whatever harm was upon him. And We gave him his family and, with them, the like of them—a mercy from near Us and a reminder for the worshippers.* (21:83–84)

The Quran, moreover, describes God's answer to Job's plea and the means by which God returned him to health. God commanded him to strike the earth with his foot where he lay or stood; thereupon a fountain sprang forth as a remedial bath and a curative drink:

> *˹Allah said,˺ "Stamp with your foot. This is a cool bath and drink." And We granted to him his family and, with them, the like of them—a mercy from Us and a reminder for people possessed of understanding.* (38:42–43)

وَأَيُّوبَ إِذْ نَادَىٰ رَبَّهُ
أَنِّي مَسَّنِيَ الضُّرُّ وَأَنتَ أَرْحَمُ الرَّاحِمِينَ

And ˹remember˺ Job, when he called out to his Lord: "Surely harm has touched me, and You are the most merciful of the merciful!"

— The Quran, 21:83

But if you patiently persevere, it is surely better for those who are patient. And be patient. And your patience does not endure except by God.

— The Quran, 16:126–27

God, the All-Merciful, restored Job's health and bestowed upon him more blessings than he had held prior to his test.

Then God ordered Job, "*And take with your hand a bundle of basil, then strike with it; and do not violate* ⌜*your oath*⌝" (38:44). This verse suggests that during the distress of his illness Job had made an oath to punish his wife for some offense. But God instructed him instead to keep his oath by brushing his wife with a bundle of basil, in order not to inflict pain on her. Some Muslim commentators have elaborated dramatically on this incident (most probably based upon the Old Testament narrative, the account of which differs markedly in both focus and length from that of the Quran). It is noteworthy that the Quran did not specify the circumstances that provoked Job's solemn resolution; for the point of recounting this aspect of Job's story is not to transcribe events or satisfy curiosity, but to emphasize the importance of maintaining peace and harmony within the family and the sanctity of a sacred oath.

The Quran emphasizes that trials are an inherent part of earthly existence, by which the patient are elevated as enduring models for others to follow. It is God who *created death and life to try you, as to which of you are best in deed* (67:2). Patiently withstanding trials, therefore, leads to honor and reward from God in this life and in the Hereafter.

Every circumstance in life—whether of hardship or leisure, sickness or health, poverty or wealth, weakness or empowerment—constitutes a kind of trial. So tribulations should not be viewed as a sign of God's wrath or as forerunners of eternal misery. God has promised that no single circumstance, especially those entailing difficulty, shall endure permanently. *So indeed, with hardship, there is ease. Indeed, with hardship, there is ease* (94:5–6). All the prophets displayed unsurpassed trust in this principle, irrespective of the varied episodes and contingencies they faced.

God affirmed Job's patience and praised him in the Quran in the same manner He did Solomon, as a *commendable servant. Indeed, he was ever penitent* (38:30, 44). Just as Solomon's miraculous powers and vast kingdom did not cause him to transgress or forget the remembrance of his Lord, neither did Job's grave affliction and loss of worldly possessions break his spirit of trusting and relying upon God.

To an important extent, moreover, the stringency of a test resides in one's ability to bear its burden, as well as in the circumstances with which one is faced at the time—

If you are thankful, I shall increase you ⌜in goodness⌝.

— The Quran, 14:7

Indeed, humankind is in utter loss—except those who believe and do righteous deeds, and exhort one another to the truth and exhort one another to patience.

— The Quran, 103:2–3

though there is no difficulty or condition beyond the help of God. Indeed, God's deliverance from trial comes in varied ways and is nearer than perceived. Further, the Quran's narrative of Prophet Job highlights the importance of the human role in bringing about relief from trial. God did not directly remove Job's sickness instantaneously; instead, He commanded Job to take the first step, as it were, by striking the ground with his foot, whereupon, by the command of God, the curative waters gushed and the delightful drink streamed.

Deliverance from trial, for the believer, occasions profound gratitude to God, who alone brings relief and repose. Yet one should never neglect turning to God in times of ease, for the Prophet ﷺ said, "Whoever would be gladdened by God's answer to his pleas in moments of hardship or affliction, let him pray much in calm."[30]

• Shuʿayb •

THE PROPHET SHUʿAYB ﷺ was commissioned by God to warn and guide the Arabs of Midian, of the northwestern region of the Arabian peninsula. He most likely lived after Joseph, and before Aaron and Moses.[31]

Shuʿayb's people had abandoned the monotheism taught by the Father of the Prophets, Abraham. They took to worshipping a tree known as al-Ayka, to which they paid ceremonious homage. The leaders of Midian required every member of the community to perform the rituals that had evolved through the generations in veneration of al-Ayka, and they strictly forbade the free practice of religion. Worship of any other kind, in fact, was considered heresy, that is, against the ways of their forefathers.

For all their strictness about maintaining the purity of their animist customs, the people of Shuʿayb showed no ethical restraint in their material lives or in their treatment of the natural environment. Like the people of Sodom to whom Lot was sent (and whose story invariably precedes the mention of Shuʿayb throughout the Quran), the

So when Our command came to pass, We delivered Shuʿayb and those who believed with him with mercy from Us. And the Shout seized those who did wrong; thus they became prostrate in their dwellings, as though they had never flourished therein. Most surely, away with Midian!

— The Quran, 11:94–95

Midianites had institutionalized corruption to such a degree that their iniquitous behavior became the societal norm, while righteousness was an offense punishable by banishment and ruin. In their transactions, they gave neither full measure nor whole weights. They also withheld goods that were the lawful property of others. They corrupted the natural purity of things upon the earth, robbed travelers along the road, and deterred people from the straight path of God.

Bearing the same message of every prophet of God before and after him, Shuʿayb called the Midianites to "*worship Allah. You have no other God but Him*" (7:85). He called them to halt the spread of corruption throughout the land and to desist from plundering wayfarers on the highway. He admonished them to be fair in their commercial transactions, to ensure that their standards and scales registered a just balance. Most pointedly, Shuʿayb asked the powerful among his people to give others the freedom to choose faith in God, if they so desired, without threat of retribution to their persons, properties, and livelihood, and to let God be their judge.

As Lot's people decried him and his family as "*a people who purify*" (27:56), so Shuʿayb's opponents mocked his reproach of their cheating and thieving, saying, "*Indeed, you are surely forbearing and rightly guided"* (11:87), as if to impugn these virtues as naive. Nor was the Midianite solution to Shuʿayb's message less brutal than that of the Sodomites—whose chastisement, Shuʿayb warned them, had not been in the too-remote past. *The noblemen of his people, who became arrogant, said, "We shall expel you, O Shuʿayb, and those who believe with you, from our town, unless you return to our ways"* (7:88).

Such is the logic of disbelief—to silence, banish, or intimidate for the purpose of suppressing interaction. The campaign of vilification and terror began. They accused Shuʿayb of sorcery and threatened his followers, saying, "*Surely, if you follow Shuʿayb, indeed you shall then be losers*" (7:90). But the prayer of Shuʿayb had already gone forth: "*Our Lord, judge between us and our people with the truth—*

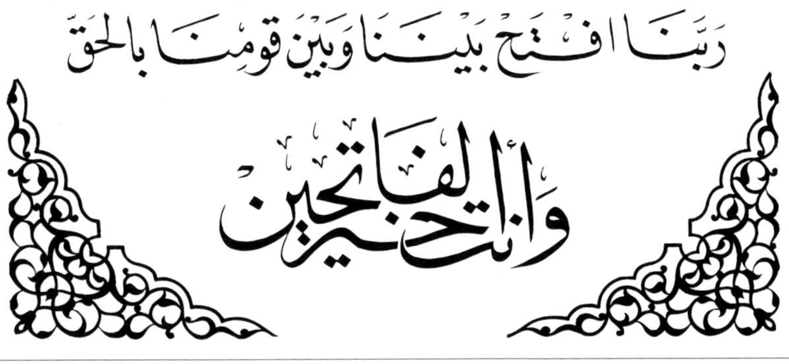

Our Lord, judge between us and our people with the truth—for You are the best of those who judge.

— The Quran, 7:89

Has not the tiding of those before them come to them, the people of Noah, and ʿÂd, and Thamûd, and the people of Abraham, and the inhabitants of Midian, and al-Mu'tafikât? Their messengers came to them with clear proofs. And it was not for Allah to wrong them. Rather, they were wronging themselves.

— The Quran, 9:70

for You are the best of those who judge" (7:89). Indeed, the judgment of God is decisive:

> *Then the convulsion seized them, and they became prostrate in their dwelling. Those who had denied Shuʿayb became as though they had never flourished therein. Those who had denied Shuʿayb, it was they who were the losers.* (7:91–92)

• Jonah •

AS STATED PREVIOUSLY, the Quran calls us to reflect on the lives of the prophets and messengers and to learn from their real-life experiences and trials. In doing so, it is important to keep in mind the following questions: What was the response of each prophet to the command of his Lord? How did each fulfill the trust of God and convey His covenant to the people? What was the response of the people to their prophets? How were the lives of the prophets and of their people affected by the call to serve the one, true Creator of the heavens and the earth?

Jonah عليه السلام, son of Amittai (Yûnus ibn Matta), is unique among the prophets. God sent him to the city of Nineveh (Nînawa) in northern Iraq, a community of a hundred thousand or more (37:147). But Jonah became embittered when his people turned away from his call and mocked him. Despairing that they would ever believe, Jonah determined to end his mission of inviting his people to serve the one and only God, and thus abandoned them. Jonah never thought that God would constrain him in any way for forsaking his people. Yet God indeed tried

> لَا إِلَٰهَ إِلَّا أَنتَ
> سُبْحَانَكَ
> إِنِّي كُنتُ مِنَ الظَّالِمِينَ
>
> *There is no God but You! Glory be to You! Indeed, I was of the wrongdoers!*
>
> — The Quran, 21:87

Jonah with a test more difficult than the rejection he had received from his people. Though it put his life in peril, it saved him, and the inhabitants of Nineveh, from incurring God's displeasure.

Having renounced his mission to the people of Nineveh, Jonah boarded a ship for a distant shore. Thereafter, storm clouds gathered; the wind blew violently, and the waves of the sea swelled like mountains. The people on board the ship regarded the sudden tempest as an ill-omen, so they cast lots and finally determined to throw Jonah into the sea. The Quran relates that a *whale gulped him—and he was blameworthy* (37:142). In the deep of the water—and in the belly of the whale—Jonah did not cease turning to God, beseeching Him and seeking His help:

> *Then [Jonah] called out in the darknesses, "There is no God but You! Glory be to You! Indeed, I was of the wrongdoers!" Then We answered him and delivered him from anguish. And thus do We deliver the believers.* (21:87–88)

Indeed, in answering Jonah's prayer, God not only delivered him from the belly of the whale and from drowning at sea, but He saved Jonah's community as well, sparing them from the devastation He had sent upon their predecessors; for after Jonah returned to them, they believed and turned to God:

> *If only there had been a town that believed, so its faith would have benefited it, besides the people of Jonah! When they believed, We removed from them the torment of disgrace in the life of this world, and We gave them enjoyment for a time.* (10:98)

It is noteworthy that very early in the mission of Prophet Muḥammad, God's peace and blessings be upon him, the Quran mentions Jonah's story as an exhortation to the Prophet ﷺ to remain steadfast and to persevere in the face of the rejection of his people and their belying of him. God forbade the Prophet ﷺ from repeating what his brother Jonah had done:

> *So be patient for the judgment of your Lord. And do not be like the Companion of the Whale, when he called out while he was distressed. Had not a blessing from his Lord reached him, he would have been cast into the wilderness, being condemned. But his Lord had chosen him, and He placed him among the righteous.* (68:48–50)

Jonah's experience ultimately admonishes believers of every era not to despair of inviting others to God; for those who at first oppose faith may be destined to become adherents of its way and bearers of its message. His life serves to remind people not to give up in calling others to belief, and to do so with open hearts and minds,

And indeed Jonah is surely of the messengers. When he ran away to the laden ship, he then partook in drawing lots. Thus he became of the castaways. Then the whale gulped him, and he was blameworthy. Yet had he not been of those who give glory, he would have remained in its belly until the day all are raised up. Then We hurled him into the wilderness while he was sick. And We caused to grow over him a tree of gourds. And We sent him to a hundred thousand, or they were more. Then they believed; thus We gave them enjoyment for a time.

— The Quran, 37:139–48

Then We shall deliver Our messengers and those who believe. And it is indeed a right upon Us to deliver the believers. Say, "O you people, if you are in doubt about my religion, then I shall not worship those whom you worship apart from God. But rather, I worship God who takes your souls, and I have been commanded to be of the believers."

— The Quran, 10:103–04

never doubting the human capacity to awaken at any moment and turn to God. In this light, the Companion Ibn ʿAbbâs related that once in his youth he was instructed by the Prophet ﷺ :

> Young man, indeed, I shall teach you words ʿof wisdomʾ: Be mindful of Allah, and Allah will protect you. Be mindful of Allah, and you will find Him in front of you. If you ask, ask of Allah; if you seek help, seek help of Allah. Know that if the Community were to gather together to benefit you with anything, it would benefit you only with something that Allah had already prescribed for you, and that if it gathered together to harm you with anything, it would harm you only with something Allah had already prescribed for you. The pens have been lifted and the pages have dried.[32]

In another transmission it is reported as follows:

> Be mindful of Allah, and you will find Him before you. Know Allah in prosperity, and He will know you in adversity. Know that what has passed you by was not going to befall you, and that what has befallen you was not going to pass you by. And know that victory comes with patience, relief with affliction, and ease with hardship.[33]

Prophet Muḥammad, peace be upon him, always remembered Jonah with respect and reverence, and he warned those deficient in understanding against any inclination to do otherwise. He said, "Let no worshipper say that I ʿMuḥammadʾ in the sight of God am better than

Jonah, son of Amittai."[34] Moreover, the Prophet ﷺ instructed the believers of every generation to avail themselves of the prayer Jonah uttered when he was in the whale's belly: "*There is no God but You! Glory be to You! Indeed, I was of the wrongdoers*!" (21:87). The Prophet ﷺ added, "For never does a Muslim ask anything of his Lord with this prayer without Allah answering him."[35]

Indeed, you are only to warn whoever follows the Reminder and fears the All-Merciful in the unseen. So give him glad tidings of forgiveness and a generous reward.

— The Quran, 36:11

Moses

THE QURAN DETAILS the significant phases of the life and mission of Prophet Moses عليه السلام in parts of at least twenty-five suras.[36] Born in Egypt when Pharaoh had condemned the infant males of the Children of Israel to death, Moses' mother, inspired by God, placed him in a basket and sent him down the River Nile. As the providence of God would have it, he was to be reared in the palace of Pharaoh himself.

By the time Moses reached young adulthood, God had blessed him with remarkable physical strength and keen intellectual discernment. Moses realized the disgrace the Israelites suffered under Pharaoh's tyranny and one day left the palace discreetly and entered the capital to see for himself the condition of the people. There he came upon an Egyptian sentinel chastising an Israelite. When the Israelite saw Moses—either recognizing his apparent strength or perhaps having heard among his people of Moses' true identity—he appealed to him for help.

Seeing firsthand the monstrous face of oppression, Moses became incensed and struck the antagonist soldier. A single blow, and the soldier fell dead on the ground. When Moses beheld the enormity of his action, he recovered his senses and realized that this confrontation had all along been the work of Satan. He turned immediately to God, seeking His forgiveness and pardon, and said, "*My Lord, I have indeed wronged myself, so forgive me*" (28:16). God answered his prayer, for indeed, He is the All-Forgiving, the Mercy-Giving.

When Pharaoh's supporters heard the news of Moses' action, they wanted revenge and feared the spread of rebellion among the long-subjugated Israelites. So they determined to eliminate Moses. One among the elite, how-

My Lord, I have indeed wronged myself, so forgive me.

— The Quran, 28:16

My Lord, by what You have graced me with, I shall never be an upholder of the trespassers.

— The Quran, 28:17

ever, sympathized with Moses and his mission (possibly the same man of Pharaoh's court who had concealed his faith in Moses and in the Lord of Moses, as mentioned in the Quran (40:28)). He hurried to Moses to warn him that Pharaoh's retainers were conspiring to kill him and advised him to leave the city, assuring Moses of his sincere counsel.

Under the threat of death, Moses readied himself to depart Egypt in stealth, fearing imminent capture and the peering eyes of Pharaoh's many informants. So he turned again to God, the source of all security, to save him from the injustice of those who had transgressed His Law: "*My Lord, deliver me from the wrongdoing people*" (28:21). God saved him, guiding him eastward through the Sinai to the northwestern part of the Arabian peninsula and the oasis of Midian.

When he reached the wells of Midian, he saw a group of shepherds watering their herds and two young women standing apart from the men, waiting to water their own flock. Moses went among the shepherds for water on behalf of the women and helped them tend their flock, learning from them that they were the daughters of an aged and noble believer. After rendering them this assistance, Moses reclined in the shade of a tree and remembered his own profound need for help. He cried, *"My Lord, of whatever good You send down to me, surely I am needful"* (28:24).

God answered his prayer. One of the women whom he had aided at the well, the Quran relates, returned walking bashfully, offering an invitation for him to meet their aged father. The patriarch listened to Moses' story and then extended asylum to him and offered him the hand of one of his daughters in marriage, thereby contracting him to shepherd his flocks for eight years. Moses accepted the offer and dwelled with them as a shepherd in Midian until God summoned him to the holy valley of Ṭuwâ, where He spoke to Moses and bestowed upon him the mantle of prophethood. God ordered him to go to Pharaoh, to summon him and his people to the worship of God alone, and to lead the Children of Israel out of bondage and into the bond of service to their Creator (28:23–28).

When Moses had received the command to invite one of the most tyrannical rulers of all time to submit to the Lord of the Worlds, he turned to God, beseeching Him for the courage, composure, and steadfastness needed to carry out this tremendous mission. He sought to face Pharaoh without trepidation and asked God to give him in his brother Aaron a true partner in his task, someone

And has the account of Moses come to you? When he saw a fire, he then said to his family, "Remain here. I have noticed a fire. Perhaps I shall bring you from it a firebrand, or I shall find at the fire guidance." So when he came to it, he was called, "O Moses! Indeed, I am your Lord. So take off your sandals; you are in the holy valley, Ṭuwâ. And I have chosen you, so hear what is being revealed: I am, indeed, I am God! There is no God but Me; so worship Me and establish the Prayer for My remembrance. Indeed, the Hour is coming—I shall keep it hidden—so that every soul is recompensed for what it strives. So let no one who does not believe in it and who follows his whim turn you away from it or you shall fall into doom."

— The Quran, 20:9–17

And Pharaoh said [to his minister], "O Hâmân, build for me a tower so that I may reach the spheres, the spheres of the heavens, so that I may rise to look upon the God of Moses. For I surely think he is a liar." And thus were Pharaoh's evil deeds made alluring to him. And he was barred from the path. And Pharaoh's scheme is in nothing but ruin. And he who believed said, "O my people, follow me. I shall guide you to the rightly guided path. O my people, this worldly life is but a passing enjoyment. And the Hereafter is the abode of permanence."

— The Quran, 40:36–39

to share in the fulfillment of the commandments of God and in the glorification and remembrance of his Lord. He said, "*My Lord, expand for me my chest and ease for me my mission; and release the knot from my tongue, so they understand my words*" (20:25–28).

Moses and Aaron confronted Pharaoh and presented him and the people of Egypt with the miraculous signs with which God had empowered them. The Quran relates the story of their dramatic challenge to Pharaoh's court magicians and how they prevailed over them by God's leave. Yet Pharaoh and his chiefs rejected their prophethood and threatened them and the Children of Israel with death. So Moses turned to God to avert Pharaoh's impending violence, acknowledging that security and safety are with Him alone. Moses said, "*On Allah do we rely. Our Lord, make us not a trial to the wrongdoing people, and deliver us by Your mercy from the disbelieving people*" (10:85–86).

Moses and Aaron led the Children of Israel out of Pharaoh's bondage to the sea, where God parted the waters to secure their safe passage. He then drowned Pharaoh and his troops, who were in swift pursuit, and saved the Children of Israel in their exodus from Egypt to the Holy Land—a destination they did not reach in

Moses' lifetime. Instead, God banished them to wander in the desert for a generation as punishment for their repeated flouting of His commandments and covenant. This they did after He had delivered them to security, freedom, and provision and had shown them great signs and miracles.

Their fatal trespass came after the exodus, when Moses entrusted Aaron to guide the affairs of the Children of Israel while he was in retreat for forty days to receive the commandments of his Lord. In his absence, they rebelled and fashioned a graven image of a calf from their gold and jewelry, ascribing divine attributes to it in defiance of God. When Aaron warned them against this heinous transgression and reminded them of God's blessings upon them, they threatened to kill him.

رب اغفر لي ولأخي وأدخلنا في رحمتك
وأنت أرحم الراحمين

My Lord, forgive me and my brother and enter us into Your mercy—for You are the most merciful of the merciful.

— The Quran, 7:151

And We caused the Children of Israel to pass through the sea. Then they came upon a people devoting themselves to some idols they had. They said, "O Moses, make for us a god as there are gods for them!" He said, "Indeed, you are a people who are ignorant!" Indeed, all that they are engaged in shall be ruined. And falsehood is what they were doing. He said, "Shall I seek for you a god other than God while He has favored you over all the world?"

— The Quran, 7:138–40

Inspired anew with the resolve to implement God's sacred law, Moses returned with the tablets of the Torah containing God's guidance for the Children of Israel. Enraged with what his eyes beheld—his newly delivered people worshipping an idol—Moses castigated the Children of Israel for breaching their covenant to worship God alone. He then cast down the tablets and seized Aaron by the beard in anger and sorrow. When it became clear that his brother had exerted his utmost and was about to be killed in trying to prevent the transgression of their community, Moses relented.

The fear that God's wrath might overtake him and his brother along with the wrongdoers welled up in Moses' heart, so he turned to God, appealing for His immeasurable clemency, "*My Lord, forgive me and my brother and enter us into Your mercy—for You are the most merciful of the merciful*" (7:151).

God, the Everlasting Refuge, answered Moses' prayer and honored his remembrance and that of Aaron for all time in the Quran. God commanded therein:

> *And mention in the Book Moses. Indeed, he was chosen, and he was a messenger, a prophet. We called him from the right side of Mount al-Ṭûr, and We brought him near for close converse. And We granted him, of Our mercy, his brother Aaron, a prophet.* (19:51–53)

• *David* •

PRAYING FOR TRANQUILITY in the heat of battle may seem unusual, if not contradictory. Yet in reality—when life and death, victory and defeat hang in the balance—it is not but a sign of courage. A party of believers among the Children of Israel voiced this special courage in an impassioned prayer before the battle between David عليه السلام and Goliath, in preparation for confronting their fearsome, heavily armed enemy. They said, *"Our Lord, pour forth upon us patience, and set firm our feet, and help us against the disbelieving people"* (2:250).

The context of this historic event explains the supplication's immense gravity. The Quran states that the Children of Israel had grown weary of oppression at the hands of an enemy who had expelled them from their homes, scattering their families widely. They appealed to a prophet among them (unnamed in the Quran) to beseech God's help in choosing from their ranks a brave and able leader to unite them against their foes.

After expressing skepticism about the sincerity of their resolve to fight, their prophet informed them that God

Our Lord, pour forth upon us patience, and set firm our feet, and help us against the disbelieving people.

— The Quran, 2:250

ربنا أفرغ علينا صبرا وثبت أقدامنا
وانصرنا على القوم الكافرين

had selected Saul (Ṭâlût) as their king—a choice, the Quran notes, that the Israelites immediately resisted. When the wise leader marshaled them into a fighting force, he informed them that God would test their loyalty and endurance at a river they would approach in their march to battle. Anyone who drank more than a handful from it, regardless of his thirst, would be repudiated and kept back. All but a few failed to heed the order. When Saul and the true believers crossed the river and beheld the great superiority of their enemy in numbers and arms, many despaired of victory and exclaimed their impotence in the face of Goliath and his mighty army.

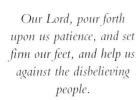

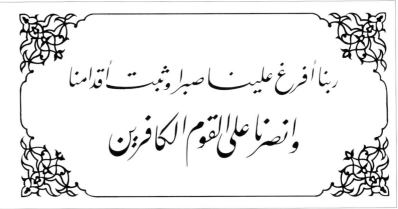

An ardent few among them, however, believed themselves to be destined by God and knew that victory and ultimate success come from Him alone, both in this world and in the Hereafter. Their undeterred faith calmed the panic in the hearts of the others, and they persuaded them that greatness in number and arms is not the true secret of victory, for God is with those who persevere and have patience. Then, turning to God, they implored, "*Our Lord, pour forth upon us patience, and set firm our feet, and help us against the disbelieving people*" (2:250).

The prayer of David and his fellows in arms echoes an extolment of the virtues of patience, perseverance, and steadfastness that pervades the entire Quran. Time and again, the Quran commends the believers to these qualities for they are central to the continuation of belief and the preservation of the godly way of life. And it is these cherished values for which David fought.

A close look at the mind-set of this band of believers shows that they had a profound consciousness of their certain return to God, along with an awareness of His presence and support. This helped them to sustain their patience and resolve. They did not view this battle as an end (to temporal life, perhaps), but rather as a final exit to their ultimate destiny before God. So they anticipated relief and did not succumb to despair. The success of their thinking—informed by, *How many a small company has tri-*

And to David We granted Solomon—a commendable servant. Indeed, he was ever penitent.

— The Quran, 38:30

The Prophet ﷺ said, "Whoever sincerely asks God for martyrdom God raises to the ranks of the martyrs, even if he dies in bed."

umphed over a ⌜more⌝ numerous company by God's permission! (2:249)—has been repeatedly borne out in history, for victory was always with those who persevered. And God indeed answered the believers' prayer as David's small company vanquished the seemingly mightier company of Goliath—a victory that has endured as the quintessential example of good triumphing over evil.

Passages throughout the Quran highlight the morals exemplified in David's story, for God promises ample recompense for the God-fearing who have patience:

> *Say, "O My servants who have believed, fear your Lord. For those who do good in this world, there is good. And the land of Allah is spacious. Indeed, those who are patient shall be rendered their reward without measure."* (39:10)

The Quran informs us that life will not be free from tests and challenges, and that whoever perseveres ultimately prevails: *We shall surely try you with something of fear and hunger and loss of wealth and life and crops. So give glad tiding to those who have patience* (2:155).

Prophet Muḥammad, God's peace and blessings be upon him, also enjoined endurance and perseverance on the believers. He said:

> One marvels at the condition of a believer. There is good for him in everything—and this is not so for anyone except the believer. When something pleasant comes to him, he is ever grateful ⌜to God⌝; and this is good for him.

> And when he is afflicted by adversity, he is ever patient; and this, too, is good for him.[37]

The Prophet ﷺ also said that there is reward even in adversity: "Whatever trouble, illness, anxiety, grief, hurt, or sorrow afflicts a Muslim—even the pricking of a thorn—God absolves with it some of the believer's misdeeds."[38]

Finally, Prophet Muḥammad ﷺ taught Muslims not to wish for death because of misfortunes and problems. He said, "Should anyone be so afflicted, let him say, 'O Allah, keep me alive so long as life is best for me, and take my soul unto Yourself whenever death is best for me.' "[39] Thus despair and suicidal tendencies are reprehensible to the believer. The essence of the Prophet's statement shows the important relationship between mental attitude and outward behavior. And in David and his small band of followers do we find penetrating proof of this relationship.

O David, indeed We have made you a successor in the land. So rule among people with the truth and do not follow whim. Indeed, those who go astray from the way of Allah, for them is a severe torment. For they have forgotten the Day of Reckoning.

— The Quran, 38:26

Solomon

GOD BESTOWED UPON Prophet Solomon عليه السلام, the son of David, great wisdom, vast knowledge, and rulership over the Children of Israel. He endowed Solomon, as well, with miraculous abilities, teaching him the languages of creatures and disclosing to him secrets of our host universe, thereby placing nature and its resources at his command.

God subordinated the wind to Solomon's will, and it blew or became still at his word. He opened Solomon's eyes to the world of living spirits, invisible to most people, and gave him authority therein. Solomon subjugated the jinn, a community of spirits created of smokeless fire, and put them to work throughout his kingdom. He employed them, for example, to mine the earth so that his people would benefit from its resources, copper in particular. Moreover, God enabled him to understand the language of birds and other animals and to communicate with them, and they too heeded his commands. Having become the heir of his father David, Solomon said, "*O you people, we have been taught the utterance of birds, and we have been given of everything. Indeed, this—it is surely a manifest favor"* (27:16). Solomon's ability to communicate with the inhabitants and forces with whom human beings share a world, but whom we often dismiss as insignificant, teaches that esteem for all life forms and natural resources is a divine imperative and that one must strive to live in harmony with all of creation, seen and unseen—all of which the Quran characterizes as *worshippers* (19:93). It also inspires the sensitive soul to study the ways of the numerous nonhuman worlds of existence.

> *And assembled before Solomon were his hosts of the jinn, humans, and birds. Then they were marshaled. When they came upon the valley of ants, an ant said, "O you ants, enter into your dwellings! Let not Solomon and his forces crush you, while they are unaware."* (27:17–18)

When an ant scurrying upon the earth drew Solomon's attention, he immediately raised his prayers of thankfulness to God, the Most High:

> *So he smiled, laughing at her statement; and he said, "My Lord, dispose me to give thanks for Your grace, with which You have graced me and my parents, and that I do righteous deeds with which You are pleased. And enter me, by Your mercy, among Your righteous servants."* (27:19)

Indeed, in this sequence of events lies a great testimony to the high eminence of knowledge and the need for people to be constant in thanking God, the All-Knowing, who

And to Solomon, 'We subjugated' the wind, with its morning course as a month and its evening course as a month. And We caused a spring of molten iron to flow for him. And of the jinn were those who worked before him by the permission of his Lord. And whoever among them swerved from Our command, We made him taste of the torment of the flaming fire. They made for him whatever he willed of sanctuaries and statues and dishes like basins and anchored pots. Work, Family of David, in thankfulness! And of My servants, few are very thankful.

— The Quran, 34:12–13

My Lord, dispose me to give thanks for Your grace, with which You have graced me and my parents, and that I do righteous deeds with which You are pleased. And enter me, by Your mercy, among Your righteous servants.

— The Quran, 27:19

رَبِّ

أَوْزِعْنِي أَنْ أَشْكُرَ نِعْمَتَكَ الَّتِي أَنْعَمْتَ عَلَيَّ وَعَلَى وَالِدَيَّ وَأَنْ أَعْمَلَ صَالِحًا تَرْضَاهُ

وَأَدْخِلْنِي بِرَحْمَتِكَ فِي عِبَادِكَ الصَّالِحِينَ

has gifted them with it. But this incident also tells of the immensity of God's gift of knowledge to Solomon and his father before him. Finally, it touches on the importance of sustaining the chain of sacred learning among all believing households, from parent to child within the bosom of the family, imparting a genuine love and esteem for true knowledge and conveying it as a cherished trust to the latter generations. In this prayer, Solomon expressed feelings of continuity, as a worshipper, with the rest of the created things of the universe. In particular, his prayer, "*My Lord, dispose me . . . ,*" is a plea to make him whole. It is as if he were saying, to use the words of Sayyid Quṭb (d. 1966):

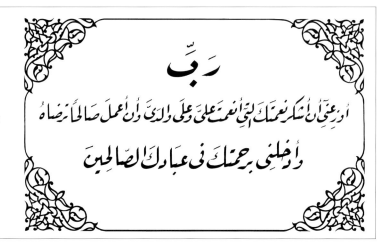

> O God, gather me together—my organs, limbs, fitness, and feelings; my tongue, mind, thoughts, and percep-

> tions; and my words, expressions, actions, and direction—gather all of them together. And, O God, marshal my energies—the first of it with the last, and the last with the first—so that I can continue being thankful for Your grace upon me and upon my parents.[40]

In Solomon's tiny ant, moreover, resounds a weighty call to refrain from violating the life we come in touch with and often exercise influence over. In this sense, God's gift to Solomon was also a test, and his instantaneous remembrance of his Lord brings to prominence one of the greatest of all virtues—gratitude. Indeed, this noble prophet was ever the thankful worshipper. The Quran records, *And indeed, We gave David and Solomon knowledge, and they said, "All praise is for Allah who has favored us over many of His believing servants"* (27:15).

This prayer of Solomon teaches that the grateful soul not only acknowledges its endowments from the Creator but seeks the continuation of His grace and His guidance, so that one may do good deeds in whatever remains of life. And it seeks more ardently still God's saving mercy in the Hereafter for entry into the Garden of Eternity.

And to each (David and Solomon) We gave wisdom and knowledge. And We subjugated the mountains—to give glory along with David—and the birds; and We are able doers. And We taught him the making of armored garments for you so that they preserve you in your battles. Will you then be thankful? And 'We subjugated' to Solomon the stormy wind running at his command to the land which We have blessed therein. And We are all-knowing of everything. And of the satans, there were those who would dive for him and do other works apart from that. And We were ever watchful of them.

— The Quran, 21:79–82

· Zechariah ·

IN THE MINDS of men and women, the hope of bringing forth children fades with advanced age and may be especially saddening to those who have not been so blessed. But God hears all prayers.

Prophet Zechariah عليه السلام understood this and knew that He who created life from nothing, bestowing it upon whomever He willed, could give the gift of children to young or old. So in old age, when Zechariah saw the miraculous and auspicious care God had conferred upon Mary—nourishing her in her prayer chamber with every provision—the longing to be blessed with a reverent child to be his own heir awakened in his heart, for he feared reaching the end of life alone with neither supporter nor successor. Then and there, on the threshold of Mary's prayer chamber, Zechariah called upon God, the Answerer of Prayer, whose will is ever done: "*My Lord, grant me from Your bounty wholesome children. Indeed, You are the hearer of prayer*" (3:38).

Mindful of life's weighty responsibilities and the human being's need to adhere to the straight way in all endeavors, Zechariah asked God for a son who would share in the blessing of faith with him and enjoy moral purity. Thus, he petitioned God not merely for a child, but for a righteous heir who would bring joy to his heart, extend the essence of his life, and carry on his message. Baring his soul in his supplication, Zechariah said, "*My Lord, leave me not alone* [*childless*], *though You are the best of inheritors*" (21:89).

Zechariah's longing for progeny, however, surpassed a mere desire to extend his lineage. Rather, it disclosed his concern for the spiritual fate of his people and for the continuation of the legacy of faith in the House of Jacob. Yet he was ever trusting in the mercy of God and expressive of his gratitude to Him:

> *He said, "My Lord, surely the bones within me have weakened and my head is lit with gray. Yet never, in praying to You, my Lord, have I been unhappy. And I fear for my kinfolk coming*

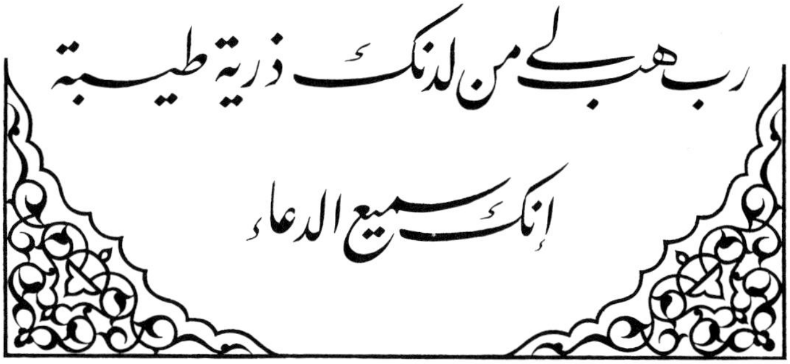

My Lord, grant me from Your bounty wholesome children. Indeed, You are the Hearer of Prayer.

— The Quran, 3:38

after me, and my wife is barren. So grant me, from Your own bounty, a successor to inherit from me and to inherit from the Family of Jacob; and make him, my Lord, well-pleasing." (19:4–6)

The angels came to Zechariah with the good tidings that his Lord had answered his prayer: God would soon bestow upon Zechariah and his barren wife a devoted son, whose name was to be "Yaḥyâ" (John), meaning "he who lives" (19:7). Gentle, benevolent, and God-fearing in nature, John عليه السلام would inherit the mantle of prophethood, be kind and dutiful to his parents, and become a pathfinder of goodness among his people.

The Quran's mention of God's grace upon Zechariah is a reminder that He indeed answers prayers. When difficulty, illness, poverty, or danger overtake us, or when wholesome desires fill us with a yearning for something that enhances the meaning of our lives in this world and the next, we should turn to the Creator—even though our appeals may relate to seemingly hopeless situations.

The Prophet ﷺ taught that a person should never despair of asking of God. Rather, one should appeal to Him and be cheered and confirmed by the unfailing responsiveness of the Most Generous, the All-Giving, for indeed He hears and has promised to answer. *Call upon Me; I shall answer you* (40:60).

> *Then the angels called to him as he stood praying in the Sanctuary, "God indeed gives you glad tidings of John, confirming a word from God, honorable and abstinent and a prophet from among the righteous." He said, "My Lord, how shall I have a boy, while advanced old age has come upon me, and my wife is barren?" He said, "So shall it be! God does what He wills." He said, "My Lord, make for me a sign." He said, "Your sign is that you shall not speak to people for three days except by gesture. And remember your Lord much and give glory in the evenings and the mornings."*
>
> — The Quran, 3:40–41

• Jesus •

THE RELATIONSHIP OF all existence with God is that of creation with Creator. Jesus, the Messiah, and his pious mother, Mary, the virgin (blessings and peace be upon both of them), are not exceptions to this eternal truth. And never would Jesus عليه السلام have claimed otherwise.

> *And when Allah shall say ⌜on the Day of Judgment⌝, "O Jesus, son of Mary, did you say to the people, 'Take me and my mother both as gods apart from Allah'?" ⌜Jesus⌝ shall say, "Glory be to You! It was not for me to say what I had no right to. If I had said it, then You truly would know it. You know what is in my soul and I do not know what is in Yourself. Indeed, You are all-knowing of all the unseen. I have not said to them, except what You commanded me with: 'Worship Allah, my Lord and your Lord.' And I was witness over them while I remained among them. Then when You took my soul, You Yourself were ever-vigilant over them. And You are witness over all things."* (5:116–17)

Jesus is a preeminent servant of God, a sign and mercy to humankind from Him, and one of the five most outstanding prophets of all time. He came to the Children of Israel with manifest proofs and wisdom, preaching the Torah and the Gospel, in order to clear up the disputes

Say: He is Allah, One.
Allah, the Everlasting
Refuge. He does not beget,
nor is He begotten.
And there is
none comparable to Him.

— The Quran, 112:1–4

that had erupted among them and to return them to the straight path.

His life is much identified with the wondrous: His conception was miraculous (19:19); he spoke at birth and again from the cradle (19:24–26, 30–33); he was the recipient of a revealed scripture (5:46); he performed miracles of life, healed the sick, and raised the dead—all by the permission of God (5:110); and, to reassure the hearts of the Disciples, he entreated God to send down to them a banquet from heaven to be a feast and celebration for all of them—and a sign (5:114–15). Moreover, he prophesied the coming of Prophet Muḥammad ﷺ after him (61:6). Jesus continued with his mission until his soul was taken by God, and he was raised to Him and purified from those who disbelieved.

The Quran states that near the end of his mission, Jesus, on whom be peace, appealed to his people to accept his message.

> *⌜He said,⌝ "Truly, I have come to you with a sign from your Lord that I indeed create for you out of mud a bird-like figure. Then I blow into it, then it becomes a bird—by Allah's permission. I cure the born-blind and the leper, and I give life to the dead—by Allah's permission. And I shall tell you what you eat and what you stock in your houses. Indeed, in that is a sure sign for you, if you are believers. And I am to confirm what has preceded me of the Torah and to make permissible some of what has*

been prohibited. And I have come to you with a sign from your Lord. So fear Allah and obey me. Indeed, Allah is my Lord and your Lord, so worship Him. This is the straight way." (3:49–51)

Yet his momentous and honorable call was lost upon many of the Children of Israel, most of whom belied his prophethood and message and the virtue of his mother.

Neither were his spectacular miracles widely believed nor his call for renewal of the covenant generally accepted. Rather, his opponents accelerated their attacks and pressure against those who believed in his message and followed him. Declaring his activities to be open rebellion against the religion they had inherited from their forefathers and the sacredness of the Torah, the rabbis and Pharisees led the opposition against Jesus. Further, they projected him as a threat to the pagan Roman political establishment in Palestine.

The Disciples, the closest supporters of Jesus and his mission, witnessed the miracles that Jesus performed—all by God's leave—as he invited the Children of Israel and their priests to accept what he had brought them from their Lord. When the pressure on the believers mounted, they yearned for God to favor them with a special miraculous sign that would support them and bring peace and resolve to their hearts. They requested Jesus to appeal to his Lord to send down a table-spread from

Indeed, those who for the fear of their Lord are cautious, and those who believe in the signs of their Lord, and those who do not associate 'gods' with their Lord, and those who in giving whatever they give their hearts are fearful because they shall return to their Lord—they rush to good works and they are the foremost in attaining them.

— The Quran, 23:57–61

heaven filled with food and drink. The Quran cites this historical event:

> *When the Disciples said, "O Jesus, son of Mary, will your Lord be able to send down to us a table from heaven?" He said, "Fear Allah, if you are believers!" They said, "We wish to eat from it and to calm our hearts and to know that you indeed have spoken the truth to us and to be among the witnesses to it." Jesus, son of Mary, said, "O Allah, our Lord, send down to us a table from heaven to be a feast for us—for the first of us and the last of us—and a sign from You. And provide for us, for You are the best of providers."*
>
> *Allah said, "Indeed, I shall send it down to you. But whoever of you disbelieves thereafter, I will torment him with a torment with which I shall not torment anyone of all the people."* (5:112–15)

When Jesus beheld the public rejection he received and the implacable disbelief in his message, he offered his followers a chance to renew their covenant with God and to pledge their full support to His messenger:

> *Jesus said, "Who will be my supporters toward Allah?" The Disciples said, "We are the supporters of Allah. Indeed, we have believed in Allah. And bear witness that we are indeed Muslims."* (3:52)
>
> *Jesus, son of Mary, said to the Disciples, "Who will be my supporters toward Allah?" The Disciples said, "We are the supporters of Allah."* (61:14)

When they declared their submission to God, with Jesus as witness over them, they prayed to God, "*Our*

When the angels said, "O Mary, indeed Allah gives you glad tidings of a word from Him; his name is the Messiah, son of Mary, eminent in this world and the Hereafter and of those brought near. And he shall speak to people in the cradle and as a grown man and shall be of the righteous." She said, "My Lord, how shall I have a son while no human being has touched me?" He said, "So shall it be! Allah creates what He wills. When He decrees a matter, He but says to it 'Be!' and so it is. And He shall teach him the Book and the wisdom and the Torah and the Gospel."

— The Quran, 3:45–48

Lord, we have believed in what You have sent down, and we have followed the Messenger. So inscribe us among those who bear witness" (3:53).

But what were the implications of the witness that the Disciples declared in the presence of Jesus? It was simply to profess that God is one, the Creator, the Sustainer, and the Judge of all. It was to attest that Jesus did indeed convey the message to the Children of Israel. It was to affirm that the great and continuous message of the prophets did not end when their appointed terms on earth expired. It was to reestablish the certainty and irrevocable nature of their commitment to God, including all He had revealed through His prophets, commanded in His scrip-

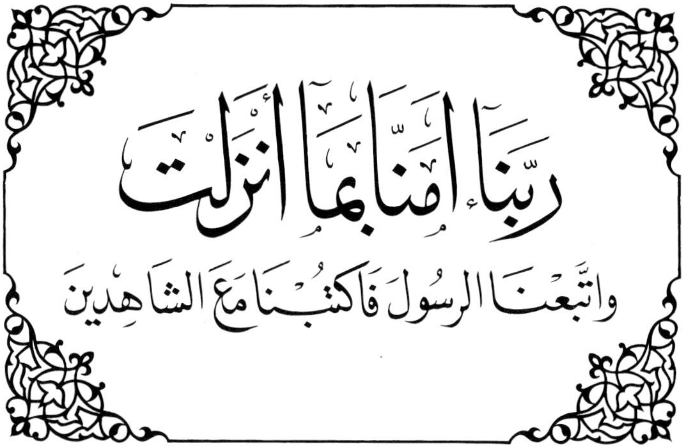

Our Lord, we have believed in what You have sent down, and we have followed the Messenger. So inscribe us among those who bear witness.

— The Quran, 3:53

tures, and promised to His worshippers. It was to strengthen the perseverance of a believer in adhering to the guidance of the Creator, enduring the difficulties and facing the challenges that come to him or her throughout life. Indeed, all of this inheres in the meaning of the Disciples' witness and in the poignancy of their prayer.

Prophet Muḥammad, God's peace and blessings be upon him, revived among Muslims the tradition that is described in the above verse, which the Disciples of Jesus articulated. He taught his followers to renew their witness with the rising of the sun and the coming of evening, giving glad tidings to whomever practiced this. A Companion of the Prophet, Anas ibn Mâlik, reported hearing the Prophet ﷺ say:

> Whoever says in the morning, "O Allah, I come to this morning calling upon You to bear witness—as I call upon Your Throne Bearers, Your angels, and all of Your creation to bear witness—that indeed You are Allah, there is no God but You, and Muḥammad is Your servant and Messenger," God will forgive their misdeeds in that day; and whoever repeats it in the evening will be forgiven for their misdeeds of that evening.[41]

The message of all the prophets, including Jesus, makes clear that Godship and divinity belong to none but God. The relationship of everything in the heavens and on earth to Him—the One, the Everlasting Refuge,

And he is a messenger to the Children of Israel: "Truly, I have come to you with a sign from your Lord that I indeed create for you out of mud a bird-like figure. Then I blow into it, then it becomes a bird—by Allah's permission. I cure the born-blind and the leper, and I give life to the dead—by Allah's permission. And I shall tell you what you eat and what you stock in your houses. Indeed, in that is surely a sign for you, if you are believers. And I am to confirm what has preceded me of the Torah and to make permissible some of what has been prohibited. And I have come to you with a sign from your Lord. So fear Allah and obey me. Indeed, Allah is my Lord and your Lord, so worship Him. Truly, this is the straight way."

— The Quran, 3:49–51

who does not beget, nor is begotten, He who is beyond all compare—is one of worshipper to the worshipped. As for Jesus' birth from a virgin mother, God says, *Indeed, the likeness of Jesus, before Allah, is as the likeness of Adam. He created him from dust; then He said to him "Be!" and so he was* (3:59–60).

• Muḥammad ﷺ •

WHEN IT COMES to the remembrance of God and prayer to Him, history records no peer for Prophet Muḥammad, God's blessings and peace be upon him. His consciousness of the Creator was unfailing, his occasion to turn to Him constant, and his beseeching of Him unsurpassed in emotional depth and eloquence. He petitioned God from the moment he awoke until the time he slept: When making ablution and dressing; while performing the ritual Prayer (*Ṣalât*) or other devotions; upon exiting or entering his home or the mosque; before or after eating and drinking; and in times of fear and joy. The opportunities for supplication in which the Prophet ﷺ invoked God number no less than the circumstances of life. And many are the souls for whom he regularly prayed, asking God to bless and forgive his family, his Companions, and the believers of every generation and locality.

Second to the divine revelation of the Quran, it is the prayers of the Prophet ﷺ that confirm for us his inspired awareness of the Lord of all being. They express the ideal intimacy between a worshipper and God, not simply because he was a prophet, but because he recognized the human being's vital need for God's guidance, help, protection, provision, mercy, and enlightenment—the very blessings that enable one to continue life on the straight path in the face of temptation and intimidation. The Prophet's ﷺ supplications juxtapose the longings and limitations of human nature with the munificence and limitlessness of God, and thereby bring into clear relief God's absolute right to and worthiness of our veneration and worship.

The Messenger of God ﷺ said, "Whoever seeks forgiveness often, God shall make for him a relief from every worry, and a way out from every distress, and shall provide for him from where he does not anticipate."

Through the divine utterances of revelation, God gradually taught His unlettered messenger the truths of the human heart and the objective universe, of this life and the Afterlife, and of the various conditions that define existence on earth. These truths are like threads of guiding light woven into the supplications and remembrances of Muḥammad, peace be upon him. Thus, those who internalize these prayers illuminate their own hearts with the values and priorities by which God intended human beings to live, die, and come before His judgment. Such people become luminaries toward God and sources of knowledge for others.

One learned in sacred knowledge understands and

O Allah, put light in my heart, light in my sight and light in my hearing; light to my right, light to my left; light above me and light beneath me; and light before me and light behind me. And grant me light.

— Prophet Muḥammad ﷺ

values the fact that only God's knowledge is complete, encompassing time, space, and dimensions untold. Thus did God instruct the Prophet ﷺ not to hasten anxiously after the Quran's inspiration, but rather to pray, "*My Lord, increase me in knowledge*" (20:114). The Prophet ﷺ persisted in seeking enlightenment from God in all affairs. Whenever he faced an issue of concern, he petitioned God's guidance, for he recognized that even a prophet's knowledge is circumscribed, while God is all-knowing. So he would turn to God in an act of worship known as the Prayer of Selection (*Ṣalât al-Istikhâra*) before proceeding in any matter, great or small, often concluding with this entreaty:

> O Allah, enable me through Your knowledge to choose what is best, and empower me through Your power. I ask You of Your vast bounty, for truly You have power, and I have no power, and You know, and I do not know. You are truly the Knower of the Unseen.
>
> O Allah, if You know this matter to be best for me in my religion, livelihood, and ultimate end,[42] then decree it for me. And if You know this matter to be evil for me in my religion, livelihood, and ultimate end,[43] then turn it away from me and turn me away from it, and decree for me what is best, wherever it may be; then make me pleased with it.[44]

Similarly, the Prophet ﷺ regularly asked God for beneficial knowledge, and requested that He protect him from the harm of ineffectual knowledge, which does not inspire one to do good or to stand against evil. He asked God to preserve him from pride and from using knowledge to exploit or oppress others. He prayed:

> O Allah, I seek refuge in You from knowledge that does not benefit, from a heart that is not humble, from a soul that is never satisfied, and from any prayer that is not answered.[45]

The Revelation and Refuge of the Quran

God opened the gates of immeasurable stores of knowledge to the world by revealing the Quran to the Prophet Muḥammad ﷺ; for the Quran is the last of the divine revelations to humanity and the most enduring reply to the questions that stir in the human soul. God, the All-Knowing, directed Muḥammad ﷺ to promulgate the Quran's message to all. So he began with the members of his family and his community, the Qurayshite Arabs of Makkah.

But the leaders of Quraysh rejected his call, as preceding communities had rejected the messages of the prophets sent to them by God. They adhered blindly to the heritage of their forefathers—polytheism, superstition, rituals performed in ignorance, tribalism, oppression of the weak, and other transgressions—and they denounced the

By the morning sunshine! And the night when it overspreads! Your Lord has not deserted you, nor is He displeased. And surely the last will be better for you than the first. And surely shall your Lord give you, until you become well-pleased. Has He not found you an orphan and sheltered you? And found you astray and guided you? And found you needy and enriched you? Then as for the orphan, do not aggrieve ˹him˺. And as for the beggar, do not rebuke ˹him˺. And as for the grace of your Lord, do speak out.

— The Quran, 93:1–11

> *Have We not expanded for you your chest, and relieved from you your burden—which had weighed down your back—and raised for you your renown? So indeed, with hardship, there is ease. Indeed, with hardship, there is ease. So whenever you have leisure, then exert yourself ⌜in worship⌝, and to your Lord alone turn imploring.*
>
> — The Quran, 94:1–8

Prophet ﷺ as insane or possessed and decried the unfolding Quran as a book of fables.

In the Quran's twenty-third chapter, "al-Mu'minûn" (The Believers), God warned the disbelievers that if they persisted in denying the Prophet's ﷺ message, an imminent chastisement would overtake them, just as punishment had been meted out to the communities before them who had spurned His prophets and messengers. He also instructed the Prophet ﷺ to voice three prayers for salvation.

The first is an appeal to God for deliverance from any impending doom that might be visited upon the Quraysh: *Say, "My Lord, should You show me what they are promised—then, my Lord, let me not be with the wrongdoing people"* (23:93–94). God, the All-Merciful, would not allow His Messenger to perish amidst any destruction He sent against the deniers. Nonetheless, through this supplication He instructed the Prophet ﷺ and the believers to seek refuge in Him from every ill-fated destiny, and showed that those who entrust God with their affairs find relief and shelter in His mercy.

The value of preempting an evil that might befall one is self-evident. But the believer must also guard against unseen forces to which he or she is exposed, for assuredly the universe is alive with intelligent beings other than humans. In this light, one may understand the Quran's directive to the Prophet ﷺ in the second prayer of Sûrat al-Mu'minûn: *And say, "My Lord, I seek refuge in You from the promptings of the satans. And I seek refuge in You, my Lord, from their presence"* (23:97–98).

God sent Muḥammad ﷺ to set the standard of goodness for humanity. Yet He prescribed this prayer of protection against the forces of evil to remind people that Satan has openly sworn his enmity toward the progeny of Adam and strives relentlessly to lead them astray.

The Prophet ﷺ responded to God's bidding with earnestness. He opened his Prayers (*Ṣalât*, pl. *Ṣalawât*) by saying, "I seek refuge in Allah, the All-Hearing, the All-Knowing, from Satan, the accursed" or "I seek refuge in Allah from Satan, the accursed." He also routinely repeated the invocation, "I seek refuge in the perfect words of Allah from His wrath, from His punishment, from the evil of His servants, from the promptings of satans, and from their coming near me."[46]

Indeed, the Prophet ﷺ sought to shield himself in God's protection from the approach of every kind of evil to which all who walk the earth are exposed. Addressing

Those who disbelieve and bar from the path of God, He causes their deeds to go astray. And those who believe and do righteous deeds and believe in what has been sent down to Muḥammad—and it is the truth from their Lord—He absolves them of their misdeeds and sets their minds aright. That is because those who disbelieve have followed falsehood and those who believe have followed the truth from their Lord. Thus does God put forth for all people their examples.

— The Quran, 47:1–3

And Muḥammad is no more than a messenger. Truly messengers have passed away before him. Were he to die or be killed, would you turn back on your heels? And whoever turns back on his heels shall never harm God in anything. And God shall recompense the thankful.

— The Quran, 3:144

even the land, mountains, waters, and all that constitutes this planet, he would say:

> O earth, my Lord and your Lord is Allah. I seek refuge in Allah from your harm and whatever harm is in you and the harm of what He has created in you and from the harm of whatever treads on you. And I seek refuge in Allah from lions and cobras and from serpents and scorpions, and from the dwellers of the area, and from whatever begets and whatever is begotten.[47]

Some, perhaps, might find the Prophet's direct address to "things" of creation unusual. But among the most striking features of the Prophet's outlook is his treatment of all of creation in the universe—sentient and unsentient, seen and unseen—as fellow worshippers of God. When sighting the new moon, for example, the Prophet ﷺ would ask God to make the advent of the new month a season for righteousness, safety, and calm: "O Allah, bring it forth upon us with security, peace, and Islam." Then, addressing the moon directly, he would say, "My Lord and your Lord is Allah!" He would then entreat God, "May this be a crescent of guidance and goodness."[48]

The third prayer for salvation revealed to Prophet Muḥammad, God's blessings and peace be upon him, in Sûrat al-Mu'minûn instructs the believers to reaffirm their covenant of faith in the one true God, and to seek His pardon and grace, that they may enter Paradise: "*Our*

Lord, we have believed; so forgive us and have mercy upon us, for You are the best of the merciful" (23:109).

Seeking Perfect Submission

As the truth of the Prophet ﷺ and his message became clearer, the hostility of the Quraysh grew more implacable. Ultimately, they conspired to extinguish the light of Islam with a plan to assassinate the Prophet ﷺ , a warn-

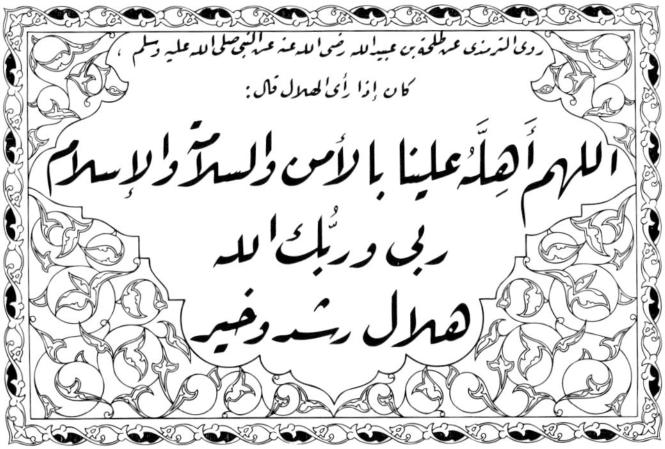

The Prophet ﷺ, whenever he saw the new moon, would say:

O Allah, bring it forth upon us with security, peace, and Islam. My Lord and your Lord is Allah. May this be a crescent of guidance and goodness.

ing of which preceded his momentous migration, or *hijra* (from which comes the word "hegira" in English), from Makkah to Madinah. It was in this dire circumstance that God taught His Messenger a very special entreaty for deliverance, referred to in Sûrat al-Isrâ' (17). In consonance with the theme of refuge, the Prophet ﷺ was to beseech his Lord for triumph against evil, asking Him to make his migration to the city of Madinah proof of his submission to His command, a testimony to his faith, and a sign of the ultimate wisdom of God, "*My Lord, let me enter a sincere entry and depart a sincere departing. And grant me, from Your own, supporting authority*" (17:80).

O Allah, I ask You for firmness in my affairs and to be resolved in doing what is right. And I ask You for thankfulness for Your grace and for excellence in Your worship. I ask You for a sound heart and a truthful tongue. I ask You for the best of what You know, and I seek refuge in You from the evil of what You know. And I ask You to forgive me for what You know of me.

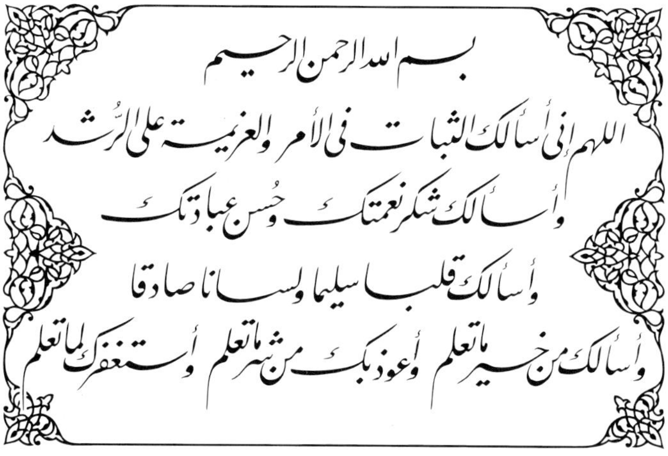

As worldly power and authority accrued to the new community founded on belief, the Prophet's recourse to taking refuge in God never flagged. Whether before battles whose outcome would determine the very fate of the young community of faith or whether deep in ritual Prayer (*Ṣalât*) in the stillness of the night, we encounter the Prophet ﷺ asking God to save and preserve him in all the conditions of life. He prayed:

> O Allah, I ask You for pardon and well-being in this world and the Hereafter. O Allah, I ask You for pardon and well-being in my religion, my life, my family, and my wealth. O Allah, cover my faults and soothe my fears. O Allah, protect me from before me and from behind me, and from my right and from my left, and from above me; and I seek refuge in You from being seized from beneath me.[49]

The Prophet ﷺ often implored God to keep even his senses obedient to Him, for it is He who had formed them, so that they would be employed exclusively in His service and not as avenues of evil. He prayed, "O Allah, I seek refuge in You from the harm of my hearing, the harm of my sight, and the harm of my heart."[50] And for each occurrence that befell him, or article that came into his possession, or journey on which he set out, or place that he came upon, the Prophet ﷺ asked God to grant him its good and protect him from its evil. When prepar-

The Prophet ﷺ said, "Do not bar the female worshippers of God from God's houses of worship [masâjid]*."*

> *Muḥammad is not a father of any of your men, but is the Messenger of God and the Seal of the Prophets. And God is all-knowing of everything.*
>
> — The Quran, 33:40

ing to embark on a journey, for example, or to fight in the path of God, he often prayed:

> O Allah, I ask You for firmness in my affairs and to be resolved in doing what is right. And I ask You for thankfulness for Your grace and for excellence in Your worship. I ask You for a truthful tongue and a sound heart. I seek refuge in You from the evil of what You know. I ask You for the best of what You know. And I ask You to forgive me for what You know of me. Indeed, You are the Knower of the unseen.[51]

And whenever his expeditions led him to a neighboring community, he would turn to God and say:

> O my Lord—Lord of the seven heavens and all they shade, and of the seven earths and all they carry, and Lord of the satans and all they lead astray, and Lord of the wind and all it scatters—I ask You for the good of this town, the good of its inhabitants, and the good of all that is in it. And I seek refuge in You from its evil, the evil of its inhabitants, and the evil of all that is in it.[52]

The lesson of such prayers is that God alone is the Everlasting Refuge, of whom humankind is ever in need.

Themes of Forgiveness

The Prophet Muḥammad ﷺ—the exemplar of obedience to God—repeatedly asked God for His forgiveness. This compels one to reflect on the virtue of this noble practice and its deficiency among the generality of people. The

Prophet ﷺ was well aware that human beings, even those sincere in their effort to please God, fail from time to time to fulfill perfectly or completely God's commandments. Sins, however few or small, can leave their impression upon the human heart. Thus, Satan seduces people to sin, and then uses it to burden them with guilt and gloom. But when the heart regrets its misdeeds and repents, God cleanses it, restoring it to its original state of purity. The Prophet ﷺ prayed, "*My Lord, forgive and have mercy, for You are the best of the merciful*" (23:118). In many prayers, particularly the shorter ones, the Prophet ﷺ began with an opening appeal for pardon, such as, "O Allah, forgive me my sins, make spacious for me my residence, and bless me in my provision,"[53] or as in the following prayer:

> O Allah, forgive me my misdeeds, and whatever I have done unknowingly, and any excess in all my affairs, and that of which You know better than me. O Allah, forgive me whatever I have done in earnestness and in jest, and forgive me my mistakes and my deliberate actions. And all this is with me. O Allah, forgive me whatever I may have done and whatever I may do, whatever I have concealed and whatever I have revealed, and that of which You know better than me. You are the Forwarder and You are the Delayer. You have power over all things.[54]

Often the Prophet ﷺ prefaced his invocations for forgiveness by expressing thanks to God, praising Him with His most excellent names, proclaiming His Lordship over all

Say, "O humankind, I am the Messenger of God to all of you, to whom belongs the kingdom of the heavens and of the earth. There is no God but He. He gives life and causes death. So believe in God and His Messenger, the unlettered Prophet, who believes in God and His words. And follow him, so that you may be guided.

— The Quran, 7:158

things in the heavens and the earth, and declaring his belief in all that He had revealed. The Companion Ibn ʿAbbâs reported that when the Prophet ﷺ awoke and rose for supererogatory Prayers in the night, he used to say:

> O Allah, for You is all praise! You are the light of the heavens and the earth. For You is all praise! You are the

في صحيح البخاري : حدثنا محمد بن بشار حدثنا عبد الملك بن صباح حدثنا شعبة عن أبي إسحاق
عن ابن أبي موسى عن أبيه عن النبي صلى الله عليه وسلم أنه كان يدعو بهذا الدعاء :

رب اغفر لي خطيئتي وجهلي وإسرافي في أمري كلّه وما أنت أعلم به مني

اللهم اغفر لي خطاياي وعمدي وجهلي وهزلي ، وكلُّ ذلك عندي

اللهم اغفر لي ما قدّمتُ وما أخرتُ وما أسررتُ وما أعلنتُ

أنت المقدِّم وأنت المؤخِّر وأنت على كل شيءٍ قدير

My Lord, forgive me my misdeeds, my ignorance, any excesses in all my affairs, and what You are more knowing of than me. O Allah, forgive me my sins, my deliberate actions, my mistakes, and my jesting—and all this is with me. So forgive me whatever I may have done and whatever I may do, whatever I have concealed and whatever I have revealed. You are the Forwarder and the Delayer. You are powerful over all things.

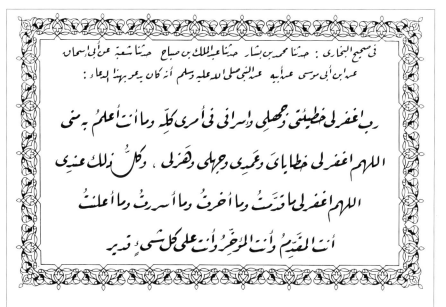

> Sustainer of the heavens and the earth. For You is all praise! You are the Lord of the heavens and the earth and all therein. You are the Truth. Your promise is the truth. Your word is the truth. The meeting with You is true. The Garden is true. The Fire is true. The Hour is true. O Allah, to You I submit. In You I believe. On You I rely. To You I repent. For You I oppose. To You I refer in judgment. So forgive me whatever I may have done and whatever I may do, whatever I have concealed and whatever I have revealed. You are my God. There is no God but You.[55]

The Messenger of God ﷺ said, "Indeed, the miser is he to whom my name is mentioned and he does not say, 'God's blessings and peace be upon him.'"

Striking are not only the pith and the beauty of the Prophet's ﷺ prayers, but also his remarkable cognizance of the human vulnerability to committing offenses unknowingly. Indeed, there are sins that one may do knowingly and bury in the recesses of the mind even as they are committed, just as there are sins that lie in plain view. Thus, the Prophet ﷺ taught us to be comprehensive in asking God's forgiveness.

Ritual Prayer and Supplication

The hallmark of worship in Islam is ritual Prayer (*Ṣalât*), an obligation upon every mature Muslim male and female five times daily, with increased blessings promised for those who fulfill them in congregation. During the obligatory Prayers—in standing, bowing at the waist, bowing down to the ground, and sitting—the Prophet ﷺ

unfailingly besought God to inspire him with adherence to the right path, asking that He illuminate for him the avenues to truth. He also frequently voiced personal appeals for clemency and direction, as in the supplication:

> O Allah, truly I have wronged myself with many wrongs, and none forgives sins but You. So forgive me with Your forgiveness and have mercy upon me. Truly, it is You who are all-forgiving and mercy-giving.[56]

The approach of each Prayer (*Ṣalât*) filled the Prophet ﷺ with a heightened sense of anticipation for the wor-

Prophet Muḥammad ﷺ often prayed:

O Allah, put light in my heart, light in my hearing and light in my sight; light to my right and light to my left; light above me and light beneath me; and light before me and light behind me. And grant me light the day of meeting You.

ship he would offer to God, the All-Praised, and for the serene petitions that his worship would occasion. With the call to Dawn Prayer, the Prophet ﷺ went out toward the congregation, saying, as he walked:

> O Allah, put light in my heart, light in my sight, and light in my hearing; light to my right and light to my left; light above me and light beneath me; and light before me and light behind me. And grant me light.[57]

And at night, he would awaken from sleep, clean his teeth, and make ablution (*wuḍû'*) in preparation for Prayer. After purifying himself, he would say:

> I bear witness that there is no God but Allah, alone; He has no partner. And I bear witness that Muḥammad is His servant and Messenger. O Allah, make me one of the oft-repentant, one of the purified.[58]

Then often the Prophet ﷺ would recite, *Indeed, in the creation of the heavens and the earth and in the alternation of night and day are signs for people of understanding* (3:190), and the closing nine verses of the Quran's third sura (Âl ʿImrân). He would then rise up to pray two *rakʿas* (each *rakʿa* being a complete sequence of prescribed rituals within the Prayer), prolonging his standing, bowing, and bowing down. He would then sleep, and repeat this process two additional times during the same night.

Before dawn, the Prophet ﷺ used also to perform what is known as the *witr,* or odd-numbered, Prayer (for it con-

Muʿâdh ibn Jabal said, "The Messenger of God ﷺ sent me to Yemen and said, 'You shall surely come to a community of the People of the Book, so invite them to bear witness that there is no God but God and that I am the Messenger of God. If they obey you in this, then make known to them that God has obliged five Prayers in every day and night. If they obey you in this, then make known to them that God has obliged them to give Zakât *[Charity] to be taken from the wealthy among them and returned to the poor among them. If they obey you in this, then avoid the choicest of their wealth. And fear the supplication of anyone who is wronged, for between that supplication and God there is no veil.'"*

Surely We have given you abundance. So pray to your Lord and sacrifice. Indeed, he who hates you will be cut off.

— The Quran, 108:1–3

sisted of an uneven number of *rakʿas*). During this Prayer, as well as the Dawn Prayer, he often concluded with a special devotional invocation (*qunût*), which he uttered before bowing down to perform his final prostrations. He made this supplication more frequently in times of hardship; raising his hands and opening his palms toward the heavens, he would say:

> O Allah, guide me among those whom You guide and grant me well-being among those whom You grant well-being. Look after me among those whom You look after, and bless for me what You have given me, and protect me from the evil of what You have decreed; for You decree and none decrees against You. And none is abased whom You uphold and none is honored whom You oppose. Blessed are You, our Lord, and exalted.[59]

The Prophet ﷺ, moreover, taught the believers to pay particular attention to supplicating God when bowing down to Him during Prayer. Among the many supplications he offered in this posture, the following are especially well known:

> O Allah, give my soul its Godfearingness and purify it. You are the best to purify it. You are its patron and its Lord.[60]

> O Allah, I seek refuge in Your pleasure from Your displeasure and in Your pardon from Your punishment. And I seek refuge in You from You. I am unable to enu-

merate the extolling of You. You are as You have extolled Yourself.[61]

As the final Messenger sent by God to all humankind, Prophet Muḥammad ﷺ is the model for modern man, having appeared in the full light of history. The Book God

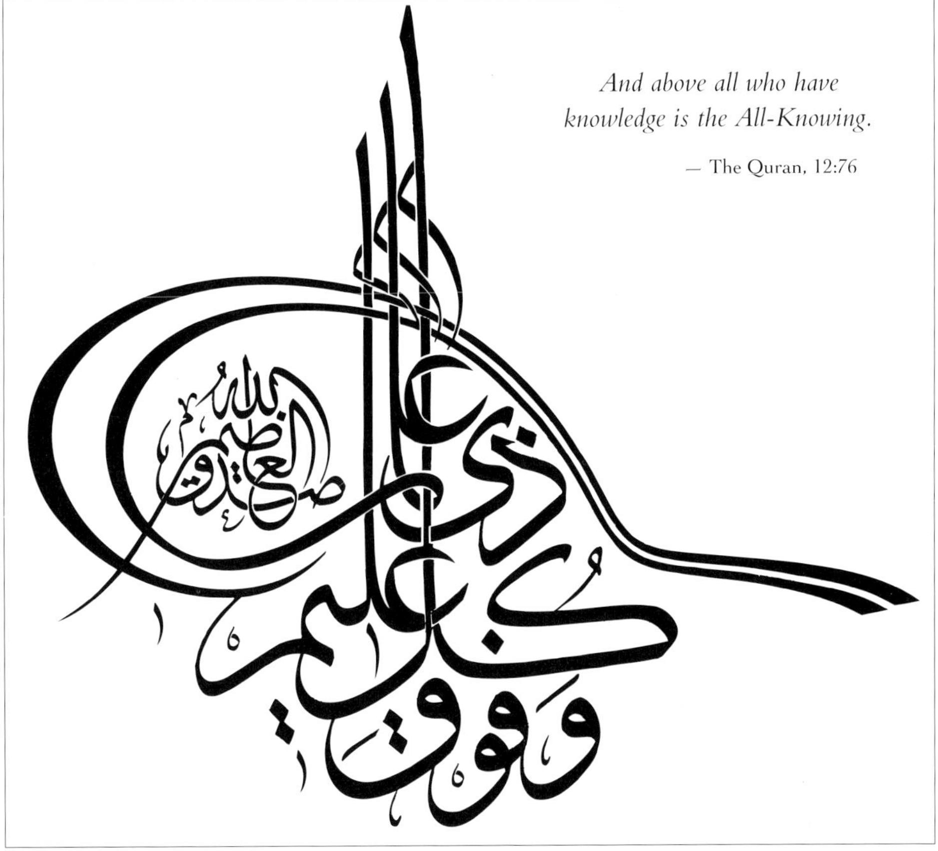

And above all who have knowledge is the All-Knowing.

— The Quran, 12:76

Truly in the Messenger of God there is for you an excellent model—for whoever is hopeful of God and the Last Day and remembers God much.

— The Quran, 33:21

revealed to him, the Quran, has been preserved, unaltered for all time. Moreover, his Companions recorded and handed down his teachings, both in deed and word—of which are the words of his prayers and remembrance of God. When one repeats them, they kindle a light of worshipfulness in the heart that is never dimmed or extinguished.

· 3 ·

Prayers of the Believers

The Human Voice of Faith: The Believers

THE SUPPLICATIONS OF the believers set down in the Quran underscore what is worthy in this life and what is vain. They lay open for reflection the frailties and strengths of the human character and reveal the leavens of success and failure. They tell of the believers' common outlook upon this world and the Afterlife, a perspective that cuts through time and across generations and speaks with one voice about sound belief in God and the human being's fundamental need for His guidance.

Thus the Quran records the utterances of believers asking God to help them perfect their worship of Him in all that they endeavor to do, striving to perform good deeds that please Him

Indeed, the Muslim men and the Muslim women, and the believing men and the believing women, and the obedient men and the obedient women, and the truthful men and the truthful women, and the patient men and the patient women, and the reverent men and the reverent women, and the charitable men and the charitable women, and the fasting men and the fasting women, and the men who guard their chastity and the women who guard ⌜theirs⌝, and the men who remember God much and the women who remember—God has promised them forgiveness and a great reward.

— The Quran, 33:35

and to abstain from that which He has prohibited. They attain to a moral character that ennobles the soul and yields happiness and security. They work to purify their hearts from doubt and malice and labor to fulfill their obligations of faith while resisting transgressions from the righteous way of life. Believers express gratitude for God's countless blessings upon them, and they petition Him to forgive their faults, errors, and sins. They savor the joy of this life when they gaze upon their wives or husbands and their sons and daughters, and when they feel the bond of pure brotherhood with those who believe in God's oneness, hopeful that He shall reward them in the Hereafter with entry into the Gardens of Delight and save them by His mercy from the torments of the Fire.

The prayers of the believers, preserved for all time in the Quran, record the human voice of faith and express the natural aspiration that God inspired in every human heart to seek His majestic Countenance.

The Servants of the All-Merciful

THE TWENTY-FIFTH chapter of the Quran, Sûrat al-Furqân (The Criterion), enumerates fourteen virtues practiced by those whom God calls the *servants of the All-Merciful*, believers of exemplary conviction, comportment, fairness, and remembrance.

The *servants of the All-Merciful* have sure faith in the oneness of God and know with certainty that He deserves obedience. While others sleep, they rise at night in worship and express their devotion in Prayer (*Ṣalât*)—standing, bowing, and prostrating. They beseech God for His blessings and assistance in their endeavor to do good and enjoin what is right, and they implore Him to make them exemplary models of goodness.

The *servants of the All-Merciful* uphold the sacredness of all existence and do not wrongfully take the life of an innocent soul. They value truth and esteem the spoken word, and thus never bear false witness. Moreover, they eschew contemptible discourse and do not debase themselves by exchanging insults with the ignorant. Yet their fear of God makes them receptive to advice and to penitence when reproved for any misdeed. The *servants of the All-Merciful* preserve the sanctity of the family and cherish the blessing of upright children. Thus they scrupulously refrain from licentiousness and obscenity. The *servants of the All-Merciful* both spend and withhold in due measure from whatever wealth God has blessed them with, an ethic that strengthens them against the covetousness of the soul and against extravagance.

The verses that characterize the *servants of the All-Merciful* impart the message that sound belief begets humility and a true understanding of one's purpose on earth, and that these two qualities have consequences in

Our Lord, turn away from us the torment of Hell. Indeed, its torment is unrelenting. It is surely an evil residence and station.

— The Quran, 25:65–66

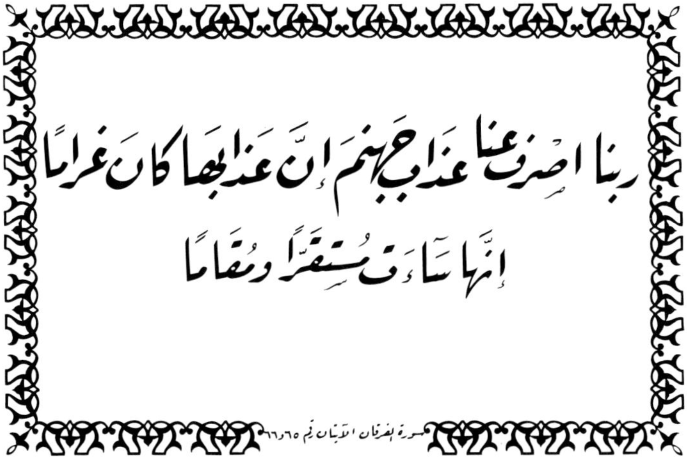

the way one conducts his or her life. Thus, the two distinguishing supplications of the *servants of the All-Merciful* recorded in the Quran hold special meaning for those wanting to be among their ranks. The first reveals their horror of the punishment in the Hereafter and their plea for God to keep it from them by His mercy: "*Our Lord, turn away from us the torment of Hell. Indeed, its torment is unrelenting. It is surely an evil residence and station*" (25:65–66).

The second prayer states their recognition of God's grace upon humankind and their aspiration to enjoy family relations that are free from marital disharmony and corrupt and irreverent offspring. "*Our Lord, grant us in our spouses and children comfort to our eyes. And make us exemplary to the God-fearing*" (25:74).

Such believers indeed serve none other than the All-Merciful, for He satisfies their yearning for real success in this world and in the Afterlife forever:

> *They shall be rewarded with the highest heaven* [al-ghurfa], *for they were patient, and they shall receive therein a greeting and "Peace!" Therein they shall dwell forever—an excellent residence and abode.* (25:75–76)

O God, bind our hearts together. Set aright relations among us. Guide us upon the way of peace. Deliver us from darkness into light. Separate us from vile deeds, whatever may be concealed of them and whatever revealed. Bless us in our hearing and our sight, our hearts and our spouses, and our children. Grant us repentance, for You are the Ever-Relenting, the Mercy-Giving. And enable us to be thankful for Your grace, and to extol ⌜*You*⌝ *for it, and to be accepting of it. And perfect it for us.*

— Prophet Muḥammad ﷺ

• A *Prayer* • *for Goodness*

GOD, THE EXALTED, ordained *Ḥajj* (Pilgrimage) as a pillar of worship, obliging every able Muslim to make the Pilgrimage to Makkah during the prescribed period at least once in a lifetime. The Quran exhorts believers to harvest the blessings of this sacred season by increasing their supplications to Him who named Himself "the Answerer of Prayer," and it urges them to beseech Him for whatever they need and hope.

During the first Pilgrimage performed by Muslims in the time of the Prophet ﷺ some pilgrims limited their supplications to asking God for worldly increase and the betterment of their condition in this life alone. The Quran, however, taught them, and succeeding generations of believers, to free their minds from the gravity of earthly life and to implore God with equal ardor for goodness in the Afterlife and salvation from chastisement. "*Our Lord, give us good in this world and good in the Hereafter, and protect us from the torment of the Fire*" (2:201).

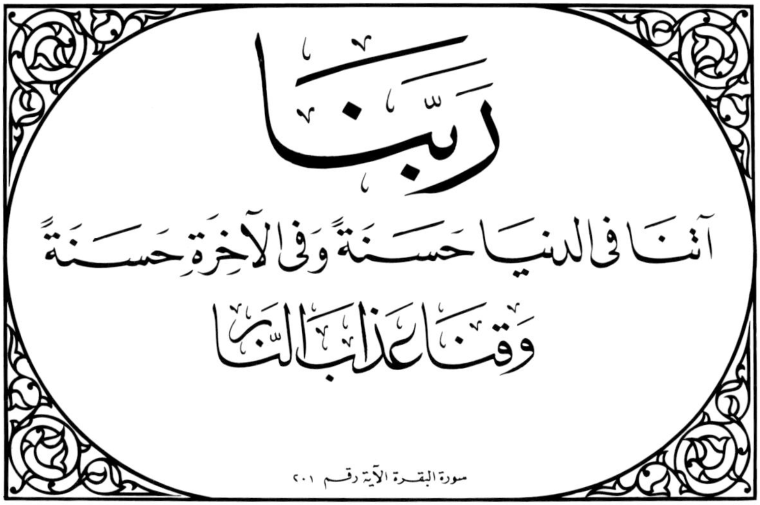

Our Lord, give us good in this world and good in the Hereafter, and protect us from the torment of the Fire.

— The Quran, 2:201

This prayer accords completely with human fate and destiny. God created people to live for a time on earth in compliance with His guidance and to follow the examples of His prophets. In the end He will resurrect us for judgment, rewarding us with either bliss or misery in the Hereafter. But even as this prayer corresponds with the two great phases of human existence, the believers themselves must strive to mirror the goodness for which they appeal, by nurturing the earth upon which they have been placed and by nourishing the souls their lives touch. During their sojourn in the world, human beings bear a

The Messenger of God ﷺ said, “Can any of you earn everyday a thousand good deeds?” One then asked him, “How could one of us earn a thousand good deeds?” He said, “When one glorifies God a hundred times, thus decreed for him is a thousand good deeds or he is disburdened of a thousand misdeeds.”

responsibility to enhance the host environment that God has made serviceable to them. They are commanded to preserve that which fosters life and to live in harmony with all things—seen and unseen—with which they share existence and the worship of God.

This weighty trust requires help from the originator of the heavens and the earth; so one must turn for guidance to the Book He has revealed, while constantly entreating His forgiveness and favor. The worshipper appeals to the source of all bounties for the goodness that benefits one in this life and for that which is better and more abiding in the life to come. The believer prays for this condition of eminence with the understanding that God’s blessings upon him or her should serve all people, transcending color, gender, geography, culture, and the like. Thus the Prophet Muḥammad ﷺ often repeated the essence of this prayer—*“Our Lord, give us good in this world. . .”* (2:201)—in different forms, especially when circumambulating the Kaʿba in Makkah, and he encouraged others to make frequent mention of it as well.

Once the Prophet ﷺ visited a Companion who had grown weak from illness. “Do you implore God with a particular prayer?” the Prophet ﷺ asked him.

“Yes,” the Companion said. “I say, ‘My Lord, advance

for me [now] whatever punishment You hold for me in the Hereafter.'"

"Glory be to Allah!" the Prophet ﷺ said. "You cannot bear this. Will you not say, 'O Allah, give us good in this world and good in the Hereafter, and protect us from the torment of the Fire'?"[62]

O you who believe, let neither your wealth nor your children divert you from the remembrance of God. And whoever does so—then it is they who are the losers.

— The Quran, 63:9

• A Prayer • of Illumination

THE POWER OF the believer's prayer has been displayed repeatedly throughout history. Some prayers have brought about the deluge and destruction of evil nations. Others have brought victory to the few and the weak. But with the exception of Sûrat al-Fâtiḥa, "The Opening" to the Quran, no prayer illuminates hearts like that of the final verses of the Quran's second sura ("al-Baqara"), which the Prophet, peace be upon him, described as "one of the two lights" without parallel in the Torah or the Gospel.[63] It is a prayer that should be said frequently by every believer:

> *Our Lord, hold us not accountable if we forget or err. Our Lord, lay not upon us a burden like that which You have laid upon those before us. Our Lord, lay not upon us that which we do not have the strength to bear. And pardon us, and forgive us, and have mercy upon us. You are our patron. So help us against the disbelieving people.* (2:286)

The second sura begins with the declaration that the Book of God is a doubtless guide for the God-fearing, namely, those who believe in the unseen, who establish ritual Prayer in their lives, spend for the sake of God from what He has provided them, and believe in God's previous revelations and are certain of the Hereafter. Also, the closing supplication of Sûrat al-Baqara itself begins with the declaration: *The Messenger believes in what has been sent down to him from his Lord, as do the believers. All believe in Allah and His angels and His books and His messengers* (2:285). Living according to these convictions leaves an indelible impression on the heart. It instills in one the desire to observe God's commandments and kindles in the soul a sense of solemnity that on one hand

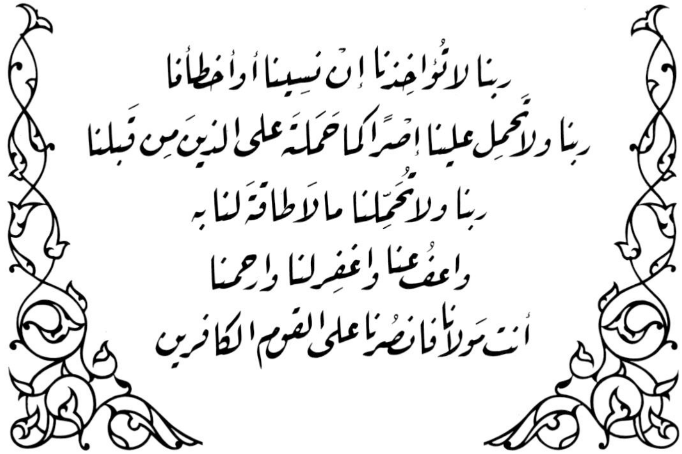

Our Lord, hold us not accountable if we forget or err. Our Lord, lay not upon us a burden like that which You have laid upon those before us. Our Lord, lay not upon us that which we do not have the strength to bear. And pardon us, and forgive us, and have mercy upon us. You are our Patron. So help us against the disbelieving people.

— The Quran, 2:286

Abû Hurayra reported that the Prophet ﷺ said, "Indeed, God, glory be to Him, shall raise high the rank of a righteous worshipper in the Garden. And he shall say, 'O my Lord, how can this be for me?' God will then say, 'By your son's asking of forgiveness for you.'"

rouses one to full consciousness, and on the other sets one at peace with the true range of human capacities. It is in this awakening that every man and woman may recognize the genuine need of the guidance and mercy of God, for it is He who created all of us from nothing and gave us life and intelligence. The believers say, "*We hear and we obey. We seek Your forgiveness, our Lord! For to You is the ultimate destiny*" (2:285).

The courage to advance good, undaunted by affliction and fear, constitutes the theme of this matchless and transcendent prayer. Through a subtle progression of alliterative and impassioned repetitions, it cites the need for asking God's help to remove, from within and without, the impediments that stand between the believer and the fulfillment of God's commandments. It is a plea to lighten the burdens that accrue in life, particularly to those who champion the cause of God in the face of obstinacy, ignorance, and resistance.

First, the prayer teaches us to ask to be absolved from the consequences of forgetfulness, error, and misjudgment. The Prophet ﷺ said, "My community has been excused from mistake, forgetfulness, and what it has been coerced into."[64] Second, the prayer directs us to beseech God not to lay upon us great encumbrances or to tax us beyond our capacity, asking Him to overlook our shortcomings. Finally, the entreaty instructs the faithful to seek God's help in overcoming those who, entrapped by base concerns, deny His signs and favors. The Prophet ﷺ often echoed these verses in his supplications. Rarely, for instance, did he rise from a gathering without offering the following prayer:

> O Allah, grant us as much reverence for You as will be a deterrent between us and sinning against You, and as much obedience to You as will deliver us to Your Garden, and as much certainty of faith as will ease for us the misfortunes of this world. Let us enjoy our hearing, our sight, and our strength for so long as You extend our lives, and make them endure after us. And set our vengeance against those who have wronged us. And give us victory over those waging animosity against us. And let not our loss be in our religion, nor let this world be the greatest of our concerns, nor the extent of our knowledge, and do not give authority over us to any who will not have mercy on us.[65]

The Messenger of God ﷺ said to his Companion, Abû Mûsâ al-Ashᶜarî, "Shall I tell you a word from the treasures of the Garden?" "Yes," said Abû Mûsâ. The Prophet ﷺ then said, "There is no strength nor might except with God."

A Prayer for Restoration

THE VICISSITUDES OF life can sometimes batter our sensibilities. Issues of all kinds may arise that confuse us about our priorities or introduce doubt into our hearts. But never does sincere prayer fail to settle a wavering sense of purpose, for it is the comforter that reassures the stirred soul. Verse eight of the Quran's third sura (Âl ʿImrân) is a most restorative prayer for the believer, for it restates one's acceptance of revealed guidance and gratitude for God's mercy: "*Our Lord, let not our hearts swerve after You have guided us, and grant us mercy from Your own ˹bounty˺. Indeed, it is You who are the All-Granting*" (3:8).

The seven verses that precede this prayer glorify God and reveal His power and all-pervasive knowledge, for *nothing in the earth nor in the heaven* is hidden from Him (3:5). He is the source of life, *who fashions you in the wombs as He wills. There is no God but Him, the Overpowering, the All-Wise* (3:6). And He has revealed the Quran to humanity, as a sure guide and criterion (3:7).

ربنا لا تزغ قلوبنا بعد إذ هديتنا وهب لنا من لدنك رحمة
إنك أنت الوهاب

Our Lord, let not our hearts swerve after You have guided us, and grant us mercy from ⌈*Your own*⌉ *bounty. Indeed, it is You who are the All-Granting.*

— The Quran, 3:8

The verses also describe two reactions to the Book's guidance and message. Some respond to the Quran by openly proclaiming their faith in the whole of it as indivisible Revelation from their Creator. They acknowledge that it affirms past revelations sent down to Moses (the Torah) and to Jesus (the Gospel) and have certainty that God—who creates human beings, grants them life, gives them form, and sustains them after birth—will receive them in the Hereafter. The Quran describes these people as *possessing sound minds* (3:7). Others, however, react to revelation by pursuing its ambiguities in order to stir up

Sufyân ibn ʿAbdullâh said to the Prophet ﷺ, "O Messenger of God, tell me of a statement in Islam such that I shall not have to ask anyone after you." The Prophet ﷺ said, "Say, 'I believe in God.' Then follow the straight way."

controversy and stimulate diversionary speculation. Their twisted understanding and sinister motives generate confusion and dissension. The Quran identifies such people as having *swerving hearts* (3:7).

Those well grounded in knowledge, however, benefit from revealed guidance, hold to it, and cherish it as a mercy from the originator of the heavens and the earth, praying fervently never to be like those who have swerving hearts: "*Our Lord, let not our hearts swerve after You have guided us, and grant us mercy from Your own ˹bounty˺. Indeed, it is You who are the All-Granting*" (3:8).

The Prophet, God's blessings and peace be upon him, and his Companions developed an immediate and special attachment to this verse. Abû Bakr al-Ṣiddîq, the dearest friend of the Prophet ﷺ, often recited this and the following verse in the Sunset Prayer, knowing the Prophet's frequent recitation of it. ʿÂ'isha, the wife of the Prophet ﷺ, reported that whenever he awoke at night he would say:

> There is no God but You. Glory be to You. O Allah, I seek Your forgiveness for my sins, and I ask You for Your mercy. O Allah, increase me in knowledge, and *let not our hearts swerve after You have guided us, and grant us mercy from Your own. Indeed, it is You who are the All-Granting.*[66]

The Prophet ﷺ also said:

> All the hearts of the Children of Adam are between two fingers of the All-Merciful like one heart. He changes them as He wills. O Allah, You change hearts, so change our hearts to be obedient to You.[67]

• A Prayer • for Salvation

THOSE WHO BELIEVE and trust in the Creator of the universe know they have direct communication with Him; such is the vastness of His mercy and will. While this relationship calls for fulfilling His commandments, it also warrants the ceaseless pursuit of His forgiveness, help, and guidance in every circumstance and condition. The ever-present prospect of calling upon the All-Powerful means that the believer does not face life's tests, temptations, and challenges alone, and that grace and salvation are most surely attainable: "*Our Lord, indeed we have believed; so forgive us our sins and save us from the torment of the Fire*" (3:16).

This supplication expresses the intimate nearness to God that He Himself has granted to the believers. The context in which this prayer appears in Sûrat Âl ʿImrân sets forth the irresistible allure that the enticements and adornments of life exert over people—prestige, abundance of children, and stores of gold, silver, and other objects that one covets. The Quran cautions that these are but fleeting indulgences and that the finest of pleasures are those that endure with God in the Gardens He has prepared for the believers (3:14–15).

Faith in God calls for shunning deceit, avarice, and impulsiveness in order to ascend to the rigorous and edifying virtues of truthfulness, perseverance, self-sacrifice, and generosity. These virtues bring about the moral rectitude that enables one to adhere to God's commandments and spend freely of His bounties for His cause. They help one, moreover, to become steadfast in seeking God's forgiveness, especially at those moments when the heart is receptive and tender and is aware that God has promised to answer the prayers of the believers. The Prophet ﷺ stated that God has said:

> O Son of Adam, so long as you call upon Me and request of Me, I shall forgive you despite what you have done,

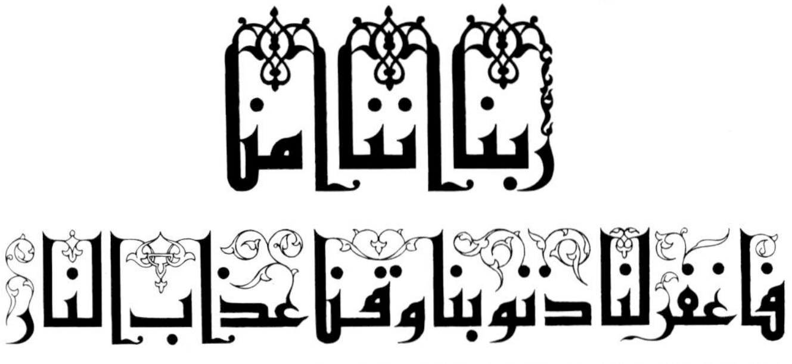

Our Lord, indeed we have believed; so forgive us our sins and save us from the torment of the Fire.

— The Quran, 3:16

The Prophet ﷺ said, "Virtuousness is good morality, and sinfulness is what agitates your soul and what you would dislike people knowing of."

> and I shall not mind. O Son of Adam, were your sins to reach the heights of the sky and were you then to seek forgiveness from Me, I would forgive you, and I shall not mind. O Son of Adam, were you to come to Me with sins nearly as great as the earth and were you then to come before Me—associating nothing with Me—I would bring you forgiveness nearly as great as the earth.[68]

There is no greater honor and expression of mercy than God's granting the Children of Adam the blessing of freely addressing and asking of Him without intermediary.

• The Kinship • of Faith

RELATIONS RUN DEEP for those who meet upon the creed of God's oneness and share a common outlook about the purpose of human existence on earth and its consequences in the world to come. The Quran calls the fraternity of faith that springs from this communion a brotherhood: *Indeed, the believers are brethren* (49:10).

This fellowship of belief draws its mantle over space and time, establishing rights and moral obligations among its members. One such duty requires us to pray for earlier believers who strove in the face of hardship to deliver the message of faith to their heirs. These forerunners in faith have departed this life, but death has not ended their presence. They endure in the hearts and prayers of those who ask God to forgive the believing generations that have passed away.

Thus, the Quran has forever preserved the model of those who lived and practiced this elevated sense of brotherhood. They prayed, *Our Lord, forgive us and our brethren who preceded us in faith, and let not into our hearts malice for those who believe. Our Lord, indeed You are all-kind, mercy-giving* (59:10). This entreaty holds a great lesson for the believers of every generation; it encourages one to seek to ennoble his or her soul by transcending the selfishness, malice, or rancor that pulls one's clay nature earthward. The Prophet ﷺ said:

> Do not envy one another; do not bid up one another deceitfully; do not abhor one another; do not turn away from one another; and do not undercut the transactions of one another. But be, O servants of Allah, brethren. A Muslim is the brother of a Muslim; he neither wrongs him, nor holds him in contempt, nor fails him. The fear of God is here [and he pointed to his chest three times]. It is

Our Lord, forgive us and our brethren who preceded us in faith, and let not into our hearts malice for those who believe. Our Lord, indeed You are all-kind, mercy-giving.

— The Quran, 59:10

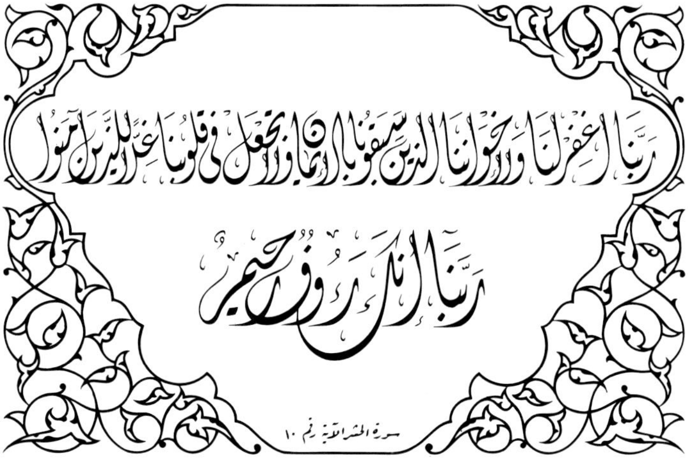

> evil enough for a person to hold his brother Muslim in contempt. The whole of a Muslim is inviolable to another Muslim—his blood, his property, and his honor.[69]

He said also, "None of you has believed until he loves for his brother what he loves for himself."[70] The Prophet ﷺ warned Muslims that discord brings about ruin and that the breakdown of cordial relations eats away at the cohesion of the community. He emphasized that a pure heart cleansed of ill will conveys one to eternal reward in Paradise.

The Prophet ﷺ said, "Let one who believes in God and the Last Day be good to his neighbor. Let one who believes in God and the Last Day be generous to his guest. Let one who believes in God and the Last Day say what is good or keep silent."

Once, the Prophet ﷺ pointed to a modest person in Madinah and said to his Companions, "Behold a man of the Garden!" Hearing this, the young ʿAbdullâh ibn ʿAmr ibn al-ʿÂṣ became eager to discover the secret of the man's success and thus stayed with him in his home for three nights to observe him. ʿAbdullâh, however, saw nothing exceptional in his practice of Islam. So he told him of the Prophet's ﷺ statement and said he desired to follow his example but found his worship ordinary. "I do nothing other than what you have seen," said the man. Then he added, "But I hold no grudge in my heart against any Muslim, nor do I deceive anyone, nor do I envy anyone for the bounty God has bestowed upon him." ʿAbdullâh said, "This is what has elevated you to this rank."[71]

None of you has believed until he loves for his brother what he loves for himself.

—Prophet Muḥammad ﷺ

The Prophet ﷺ warned that the erosion of mutual consideration diminishes one's claim to Islam because it contradicts its basic principles. He said to his Companions, "Shall I tell you what is superior in rank to fasting, praying, and giving charity?" They said, "Yes!" He said, "It is the mending of relationships, for the dissolution of relationships—these are the shears. And I do not say the shearing of hair, but the shearing of religion!"[72]

Thus the Prophet ﷺ encouraged those whose hearts pang with ill feelings against others to invoke God with the prayer, "*Our Lord, forgive us and our brethren who preceded us in faith, and let not into our hearts malice for those who believe. Our Lord, indeed You are all-kind, mercy-giving*" (59:10), for it holds an antidote for the harboring of enmity.

The Believers at the Battle of Uḥud

FREEDOM TO WORSHIP God is the birthright of every human being. The Quran declares, *Whoever wills may believe and whoever wills may disbelieve* (18:29). Yet the nature and history of relations within the human race lead to a solemn fact: The preservation of this basic liberty is guaranteed only by the willingness of the believers to secure and defend it against those who deny the primacy of this right and actively seek to contravene it.

In the midst of the struggle to maintain the right to worship without coercion or restriction, the believer turns to his or her Lord and asks His help, as did an early group of believers, whose supplication the Quran records: "*Our Lord, forgive us our sins and our excesses in our affairs; and set firm our feet, and help us against the disbelieving people*" (3:147).

This prayer came as a lesson to the first generation of Muslims, though its application endures for all. During the Battle of Uḥud,[73] a rumor spread that the Prophet ﷺ

had been killed, throwing some of his Companions into confusion. This verse was then revealed, underscoring an axiom of history: Whenever the opponents of disbelief moved to repress the believers' right to worship God alone, the prophets and their followers adhered to faith and engaged in a struggle, against whatever odds, to maintain this most basic freedom.

The march of faith never halted with the death of any prophet, scholar, or leader. Rather, the good carried on the task of living the faith and sharing its guidance with others, entreating God to forgive their mistakes and to hearten and support them.

Seven years after the Battle of Uḥud, when the Prophet,

Our Lord, forgive us our sins and our excesses in our affairs; and set firm our feet, and help us against the disbelieving people.

— The Quran, 3:147

God's peace and blessings be upon him, did depart from this life, the first caliph, Abû Bakr, called the stunned and grief-stricken community to remember its mission by reciting from the Quran the verses revealed at Uḥud that introduce the above supplication:

> *And Muḥammad is no more than a messenger. Truly messengers have passed away before him. Were he to die or be killed, would you turn back on your heels? And whoever turns back on his heels shall never harm Allah in anything. And Allah shall recompense the thankful.* (3:144)

The Prophet ﷺ said, "Do you know what backbiting is?" They said, "God and His Messenger know best." He said, "It is to mention about your brother what he dislikes." It was said, "Even if what I say about my brother is true." The Prophet ﷺ said, "If what you said about him is true, then you were backbiting him. And if what you say ⌜about him⌝ is not so, then you have charged him falsely."

• Dialogue with the • Disbelievers in the Afterlife

DISCOURSE ABOUT FAITH and disbelief in God will continue in the Afterlife, although the nature of the debate will differ greatly from its character in this life. In the disputations of this world, any human being may assert his or her position, and others have the right to accept or reject. Anyone who chooses to oppose another's stand has the option of contending the matter gently or harshly. Some become convinced with arguments in favor of faith and thus choose to believe in the true and only God and His religion. Yet others dismiss faith in the Creator as naive, irrational, or ancient.

A like discussion will convene in the Hereafter under very different circumstances. Every person will have been resurrected from his or her grave and each will have been recompensed according to his or her beliefs and deeds on earth: Those who excelled in faith shall be rewarded with joy and the deniers and wrongdoers with torment. The Quran gives a glimpse of the believers, delighted in Paradise, inquiring of one another and questioning their former opponents now steeped in misery:

> *And some of them shall turn to others, asking one another questions. One of them shall say, "Once I had a close friend who would say, 'Do you hold this to be true that when we are dead and have become dust and bones, we will indeed be judged?'"*
>
> *He shall say, "Will you ⌜People of the Garden⌝ look?" So he shall look and see ⌜his close friend⌝ in the midst of Hellfire. He shall say, "By God, you ⌜my former friend⌝ very nearly doomed me! Had it not been for the grace of my Lord, surely I would have been of those brought there ⌜in the Fire⌝. Do we not, then, die except for our first death and shall we not be tormented?" This is indeed the great success, and for the like of this ⌜reward⌝ let the workers work.* (37:50–61)

The denizens of the Fire will bicker among themselves, beg for cool drink from the believers, and implore the angels who guard Hell (called *zabâniya*) to intercede with God on their behalf to alleviate their suffering. But all shall be refused. They will then turn to their Lord imploring Him for His mercy and deliverance from Hellfire. The Quran states that on the Day of Judgment, God will address all His servants and speak specifically to the wrongdoers. He will confront them with their denial of Him in this life and then disclose their misdeeds, reminding them of how they laughed at those who upheld belief

The Companion of the Prophet, ʿUmar ibn al-Khaṭṭâb, related that a woman was running ⌜to and fro⌝ in search of her baby. When she found him, she drew him close to her body and suckled him. The Messenger of God ﷺ then said to his Companions, "Can you envision this woman throwing her son into the fire?" We said, "By God, no, as long as she has the power not to throw him in to it." The Prophet ﷺ said, "God is more merciful toward His servant than this woman is toward her child."

in God and how they mocked those who asked Him for pardon and grace. He shall say to the wrongdoers:

> *And do not speak to Me. Surely there was a party of My servants who said, "Our Lord, we have believed; so forgive us and have mercy upon us, for You are the best of the merciful." But you took them as a mockery—until your mockery of them caused you to forget My remembrance—and you were laughing at them.* (23:108–10)

The Quran recounts the culminating discourse about faith between believers and wrongdoers in the Hereafter to remind humanity that this world is the real arena of performance and the appropriate place to beseech God for His mercy and forgiveness and for peace and bliss in the Hereafter. Moreover, this narration warns all who

Our Lord, we have believed; so forgive us and have mercy upon us, for You are the best of the merciful.

— The Quran, 23:109

would ridicule a believer's devotion to God: Reconsider your own soul's eternal destiny before death bars you evermore from readying yourself to meet the Lord of the Worlds with righteous deeds and a sound heart.

The Companion Samura ibn Jundub wrote to his son, "Now then, the Messenger of God ﷺ commanded us to have mosques, to make them in our dwellings [diyârinâ], *to take suitable care of them, and to clean them."*

The People of "The Heights"

GOD WILL RESTORE the life of every member of the human family in the Hereafter. The Quran states this with certainty. The mention of the stages of the Last Day and many of its details occurs in hundreds of verses, for belief in the Afterlife—the Resurrection, the Standing, and the Judgment—is a cardinal tenet of Islam. It is the promise of God and His Messenger that it will be a fearsome event.

The Quran's seventh sura, known as "al-Aʿrâf" or "The Heights," gives a unique account of one phase of the Last Day when God will sort people into three groupings—after which a dialogue between them shall emerge (7:37–58).

The uppermost group is called "the People of the Garden" and the lowermost party, "the People of the Fire." A veil set between them prevents the blessed light of the Garden dwellers from reaching the inmates of Hell and stops the woeful misery of the inhabitants of the Fire from coming near those of the Garden. The veil does not, however, prevent conversation between the two assemblages concerning matters of faith and the acts that they each used to pursue in the course of their brief lives on earth. It is a discourse that will finally resolve their former disputes about believing in one God and the Last Day, for which the denizens of Hell had formerly oppressed and mocked the believers.

It is the third group, however, that these verses of "The Heights" center on, and from which the sura takes its name, for these are the People of the Heights, that is, the people assembled on a plateau from which they await God's decree and are able to see and communicate with

Our Lord, let us not be among the wrongdoing people.

— The Quran, 7:47

The Prophet ﷺ related: "God the Exalted, the Majestic has said, 'I have prepared for My righteous servants what no eye has seen and no ear has heard, and what has never occurred to a human heart.' The confirmation of this is in the Book of God: 'So not a soul knows what has been hidden for it from what shall comfort the eyes—a reward for what they have been doing' (32:17)."

both the People of the Garden and the People of the Fire. The People of the Heights have not yet entered the Garden and hope with great anxiety that they will be delivered to this final destination. They fear with terrible trepidation the torment and suffering of the People of the Fire, whom they see and hear. Thus, they cry out to their Lord whenever they behold the People of the Fire, *"Our Lord, let us not be among the wrongdoing people"* (7:47).

This prayer reminds the believer of the spectacle of the Hereafter and its awesome events. In so doing, it also inspires one to consciously avoid, in this life, the ways and actions of those who wrong themselves and do evil to others. It heartens one to persevere in the performance of righteous deeds—even in the face of threat and ridicule—keeping always before one the image of the People of the Garden and their light and felicitous ends in Heaven. Those adhering to goodness shall ultimately express their gratitude to their Lord:

> *And they shall say, "All praise is for Allah, who has guided us to this, and we would not have been guided had not Allah guided us. Truly, the messengers of our Lord came with the truth." And they shall be called: "This is the Garden you are given to inherit for that which you have done."* (7:43)

The Believers of Reflection

THE QURAN SAYS that the most reflective believers are moved by their meditations upon creation to a profound remembrance of God. In fact, the Quran welcomingly invites such reflection.

> *Indeed, in the creation of the heavens and the earth, and in the alternation of night and day are signs for people of understanding, those who remember Allah while standing and sitting and lying on their sides, and they reflect on the creation of the heavens and the earth.* (3:190–91)

In their contemplation of creation, such believers become acutely aware of its significance as both a bountiful blessing and a school of signs pointing to the mighty Hand of the all-powerful Creator. They pray:

> *Our Lord, do forgive us our sins, and absolve us of our misdeeds, and take our souls with the virtuous. Our Lord, and give us what You have promised us through Your messengers, and do not disgrace us on the Day of Resurrection. Indeed, You do not fail the promise.* (3:193–94)

The verses that make up the context of this supplication address the relationship between the human being's

The Messenger of God ﷺ said to his Companions, "Do you realize who is the destitute?" They said, "The destitute among us is one who has no money nor any belongings." The Prophet ﷺ then said, "Truly, the destitute of my community is one who comes on the Day of Resurrection with Prayer [Ṣalât] *and Fasting* [Ṣawm] *and Alms* [Zakât] *yet he has insulted someone and defamed someone and devoured the wealth of someone and shed the blood of someone and struck someone. Thus one of them is given of his good deeds and another is given of his good deeds, until his good deeds come to an end before what he owes has been fulfilled. Then some of their sins shall be taken and flung upon him. Then he will be flung into the Fire."*

meditative nature and the great varieties of creation in the furthest reaches of this vast universe—seen and unseen. They assert that a free mind uncluttered with prejudice and impertinence can read the countless signs and proofs in the open book of creation that clearly point to the existence and glory of its Creator.

The narrow and flawed premises based on the dismissal of revealed knowledge attempt to cast nature, its wonders and signs, into a mold that points to the glorification of the human being. But tension and contradiction inhere in these ideologies, for the human being has been fashioned to glean from nature the higher principles of divine purpose. In the planets, stars, and galaxies; in light and darkness; in the oceans and continents; in the mountains and valleys; in meadows and rivers—the great diversity of terrain and life is unmistakable evidence for people of understanding. Thus the mindful believer remembers God in labor and in repose, and reflects on the creation of the heavens and earth. The meditations of the sound mind naturally lead it to the important questions of life, among them, *What is the significance of existence and the ultimate end of every being?* The response culminates in the joy of glorifying the originator of the heavens and the earth, the All-Wise and the Almighty, and to the rejection of the notion of life as frivolous play or the result of some random occurrence or chaos. "*Our Lord, You have not created this ˹world˺ falsely. Glory be to You*" (3:191). The reflective believer searches for the words to express his or her hopes for God's reward for having answered the call of His messengers and prophets.

> *Our Lord, we have heard a caller calling to faith, "Believe in Your Lord!" So we have believed. Our Lord, do forgive us our sins, and absolve us of our misdeeds, and take our souls with the virtuous. Our Lord, and give us what You have promised us through Your messengers, and do not disgrace us on the Day of Resurrection. Indeed, You do not fail the promise.* (3:193–94)

God, the All-Granting, responds by assuring the believers that He does not neglect the good works of anyone. It is invaluable to ponder the deep effect these verses had on the Prophet ﷺ when revealed to him in Madinah. His wife ʿÂ'isha reported:

> One night the Prophet ﷺ said, "O ʿÂ'isha, allow me to worship my Lord tonight." I said, "By Allah, I love being near you, yet I equally love what pleases you." Then he

ربنا فاغفر لنا ذنوبنا وكفر عنا سيئاتنا

وتوفنا مع الأبرار

Our Lord, do forgive us our sins, and absolve us of our misdeeds, and take our souls with the virtuous.

— The Quran, 3:193

The Companion ʿAbdullâh ibn Busr said, "I have heard a report since long ago that if ever you are amidst a group of twenty men, or somewhat more or less, and you look into their faces and find no one among them who is esteemed for the sake of God, then know that the state of affairs ˹of the community˺ has indeed become fragile."

left his bed, performed ablution, and stood in Prayer, crying continuously until his clothes became wet. Then he sat down ˹in Prayer˺ upon the ground, crying until his beard became wet. When Bilâl [a close Companion of the Prophet and the Caller to Prayer] came to inform him of the coming of Dawn Prayer, he saw him crying and said, "O Messenger of Allah, do you cry though Allah has forgiven you whatever you may have done and whatever you may do?" The Prophet ﷺ said, "Shall I not then be a grateful worshipper? Tonight, verses have been revealed to me [referring to the closing verses of the Quran's third sura (Âl ʿImrân)]—and woe to those who recite them without reflecting on them!"[74]

Whenever he recited these verses, the Prophet ﷺ asked God to enlighten his heart and guide his thinking. The Companion ʿAbdullâh ibn ʿAbbâs said that he spent one night with the Prophet ﷺ and saw him arising for Prayer (*Ṣalât*) before dawn and heard him reciting these same verses. Then on the way to the mosque, he lifted his gaze toward the heavens and prayed, "O Allah, let there be light in my heart, light on my tongue, light in my ears, light in my eyes, light before me, light behind me, light above me, and light beneath me. O Allah, give me light."[75]

· The Believers · of Thanksgiving

THE UNDERPINNINGS OF Muslim belief entail certain responsibilities and imply that one must acquire the will to fulfill them. This calls for the moral drive to carry one through to the goals of faith and to enable one to overcome obstacles along the way. The believer derives this spiritual energy by turning to God, the source of all power and all blessings:

> *My Lord, dispose me to give thanks for Your grace, with which You have graced me and my parents, and that I do righteous deeds with which You are pleased. And make righteous for me my children. Indeed, I have repented to You, and surely I am of the Muslims.* (46:15)

There is something subtle and beautiful about asking God to help one nurture feelings of gratitude to Him for the abundant favors He has bestowed. It testifies that the servant recognizes that his or her Lord's blessings must not be employed in ways that displease Him. When one's heart yearns with so elevated an aspiration as to be always a mindful worshipper, it is instinctive for one to entreat God for the inspiration to labor for His love and pleasure alone ("*Dispose me that I do righteous deeds with which You are pleased*").

Then, like the prophets and the believers of the past, one desires in the recesses of the soul to see this passion for good works perpetuated into the future ("*And make righteous for me my children*"). Moreover, the awakened worshipper apprehends that when one submits to God alone and diligently nurtures an ethic of turning to Him for forgiveness, such a person is given hope for success in this world and in the Afterlife ("*Indeed, I have repented to You, and surely I am of the Muslims*").

My Lord, dispose me to give thanks for Your grace, with which You have graced me and my parents, and that I do righteous deeds with which You are pleased. And make righteous for me my children. Indeed, I have repented to You, and surely I am of the Muslims.

— The Quran, 46:15

رَبِّ

أَوْزِعْنِي أَنْ أَشْكُرَ نِعْمَتَكَ الَّتِي أَنْعَمْتَ عَلَيَّ وَعَلَى وَالِدَيَّ

وَأَنْ أَعْمَلَ صَالِحًا تَرْضَاهُ

وَأَصْلِحْ لِي فِي ذُرِّيَّتِي إِنِّي تُبْتُ إِلَيْكَ وَإِنِّي مِنَ الْمُسْلِمِينَ

سورة الأحقاف الآية رقم ١٥

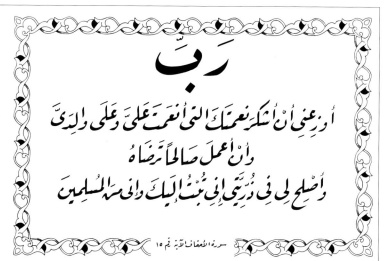

Thus the Prophet ﷺ taught his Companions to say the following supplication at the end of every Prayer (*Ṣalât*):

> O God, bind our hearts together. Set aright relations among us. Guide us upon the way of peace. Deliver us from darkness into light. Separate us from vile deeds, whatever may be concealed of them and whatever revealed. Bless us in our hearing and our sight, our hearts and our spouses, and our children. Grant us repentance, for You are the Ever-Relenting, the Mercy-Giving. And enable us to be thankful for Your grace, and to extol You for it, and to be accepting of it. And perfect it for us.[76]

Further, the Prophet ﷺ taught his Companions to constantly seek God's protection against thoughts, characters, conditions, and ailments that impede one from doing righteous deeds, and to ever turn to God for refuge against insufficiency, humiliation, the commission of injustice, or being subjected to injustice:

> O Allah, I seek refuge in You from the harm of what I have done and the harm of what I have not done. I seek refuge in You from disbelief and poverty and the torment of the grave. And I seek refuge in You from feebleness and laziness. And I seek refuge in You from cowardliness and avarice. And I seek refuge in You from overwhelming debt and overpowering men. O Allah, suffice me with what You have made lawful against what is unlawful, and enrich me with Your favor against Your disfavor.[77]

"Why should we not believe in God and the truth that has come to us and long for our Lord to enter us with the righteous people." So God has rewarded them for what they have said—Gardens beneath which the rivers flow, abiding therein forever. Such is the reward of those who excel in good.

— The Quran, 5:84–85

• The Believers' • Perfect Light

THE UNIVERSAL ORDER we ponder and in which we live, the mysteries and majestic balance of which we seek to understand, shall not last forever. The Quran foretells the annihilation of creation and the dramatic tribulations of a day when the mountains are swept away, the seas boil over, the sun and the moon enfold, the stars collapse, and the skies are stripped away. These events will mark the end of an existence we have only begun to better understand and the beginning of an everlasting one that the Quran repeatedly describes and brings to our attention.

Every human being who has ever lived will pass through certain stages in the Afterlife along the way to his or her final dwelling place. God will resurrect us from the dead and summon us to the great Plain of the Standing, where we will assemble, abide in awesome anticipation, and tarry in our sweat, until the Balance in which our deeds will be weighed is established and the Traverse across Hellfire is laid. There we will await God's judgment, at which time He will speak to each individual and pass perfect and just judgment over each: Paradise or Hell.

In each phase, one will be enshrouded in horror and fear, and feel in desperate need of assistance and guidance. Parents and children, husbands and wives, friends and brothers will flee from one another, distressed over the state of their own souls. But God, the Exalted, will command the angels to lower their wings upon the believers and calm their fears. They will guide them through the trials of this day, speaking words of comfort to them, saying, *"This is your day, the day you have been promised"* (21:103).

The believers will see and realize the fulfillment of all the conditions that their Lord had promised them in His Book and through the words and teachings of His messengers. They will long to reach the end of judgment and ardently appeal to the Master of that day to complete His favor upon them, pardon them, and grant them the blessing of guiding them to eternal serenity and delight. They will cry out, *"Our Lord, perfect for us our light, and forgive us, for surely You are powerful over all things"* (66:8).

This prayer in Sûrat al-Taḥrîm constitutes a special call to people to guard themselves and their families against

رَبَّنَآ أَتْمِمْ لَنَا نُورَنَا وَٱغْفِرْ لَنَآ
إِنَّكَ عَلَىٰ كُلِّ شَىْءٍ قَدِيرٌ

Our Lord, perfect for us our light, and forgive us, for surely You are powerful over all things.

— The Quran, 66:8

Three Men in a Cave

The Prophet ﷺ once told his Companions:

ONCE THREE MEN went out for a walk, and a rainstorm overtook them, so they took shelter in a mountain cave. But then a boulder slid down the mountain and blocked the entrance of the cave, shutting them in. So they said to one another, "By God, nothing will deliver you but the truth! So let each of you recall righteous deeds—the best of what you have done sincerely for the sake of God—and implore God by them. It may be that God will remove it from your way."

So the first of them said, "O God, I had parents, aged and advanced in years, and my wife and young children, all of whom I attended. And whenever I returned with my herd, I would milk the herd and begin by offering my parents to drink before my children. One day, I ranged far away for pasturage and did not return until evening and found my parents sleeping. I milked the herd as I usually did, and I brought in the milk vessel and stood beside their heads. I did not like to wake them from their sleep, nor did I like to give milk to the children before them, though the children were clamoring at my feet. And this situation continued until the break of dawn. Then they awoke and drank their milk. So if You know that I have done this seeking Your Countenance, then make for us an opening through which we may see the sky."

So it opened somewhat, but still they were not able to go out.

Another said, "O God, I had a cousin whom I loved as ardently as a man can love a woman. And I solicited her to have her, but she refused and kept herself from me, until she was stricken one year with famine. Then she came to me, and I gave her 120 gold coins, on the condition that she would yield herself to me. She conceded. Then when I had power over her, she said, 'I deem it not permissible for you to break the seal without due right ⌜of marriage⌝.' So I refrained from coming upon her, and I turned away from her, even though she was, of all people, the most beloved to me. I left for her the gold that I had given her. So if You know that I have done this out of being fearful of You, then relieve us."

So it opened somewhat, but still they were not able to go out.

Then the last one said, "O God, I hired a workman for a bushel of rice. When I showed him his bushel, he disliked it and went away leaving it behind. So I kept replanting it until I accumulated enough from it to buy cows. ⌜Years later⌝ he returned and demanded of me his wages, and said, 'Fear God and do not deprive me of my right.' I told him, 'Proceed to these cows and take them.' He said, 'Fear God and do not mock me!' I said, 'I am not mocking you. Take these cows.' So he took them, and went on his way. So if You know that I have done this out of seeking Your mercy and fearing Your punishment, then relieve us."

Thus God relieved them and they departed the cave.[78]

And when they hear what has been sent down to the Messenger, you see their eyes overflowing with tears because of the truth which they recognize. They say, "Our Lord, we have believed; so inscribe us among those who bear witness."

— The Quran, 5:83

any deed that displeases God and the recompense of which lies in Hellfire. It summons them to immediately seek His forgiveness for their misdeeds and to strive to please Him, while they still have life.

The Quran provides the believers with the incentive to meet the rigors of this life in order to enjoy the peace of the next, that God may forgive them on the Day of Judgment and grant them an unfailing light that will ease their way to the eternal Garden. When they see their light running before them and about them, they will yearn to behold God's perfect light, and ask the Deliverer to convey them to endless joy.

The Universality of Belief

THE EARLY REVELATIONS of the Quran directed the Prophet ﷺ to worship none other than God, the Lord of the Worlds, and to invite people to worship their Creator and prepare to stand before His judgment in the Hereafter. The Prophet ﷺ fulfilled this imperative in part by advising a group of his earliest followers to migrate under the leadership of Jaʿfar ibn Abî Ṭâlib to another continent and society. The company of Muslims, numbering less than a hundred men and women, crossed the Red Sea to Abyssinia in East Africa, for there reigned "a king under whose rule people were not oppressed," the Prophet ﷺ said.[79] The Negus (al-Najâshî) was indeed a just monarch, and his people were devout Christians loyal to their clergy.

The idol-worshipping Quraysh, however, resolved to cut the promising relations growing between the Negus and the Muslim émigrés. They dispatched emissaries to the king seeking the extradition of the Muslims. When

O Allah!

their initial attempts to gain custody of the Muslims failed, the Makkan opposition claimed that the followers of the new faith repudiated Jesus and did not revere Mary, the mother of Jesus, or the Christian scripture. The Qurayshite emissaries portrayed them as rebellious youths and petitioned that they be returned to Makkah, suggesting that they knew best how to recompense their own.

Jaʿfar ibn Abî Ṭâlib was summoned by the Negus to answer these charges. He stood before the king and the attendant bishops of the court defending the case of Islam and that of the believers. He said:

> O King, we were a people steeped in ignorance, worshipping idols, eating carrion, committing abominations, severing relations with kinship and ill-treating our neighbors. The strong among us devoured the weak. This has been our way until God sent us a messenger from our midst. We know his lineage, his truthfulness, his trustworthiness, and his integrity. He called us to God—to believe in Him alone and worship Him—and to renounce what we and our fathers used to worship apart from Him, of stones and idols. He commanded us to speak the truth, fulfill trusts, be dutiful to kinship, be good to our neighbors, and to refrain from what is forbidden and from bloodshed. And he has forbidden us from obscenities, from speaking falsehoods, from devouring the property of the orphan, and from vilifying virtuous women. And he has commanded us to worship

> God alone, and never associate anything with Him. And he has commanded us to establish Prayer, Charity, and Fasting. [Then Jaʿfar listed the tenets of Islam.] So we accepted his truth, and we have believed in him. And we have followed what he has brought from God. Thus we worshipped God alone and we did not associate anything with Him. And we held as forbidden what He has forbidden and lawful what He has made lawful.
>
> Then our people turned against us and tormented us and persecuted us, to ⌜compel us to⌝ forsake our religion and revert back to the worship of idols instead of the worship of God, the Exalted, and to ⌜compel us to⌝ indulge in the evil deeds we used to indulge in. So when they oppressed us and treated us unjustly and constrained our lives and denied us our religion, we came to your land and have chosen you above all others. And we are hopeful for your protection, and request that we not suffer injustice with you.[80]

Then Jaʿfar recited verses from Sûrat Maryam that tell of the miraculous birth of Jesus. After its translation by the court interpreters, the Negus and his Bishops immediately rejected the designs of the Makkans to stir up enmity between the believers and their Abyssinian, Christian hosts. The Negus said, "This has truly come from the same source as that which Jesus brought. . . . What do you say of Jesus?"

Jaʿfar said, "We say of him what our Prophet brought to us, that he is the servant of God, and he is His messen-

Umm Kulthûm bint ʿUqba, may God be pleased with her, stated that the Prophet ﷺ said, "The best of charity is beneficence to a resentful relative."

ᶜAbdullâh ibn Masᶜûd reported that the Prophet ﷺ said, "Each loan is an act of charity."

ger and His spirit and His word which He cast unto Mary, the virgin."

The Negus picked up a splinter of wood and said, "Jesus, the son of Mary, does not exceed what you have said by the length of this stick."

Nearly fifteen years later, in the eighth year of Hijra, Jaᶜfar and the Muslims returned to the Prophet ﷺ and the swelling community of Madinah. The Negus sent a delegation of clergy with them. The Prophet ﷺ received them and recited to them the Quran. Their eyes welled up with tears, and they echoed the words spoken by the disciples of Jesus six centuries before, when they had seen a great sign from God (3:53). The Quran itself hallowed the response of the Abyssinian envoys and preserved it in its verses:

> *And when they hear what has been sent down to the Messenger, you see their eyes overflowing with tears because of the truth which they recognize. They say, "Our Lord we have believed; so inscribe us among those who bear witness. Why should we not believe in Allah and the truth that has come to us and long for our Lord to enter us with the righteous people." So Allah has rewarded them for what they have said—Gardens beneath which rivers flow, abiding therein forever. Such is the reward of those who excel in good.* (5:83–85)

• Women • of Prayer

WOMEN AND MEN are equal worshippers before God, and they shall be rewarded equally for doing and advocating good and standing against evil. This is explicit in the Quran:

> *Indeed, the Muslim men and the Muslim women, and the believing men and the believing women, and the obedient men and the obedient women, and the truthful men and the truthful women, and the patient men and the patient women, and the reverent men and the reverent women, and the charitable men and the charitable women, and the fasting men and the fasting women, and the men who guard their chastity and the women who guard 'theirs', and the men who remember Allah much and the women who remember, Allah has promised them forgiveness and a great reward.* (33:35)

> *Thus has their Lord answered them. For indeed, I do not waste the deed of any doer of you, whether male or female. You are of one another.* (3:195)

> *And whoever does righteous deeds—whether male or female—and is a believer, they then shall enter the Garden, and they shall not be wronged in the least.* (4:124)

ᶜÂ'isha, may God be pleased with her, said, "The Messenger of God ﷺ never exceeded ˹in Prayer [Ṣalât]˺, during Ramadan or other months, more than eleven cycles [rakᶜas]. *He used to pray four—and do not ask of their beauty and their length. Then he would pray another four—and do not ask of their beauty and their length. Then he would pray three. I said ˹once˺, 'O Messenger of God, do you sleep before praying the concluding* [Witr] *Prayer?' He said, 'O ᶜÂ'isha, my eyes sleep, yet my heart does not sleep.'"*

Eve, the Mother of Humanity

Among the supplications of the believers that the Quran immortalizes are a number issuing specifically from believing women throughout the course of human history, beginning with Eve, the first woman and the mother of humanity. When she realized the enormity of disobeying the command of God after she and her husband had eaten from the forbidden tree, both she and Adam cried out to their Lord: *Our Lord, we have wronged ourselves, and if You do not forgive us and have mercy upon us, we shall surely be of the losers* (7:23).

As she was a participant in the act of disobedience, so too was she a partner in regretting her misdeed and an equal in voicing the first human entreaty for pardon and clemency from God for what she and her husband had done and for which each was forgiven.

Âsiya, the Wife of Pharaoh

The Quran exalts the example of Âsiya, the believing wife of the foremost human symbol of tyranny and disbelief for all time, Pharaoh. Âsiya retrieved the infant Moses from the Nile and thus spared him from the fate of Pharaoh's decree of death for all newborn males of the Children of Israel, and she reared him as a son in the palace. Then, when Moses had reached full maturity, God chose him, bestowing the honor of prophethood upon him. Thus Moses went forth to Pharaoh, calling him to abandon his false claims to divinity and Lordship, to rid himself of arrogance, to become a servant of the true God, and to free the Children of Israel from slavery and to allow them to depart for the sacred land of Palestine. But Pharaoh rejected Moses' call and accused him of sorcery and fabrication, condemning to death any who believed in Moses and ordering the crucifixion of any who abandoned allegiance to himself.

Âsiya, however, knew well the truthfulness of Moses and answered his call. In the face of Pharaoh's persecution, she turned to the God of Aaron and Moses for refuge in this life and asked Him to prepare a dwelling for her near Him in Paradise:

> *And Allah has set forth an example, for those who believe, the wife of Pharaoh, when she said, "My Lord, build for me near You a house in the Garden. And deliver me from Pharaoh and his doings, and deliver me from the wrongdoing people."* (66:11)

God, the Answerer of Prayer, did indeed deliver her and all those persecuted by Pharaoh, for God overwhelmed Pharaoh and his hosts in the sea. As for Âsiya, God has preserved her prayer as a symbol of courage

رب ابن لي عندك بيتا في الجنة
ونجني من فرعون وعمله ونجني من القوم الظالمين

My Lord, build for me near You a house in the Garden. And deliver me from Pharaoh and his doings, and deliver me from the wrongdoing people.

— The Quran, 66:11

and belief and as an exhortation to heed the call of reason and faith even against the coercion inherent in the culture of disbelief and intimidation.

Balqîs, the Queen of Sheba

Generations after the time of Âsiya, a wise woman, named Balqîs, ascended to the throne of the wealthy, though idol-worshipping, kingdom of Sheba in southern Arabia (which encompasses present-day Yemen). Balqîs ruled her people on the basis of consultation, and she was a contemporary of Solomon, to whom God had given a kingdom the like of which He has not bestowed upon anyone after him. Solomon called for people to

[Balqîs] said, "My Lord, I have indeed wronged myself, and I submit myself, together with Solomon, to Allah, Lord of the Worlds."

— The Quran, 27:44

قَالَتْ رَبِّ إِنِّي ظَلَمْتُ نَفْسِي
وَأَسْلَمْتُ مَعَ سُلَيْمَٰنَ لِلَّهِ رَبِّ ٱلْعَٰلَمِينَ

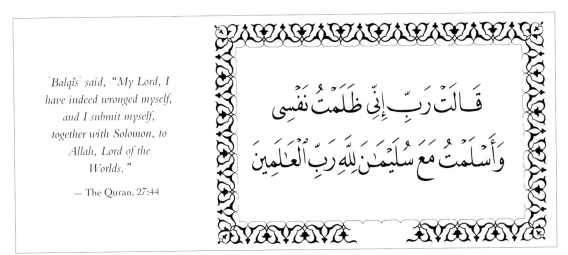

abandon the worship of idols and to come to believe in the Creator alone. When he learned of the Queen and her errant beliefs, he sent to her a brief and forceful letter:

> *She said, "O noblemen, an honorable letter has been cast down to me. And it is from Solomon, and it is, 'In the name of Allah, the All-Merciful, the Mercy-Giving. Do not exalt yourselves above me, and come to me in submission.'"* (27:29–31)

The Queen truly loved her people and wanted neither to bring destruction upon them nor to hastily declare war upon Solomon and his hosts. The Quran tells us, however, that her blind adherence to the ways of her forefathers turned her away from Solomon's call to worship God alone. Rather, she sought to pacify Solomon through diplomacy and dispatched valuable gifts to him. Solomon, however, spurned the gifts, saying that what God had bestowed upon him was better than the treasures of the world.

Later, when she came to Solomon, she beheld with her own eyes all that God had granted him. She saw, as well, how a faithful sovereign endowed with great fortunes remained firm in belief of his Maker. When all of this became manifest to her, she declared her faith in the true and only God and sought forgiveness for her misguided ways. *She said, "My Lord, I have indeed wronged myself, and I submit myself, together with Solomon, to Allah, Lord of the*

غافر الذنب وقابل التوب
شديد العقاب ذي الطول
لا إله إلا هو
إليه المصير

The forgiver of sin, accepter of repentance, severe in punishment, all-reaching! There is no God but He. To Him is the ultimate destiny.

— The Quran, 40:3

Worlds" (27:44). God accepted her prayer and preserved her memory for us, that we may not permit ambition, position, or wealth to deprive us of choosing devoted service to the Lord of the Worlds.

Prayerful Mother and Daughter

God has conferred His blessings upon many people throughout time. But among the loftiest examples of His favor is that which He bestowed upon the wife of ʿImrân, whose life was rich with abiding lessons.

When she perceived the presence of a child in her womb, she became concerned for the future of this growing life. She aspired in her heart to have a son who would bear the mission and message of his forefathers from among the Children of Abraham, invite people to the oneness of God, the Most High, and live a devout and pure life. So she turned to her Lord: *"My Lord, I have dedicated to You in devotion what is in my womb. So accept it from*

رب إني نذرت لك ما في بطني محررا فتقبل مني إنك أنت السميع العليم

My Lord, I have dedicated to You in devotion what is in my womb. So accept it from me. Indeed, You are the All-Hearing, the All-Knowing.

— The Quran, 3:35

me. Indeed, You are the All-Hearing, the All-Knowing" (3:35). God willed, however, that the new life be a female. So when the wife of ʿImrân delivered her and named her "Mary," she poured out her heart to her Lord, with reverence and devotion, entreating God to protect her daughter and her daughter's children as well from evil and the promptings of Satan. God answered her prayer:

> *She said, "My Lord, indeed I have delivered her, a female"—and Allah knows best what she delivered. "And the male is not like the female. And I have named her Mary. And I seek refuge for her and her children in You from Satan, the accursed." Thus her Lord accepted her with a good acceptance and made her to grow with a good growing.* (3:36–37)

Thus, Mary grew in the footsteps of her pious mother. The Quran records that she was given into the care of Prophet Zechariah, who would find her in her sanctuary in constant remembrance of her Lord, placing her every need before Him for fulfillment, offering thanks to Him, and celebrating His praises for His blessings upon her and her family. It was there in her sanctuary that an angel came to her in human form to give her the glad tidings that she would bear a child in a miraculous manner, that her son would be born without a father, by the command of God and in accordance with His will. She was terrified

> *God bears witness that surely there is no God but He—as do the angels and those with knowledge—upholding justice. There is no God but He, the Overpowering, the All-Wise.*
>
> — The Quran, 3:18

Bahz bin Ḥakîm reported from his father, that his grandfather, may God be pleased with him, stated, "I said, 'O Messenger of God, to whom shall I be most dutiful?' He said, 'Your mother. Then your mother. Then your mother. Then your father. And then your next of kin.'"

at the presence of this extraordinary messenger who brought still more extraordinary news:

> *And mention in the Book Mary when she withdrew from her family to an eastward place, and she placed a veil between herself and them. Then We sent to her Our Spirit, who thus appeared before her as a complete human being. She said, "I seek refuge in the All-Merciful from you, if you are God-fearing!" He said, "Indeed, I am only a messenger of your Lord to grant to you a pure boy." She said, "How can I have a boy while no human being has touched me, nor have I been unchaste?" He said, "So shall it be! Your Lord has said, 'This is easy for Me. And We shall make him a sign for all people and a mercy from Us. And it is a matter decreed.'"* (19:16–21)

Fearing disgrace among the people, Mary, in the throes of childbirth, wished to have died before or to have never even existed. At that instant, Jesus, the miraculous newborn, called upon her from beneath her:

> *And the birth pangs drove her to the trunk of a date-palm. She said, "Oh, if only I had died before this and become something utterly forgotten!" Then he called to her from beneath her, "Do not grieve. Indeed, your Lord has placed beneath you a streamlet. And shake toward you the trunk of the date-palm, and it shall drop upon you dates, ripe and fresh. So eat and drink and cool your eyes. And should you see any human being, then say, 'I have vowed to the All-Merciful a fast. Thus I will not speak to any person today.'"* (19:23–26)

When Mary returned with the newborn to her people, they expressed shock and dismay at the thought that one so pure and devout—the descendant of prophets—could have conceived a child in violation of her chastity and in any circumstance other than that of lawful marriage. In the face of these imputations, she refrained from speech, turning only to her Lord for help. She then pointed to the infant, and God aided her with the miracle of Jesus speaking in the cradle:

> *Then she came with him to her people, carrying him. They said, "O Mary, you have indeed brought something outrageous! O sister of Aaron, your father was not an evil person, nor was your mother unchaste." Then she pointed to him. They said, "How can we speak to one who is a child in the cradle?"*
>
> *He said, "Indeed, I am a servant of Allah. He has given me the Book ˊof the Lawˋ and has made me a prophet. And He has made me blessed wherever I may be; and He has charged me with Prayer and Charity, as long as I am alive, and being virtuous to my mother; and He has not made me overbearing, wretched. And peace be upon me the day I was born, and the day I die, and the day I am raised to life."* (19:27–33)

Two millennia later, we still send salutations of peace upon Jesus, upon his mother, upon his true brothers—the honorable prophets—and upon all, from every generation, who believe in his message and his worshipfulness of God.

• 4 •
Prayers of Angels

Beings of Light and Love: The Angels

ANGELS ARE BEINGS of perfect obedience to God, who created them from light, whereas He created humankind from clay and jinn from smokeless fire. The Quran states that the existence of angels preceded that of humanity. Angels, who are genderless beings, neither marry nor bear children. Belief in them (their existence, worshipfulness to God, and role in the scheme of things) is one of the main tenets of faith.

On occasion, angels manifest themselves to human beings in various forms, including human likeness, as did the angel who gave Mary the glad tidings regarding her conception of Jesus, or the two angels who came to Abraham as travelers, foretelling the birth of his son Isaac from Sarah—the very angels who then went to Lot and his community of Sodom bearing destruction.

Numerous angels reside in Heaven, from where they descend to earth to carry out the commands of God. They vary in rank and duty, a fact that is often reflected in their physical states; God has distinguished them by the various numbers of their wings: Two, three, four, or many more (35:1).

Some among them bring revelation from God to His messengers, Gabriel عليه السلام being the most well known of them. One of them is entrusted with taking the souls of the living at the moment of death; he is known as the Angel of Death (*Malak al-Mawt*). Another, Isrâfîl, will blow the horn blast that signals the end of earthly time and the coming of the Day of Judgment.

Others perform varied functions. Those who carry the Throne of God are known as the Throne Bearers. Some watch over the gates of Paradise and will give those who shall dwell therein salutations of peace. Others guard Hell and will reprimand its denizens. Still others accompany human beings upon earth, recording their every word and deed and supporting them in times of tribulation. Angels also pray for believers who gather to worship God or who learn sacred knowledge, giving those present good tidings of a felicitous reward.

Being conscious of the existence of angels—their

And they appointed for Allah associates from among the Jinn—though He created them. And they impute to Him sons and daughters without any knowledge. Glory be to Him, and exalted is He over what they claim.

— The Quran, 6:100

The Messiah shall never disdain to be a servant of God, nor shall the angels who are brought near.

— The Quran, 4:172

mission and unfailing obedience to God—increases one's awareness of God's glory and mercy, for He has commanded the angels also to pray for the believers. Thus they counsel the believers, in ways mysterious to humans, against indulgence in sin, and they implore God to forgive them.

Calling to mind the presence of angels, these wonderful beings, and the fact that they record each action, inspires one to keep to the straight way and avoid errant deeds, words, and even thoughts. Reflecting upon these fellow creatures of exemplary obedience—who, like human beings, possess rational intelligence—strengthens in one the resolve to work righteousness, being hopeful of God's mercy and help.

The Friendship of Angels with Humanity

THE ABOUNDING PRESENCE of angels in the universe bears witness that the range of creation and the splendor of its Creator far surpass the perimeter of human knowledge. What a tragedy it is, then, for so much of humanity to be subjected to doubt and misconception about angels and their relationship to God and humankind, and about the great variety and diversity of creation! Yet the Quran, which remains the mirror of reality, gives prominence to sound belief in angels as a constituent of genuine faith.

The Quran introduces angels in the course of recounting God's proclamation that He would settle the human family upon the earth and give them authority in it:

> *And when your Lord said to the angels, "I am placing upon the earth a successor." They said, "Will You place therein one who will do corruption therein and shed blood while we glorify Your praise and extol You?" He said, "I know what you do not know."* (2:30)

The angels, intelligent beings whom God created from light, experienced perhaps a sense of disinclination

Those who say, "Our Lord is Allah," and continue upon the straight way, the angels descend upon them: "Do not fear, nor be grieved, and receive glad tidings of the Garden which you were promised. We are your supporters in this world and in the Hereafter. And for you therein is whatever your souls desire, and for you therein is whatever you ask for—a hospitality from one who is all-forgiving, mercy-giving."

— The Quran, 41:30–32

إِنَّ ٱلَّذِينَ قَالُوا۟ رَبُّنَا ٱللَّهُ ثُمَّ ٱسْتَقَـٰمُوا۟ تَتَنَزَّلُ عَلَيْهِمُ
ٱلْمَلَـٰٓئِكَةُ أَلَّا تَخَافُوا۟ وَلَا تَحْزَنُوا۟ وَأَبْشِرُوا۟ بِٱلْجَنَّةِ
ٱلَّتِى كُنتُمْ تُوعَدُونَ ﴿٣٠﴾ نَحْنُ أَوْلِيَآؤُكُمْ فِى ٱلْحَيَوٰةِ
ٱلدُّنْيَا وَفِى ٱلْـَٔاخِرَةِ ۖ وَلَكُمْ فِيهَا مَا تَشْتَهِىٓ أَنفُسُكُمْ
وَلَكُمْ فِيهَا مَا تَدَّعُونَ ﴿٣١﴾ نُزُلًا مِّنْ غَفُورٍ رَّحِيمٍ ﴿٣٢﴾

because they recognized that the new creature had in its very nature the potential to disobey God, while they themselves were predisposed to purity, and so knew only obedience, ceaseless worship, and glorification of Him. Their compassion for creation and their inherent aversion to evil impelled them to exclaim their revulsion to corruption. The angels, perhaps naturally, expected humanity to be as they themselves are, constantly celebrating the praise of God, grateful, obedient, devoted to goodness, and displaying respect for the whole of creation.

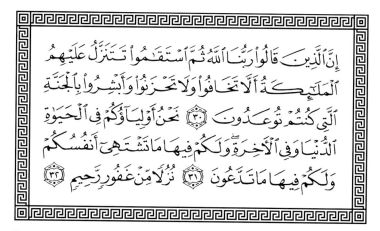

Yet God, the All-Knowing, demonstrated to the angels, after teaching Adam, the father of humanity, "the names, all of them" (2:31), that though He had fashioned humans from the elements of the earth, He nevertheless endowed them with the capacity to transcend the angels in knowledge and eminence. So God commanded the angels to honor Adam by bowing down before him and to extend their help to him, his wife, and their progeny.

Thus, since the dawn of human existence, angels have shown goodwill to human beings. God decreed that they convey His revelations and commandments to the prophets. Moreover, God instructed them to support those striving to adhere to His way by easing their difficulties in this life and sharing with them the tidings of a great reward near their Lord in the Hereafter:

> *Those who say, "Our Lord is Allah," and continue upon the straight way, the angels descend upon them: "Do not fear, nor be grieved, and receive glad tidings of the Garden which you were promised. We are your supporters in this world and in the Hereafter. And for you therein is whatever your souls desire, and for you therein is whatever you ask for."* (41:30–31)

The angels hearten the believers in their obedience to God and encourage them to venerate Him, glorify His name, and recite His Book. They observe and record the intimate moments of human devotion and nearness to the Creator, and thus they appeal to God to forgive and have mercy on His servants. The Prophet ﷺ said:

> When one of you performs ablution, doing so in an excellent manner, then goes out to the mosque—moved only

The Prophet ﷺ said, "When you hear the crowing of a rooster, ask God for His favor, for it has seen an angel. And when you hear the braying of a donkey, seek refuge in God against Satan, for it has seen a devil."

The heavens nearly burst from above them, and the angels glorify the praise of their Lord and seek forgiveness for those on the earth. Surely it is God who is the All-Forgiving, the Mercy-Giving.

— The Quran, 42:5

> by the desire to pray—one does not take a step save that he is elevated one degree and one of his sins is removed until he enters the mosque. And when in the mosque awaiting the Prayer—with patience and in remembrance of God—one is regarded as in Prayer for the duration. So long as he remains in the place of Prayer, the angels implore God for him, saying, "O God, have mercy on him! O God, forgive him! O God, grant him repentance!" as long as one commits no harm therein and maintains ablution.[81]

The Prophet ﷺ also said that there are companies of angels who descend to earth to seek out gatherings of believers engaged in the remembrance of God. When they ascend to heaven, God addresses them:

> Allah says, "What are My worshippers saying?"—and He knows best of them. They say, "They glorify You, magnify You, praise You, and extol You." He says, "Have they seen Me?" They say, "No. By Allah, they have not seen You." He says, "And how would it be were they to see Me?" They say, "If they were to see You, they would be more diligent in worshipping You, more diligent in extolling You, and would glorify You more."
>
> Then He says, "So what is it they ask of Me?" They say, "They ask of You the Garden." He says, "Have they seen it?" They say, "No. By Allah, O our Lord, they have not seen it." He says, "And how would it be were they to see it?" They say, "If they were to see it, they would strive for it more, seek it more, and would have a more ardent desire for it."
>
> He says, "From what do they seek refuge?" They say,

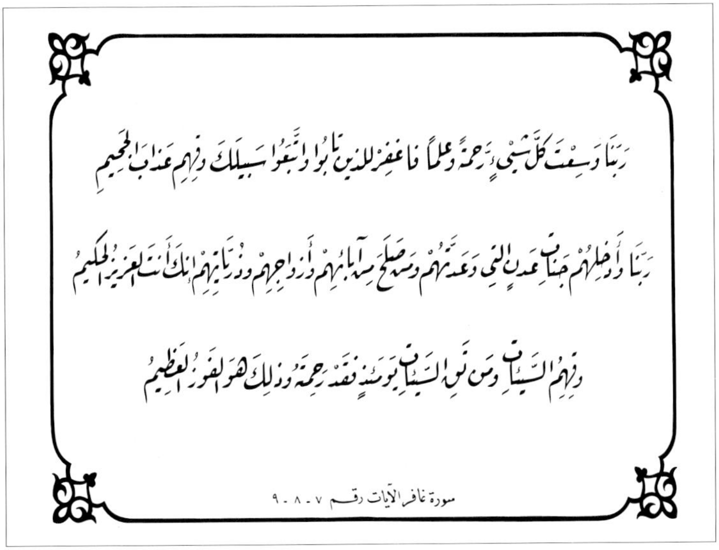
ربنا وسعت كل شيء رحمة وعلما فاغفر للذين تابوا واتبعوا سبيلك وقهم عذاب الجحيم
ربنا وأدخلهم جنات عدن التي وعدتهم ومن صلح من آبائهم وأزواجهم وذرياتهم إنك أنت العزيز الحكيم
وقهم السيئات ومن تق السيئات يومئذ فقد رحمته وذلك هو الفوز العظيم
سورة غافر الآيات رقم ٧ - ٨ - ٩

> "They seek refuge from the Fire." Then He says, "Have they seen it?" They say, "No. By Allah, O our Lord, they have not seen it." He says, "And how would it be were they to see it?" They say, "If they were to see it, they would flee from it more and fear it more." Then He says, "Bear witness that I have forgiven them." One of the angels then says, "Among them is so and so. He is not one of them, but came to them for some other need." Allah says, "They are a gathering, none of whose company shall be aggrieved."[82]

God entrusted other angels to transmit His revelations to the prophets. Gabriel, the Angel of Revelation, used to descend with the verses of the Quran and impart them to Muḥammad ﷺ. On one occasion, he appeared before the

Our Lord, You have embraced everything with mercy and knowledge, so forgive those who have repented and followed Your way. And save them from the torment of Hellfire. Our Lord, and enter them into the Gardens of Eden that You have promised them, as well as whoever is righteous among their forebears and their spouses, and their children. Indeed, You are the Overpowering, the All-Wise. And save them from misdeeds, for whomever You save on that day from misdeeds, then surely You have shown him mercy. And this is surely the great success.

— The Quran, 40:7–9

A Test of Gratefulness

The Prophet ﷺ once told his Companions

GOD DECREED TO test three people of the Children of Israel—a leper, a person balded by a scalp disease [*aqraʿ*], and a blind man. So he sent an angel to them.

The angel went to the leper and said, "Of all things, what would you love most?" The leper said, "Beautiful complexion, beautiful skin, and the removal of that for which people shun me." So the angel passed his hands over the man, and his affliction was removed, and he was given beautiful complexion and beautiful skin. Then the angel said, "Of all possessions, what would you love most?" He said, "Camels." So he was given a pregnant she-camel. And the angel said, "May God bless it for you."

Then the angel went to the scalp-diseased man and said, "Of all things, what would you love most?" He said, "Beautiful hair and the removal of that for which people shun me." So the angel passed his hands over him, and his affliction was removed, and he was given beautiful hair. And the angel said, "Of all possessions, what would you love most?" He said, "Cows." So he was given a pregnant cow. And the angel said, "May God bless it for you."

Then the angel went to the blind man and said, "Of all things, what would you love most?" He said, "That God may restore to me my sight so I can see people." So the angel passed his hands over him, and God restored to him his sight. And the angel said, "Of all possessions, what would you love most?" He said, "Sheep." So he was given a ewe with its young. And the angel said, "May God bless it for you."

All the animals multiplied exceedingly. So one of the men had a valley of camels, the other a valley of cows, and the other a valley of sheep. Later, the angel came to the leper, in the leper's previous form and condition, and said, "A poor man! Truly, I have been cut off from means in my journey, and I will not reach ˆmy destinationˇ except by God's help, then yours. I ask you by He who has given you beautiful complexion, beautiful skin, and wealth to give me a camel to ride in my journey." The man said, "My obligations are so many." The angel said to him, "I seem to recognize you. Were you not a leper whom people shunned? And were you not poor, then God gave you much?" He said, "I have inherited this wealth from a nobleman who had inherited it from a nobleman." The angel said, "If you are a liar, may God return you to the way you were."

Then he came to the scalp-diseased man, and said to him as he said to the first man. And the man answered him as the first did. And the angel said, "If you are a liar, may God return you to the way you were."

And he came to the blind man, in the blind man's previous form and condition, and said, "A poor man and homeless! Truly, I have been cut off from means in my journey, and I will not reach ˆmy destinationˇ except by God's help, then yours. I ask you by He who has restored your sight to give me a ewe to enable me in my journey." He said, "I was blind and God restored to me my sight. So take whatever you will and leave whatever you will; for by God I will not tax you for anything you take for the sake of God." The angel said, "Keep your wealth, for you were being tested. Pleasure has been dispensed to you, and displeasure to your two companions."[83]

Companions in human form so that they could see him. Gabriel عليه السلام then taught them the essence of their religion, as has been passed down in a well-known account reported by ʿUmar ibn al-Khaṭṭâb, the second Caliph, who said:

> One day while we were sitting with the Messenger of Allah ﷺ a man approached us whose clothes were exceedingly white and whose hair was exceedingly black; no signs of travel were to be seen on him and none of us knew him. He sat down before the Prophet ﷺ. Resting his knees against the Prophet's knees and placing the palms of his hands on his thighs, he said, "O Muḥammad, tell me about Islam." The Messenger of Allah ﷺ said, "Islam is to bear witness that there is no God but Allah, and Muḥammad is the Messenger of Allah, to perform the Prayers [*Ṣalât*], to pay the Charity [*Zakât*], to fast the month of Ramadan, and to make the Pilgrimage to the House, if you are so able." He said, "You have spoken rightly." And we were amazed at the man asking the Prophet ﷺ, then saying that he had spoken rightly.
>
> He said, "Then tell me about faith." The Prophet ﷺ said, "It is to believe in Allah, His angels, His books, His messengers, and the Last Day, and to believe in the Divine Measure [*al-Qadr*], the good and the evil thereof." The man said, "You have spoken rightly."
>
> He said, "Then tell me about *iḥsân* [excellence of faith]." He said, "It is to worship Allah as though you see Him. And though you do not see Him, truly He sees you."

Hudhayfa ibn al-Yamân, may God be pleased with him, reported that he heard the Messenger of God ﷺ say to his Companions, "There lived a man among the people before you. The angel came to him to take his soul. It was said to him, 'Have you done anything good?' He said, 'I don't know.' It was said to him, 'Consider!' He said, 'I do not know anything, except that I used to sell to people in the world, and I used to ask them for the due price; but I used to give respite to the affluent and forgive people in difficulties.' God then admitted him into the Garden."

> He said, "Then tell me about the Hour." He said, "The one questioned about it knows no better than the questioner." He said, "Then tell me of its signs." He said, "The slave-girl shall give birth to her mistress, and you will see the barefooted, naked, destitute shepherds competing in constructing lofty buildings."
>
> Then he departed, and I stayed for a time. Then the Prophet ﷺ said, "O ʿUmar, do you know who the questioner was?" I said, "Allah and His Messenger know best." He said, "It was Gabriel, who came to you to teach you your religion."[84]

Whoever is an enemy to Allah and His angels and His messengers and Gabriel and Michael, then know that surely Allah is an enemy of the disbelievers.

— The Quran, 2:98

Another class of angels are the mighty Throne Bearers. They carry the Throne of God and enjoy an eminent rank with Him, engaging in continuous exaltation of His name. The Quran records their concern and compassion for the believers who turn to their Lord. They implore God on behalf of the faithful:

> *Our Lord, You have embraced everything with mercy and knowledge, so forgive those who have repented and followed Your way. And save them from the torment of Hellfire. Our Lord, and enter them into the Gardens of Eden that You have promised them, as well as whoever is righteous among their forebears and their spouses, and their children. Indeed, You are the Overpowering, the All-Wise. And save them from misdeeds, for whomever You save on that day from misdeeds, then surely You have shown him mercy. And this is surely the great success.* (40:7–9)

The angels have universal concern for the needy, the indigent, those with disabilities, and all others who lack

And they said, "If only an angel had been sent down to him!" But had We sent down an angel, the matter would have been decided, then they would not have been given respite.

— The Quran, 6:8

means. Thus they ask God to aid whoever provides relief to the needy and to deprive whoever has the means but withholds from the destitute. The Prophet ﷺ said, "Each morning two angels descend ⌜to earth⌝. One of them calls out, 'O Allah, give the benefactor replacement!' And the other cries, 'O Allah, give the miser ruin!'"[85]

Angels also accompany every human being for the duration of his or her life, watch what they do, guard them, and record everything: *Indeed, over you are guardians, noble ones writing. They know what you do* (82:10–12). A believer's consciousness of angels and their watchfulness encourages him or her to do good, thus serving as a deterrent from evil. In this manner, the believer perseveres through life's adversities knowing that among God's creation one has the support and prayers of angels.

Prayers for All Times and Occasions

Prayers in Worship

Provision for This Life and the Afterlife

GOD PREPARED THE blue planet especially to host humankind. All that is in it, and in the horizons of the heavens and the universe, provide for the honorable and wholesome existence of humanity. And He endowed the human being with physical energy, a spiritual nature, and a rational capacity. He has inspired the male and female of us with creative genius and the ability to learn and teach. God has granted each of us freedom to choose in many aspects of life and has placed in us an innate sense of discernment and purpose. All this God has bestowed upon us that we may live out our lives in harmony with the vast and colorful creation around us, mindful of the great Creator who has brought all things into existence and revealed to us His guidance so that our short journey upon the earth may extend successfully into the bliss of eternal life in Paradise.

When a person recognizes his or her purpose and place within creation and establishes a sound relationship with the Creator, he or she attains the spirit of worship and thereby fulfills the aims for which he or she was created. Indeed, the message of Noah, Abraham, Moses, Jesus, and Muḥammad, peace and blessings upon them all, did not in essence extend beyond this concept of worship. Thus, the meaning of worship in Muslim life encompasses every fragment of thought, every desire, every conscious act that issues from the worshipping human being in the course of his or her life. And since worship, as Islam defines it, is not limited by the familiar dimensions of time and space, it embraces all the occasions and occurrences of life, whether of solemnity, leisure, or repose. Moreover, worship is not restricted to the habitations of humankind, but is performed everywhere upon the face of the earth, in the depths of the waters, and in the altitudes of the skies. Inherent in this type of worship is a kinship that interrelates all created beings in existence and unites them before their Creator. Indeed, from the Muslim viewpoint, the entirety of existence with its great diversity of creatures constitutes a worshipping universe glorifying the name of its one Creator.

The worshipfulness of the human being continues beyond the journey of the life we now know, when it becomes a worship unbounded by earthly obligations and free of the sense of requirement that a believer here accepts and adheres to. But for now, here on earth, we are content with being conscious of the inestimable worth and elevation that derive from a sincere and genuine relationship with creation and Creator. This relationship has the effect of refining one's very humanity and guaranteeing one's fulfillment in life.

Thus the main pillars of worship—by which Islam is generally characterized—begin with the declaration, or the witness to faith, *"There is no God but Allah, and Muḥammad is His Messenger,"* the repetition of which manifests the deep-rootedness of worship in the heart of a believer and his or her earnestness concerning it. The Islamic testament is a source of power that helps one to promote civility in life and to spread the blessings of peace, love, and universal brotherhood. It lends the believer enormous support in the struggle to stand firm in the face of all forms of corruption and obscenity that threaten the wholesomeness of life on earth.

At every moment that a believer carries out the pillars of worship—when standing before Allah in daily Prayer (*Ṣalât*), or extending the hand in charity to the poor, or during periods of special spiritual and physical exertion, such as fasting during the month of Ramadan, or embarking on the journey of Pilgrimage (*Ḥajj*)—on every such occasion that a believer performs his or her duties, thereby reaffirming the covenant with God, the meaning of worship is renewed; and then life on earth, as we experience it, comes one step closer to what we aspire for it to be.

Sustaining the kind of consciousness of worship that Islam envisions, however, requires from each of us a certain energy. It is for precisely this reason that Islam emphasizes the central importance of supplication in all its forms, as set forth in the verses of the Quran and the teachings of the Prophet Muḥammad ﷺ . In both of these sources there are explicit texts indicating that supplication is the essence of worship. The Prophet ﷺ summed this up in his statement, "Prayer *(duʿâ')* is the marrow of worship."[86] He said, as well, that prayer is the "armament for the believer"[87] and that "prayer is worship."[88] For it is the act of *supplication* that links one's entreaty, imploring, petitioning, invocation, appeal, or, the term chiefly employed here, "prayer," to irresistible power of the universe, God. Thus it is prayer that forms an undepletable reservoir of spiritual energy that enables the worshipper to live his or her worship in the widest possible sense, to maintain its vitality, and to realize its ends.

This explains the large number of prayers that are desirable (and sometimes required) for believers to repeat in the performance of obligatory acts of worship as well as in the everyday affairs of life. Whether one is proceeding to perform ablution or completing it, or moving to the place of Prayer (*Ṣalât*), or uttering the first *"Allâhu akbar"* that commences the obligatory Prayer, or standing, or bowing, or bowing down, or sitting in the midst of the performance of this pillar, or reciting remembrances of God after its completion, or performing a Prayer for a special occasion, or reaching the moment of fast-breaking, or extending a hand to give or receive *Zakât*, or arriving at any of the various circumstances or stations of *Ḥajj*—there are appropriate words of God's remembrance for each of these occasions.

Prophet Muḥammad ﷺ has consigned to us, in this regard and beyond, a treasury of compelling, beautiful prayers relating to every manner of our social interaction (both intimate and formal), our engagement with nature (observing and learning from its wonders), and our spiritual yearnings (praising God and seeking His grace and forgiveness). Yet perhaps none of these is so moving as the Prophet's ﷺ matchless expressions of thanksgiving and praise for God, the Exalted, for all that He has bestowed upon us.

The select prayers from the Quran and from the Prophet ﷺ presented in the following pages have been ordered according to the five pillars of Islam as articulated above and according to the general courses and occasions of our lives. The English translations of the verses of the Quran and of the authentic collections of the *Sunna* (the statements, deeds, and consent of the Prophet ﷺ) have been rendered from the primary and classical Arabic sources, which are cited after each supplication.

1. Prayers and the Pillars of Worship

WORSHIP PURIFIES THE heart of the believer. All good acts intended and known to be pleasing to God constitute worship—from smiling at one's brother to giving one's all for the sake of God. But it is the rituals of worship in Islam that form the edifice of religion and its worshipful rhythms of life, teach its values, and perfect one's submission to God. This is illuminated by the authentic report about Gabriel عليه السلام, the Angel of Revelation, appearing before the Companions of the Prophet in human form to teach them the essence of their religion, in which the Prophet ﷺ stated:

> Islam is to bear witness that there is no God but Allah, and Muḥammad is the Messenger of Allah, to perform the Prayers [*Ṣalât*], to pay the Charity [*Zakât*], to fast the month of Ramadan, and to make the Pilgrimage to the House, if you are so able....[89]

The rituals of worship enumerated in the above report are known as "the pillars of Islam" and are the hallmark of the Islamic observances—especially Prayer (*Ṣalât*), with its distinctive timings and postures. Invocations that the Prophet ﷺ used to say while performing these rituals of worship, or in fulfilling their preconditions, or after completing them, are presented here.

ABLUTION (*Wuḍû'*)

Before entering into Prayer (*Ṣalât*), the worshipper purifies him- or herself with water (an act known as *wuḍû'* or ablution), three times washing the hands, rinsing the mouth and nostrils, washing the face and the forearms, wiping the head, and lastly washing the feet to the ankles.

What one says before making ablution

1.1 In the name of Allah, the All-Merciful, the Mercy-Giving.

The Prophet ﷺ said, "There is no ablution for whoever does not mention the name of Allah before it." Sunan al-Tirmidhî, *1:37–39, #25 and #26, and* Sunan al-Nasâ'î, *1:61.*

What one says while making ablution

1.2 O Allah, forgive me my sins, make spacious for me my residence, and bless me in my provision.

Al-Nasâ'î, ʿAmal al-Yawm wa al-Layla, *pp. 172–73. Imâm al-Nawawî endorsed the authenticity of this* ḥadîth. *See* al-Adhkâr, *p. 24. A variant report is found in* Sunan al-Tirmidhî, *5:492–93, #3500.*

What one says after making ablution

1.3 I bear witness that there is no God but Allah, alone; He has no partner. And I bear witness that Muḥammad is His servant and messenger. O Allah, make me one of the oft-repentant and make me one of the purified.

The Prophet ﷺ stated that eight gates of the Garden shall be opened for a person who says this supplication, such that in the Hereafter one may enter the Garden through any of them. Sunan al-Tirmidhî, *1:77–78, #55, and* Ṣaḥîḥ Muslim, *1:210, #234. Al-Nasâ'î,* ʿAmal al-Yawm wa al-Layla, *p. 174.*

The Call to Prayer (*Adhân*)

At the appropriate time for each of the five daily Prayers, the *Mu'adhdhin* (or the Caller) says the following Call to Prayer (or *Adhân)*:

1.4 Allah is the greatest! Allah is the greatest!
Allah is the greatest! Allah is the greatest!
I bear witness that there is no God but Allah.
I bear witness that there is no God but Allah.
I bear witness that Muḥammad is the Messenger of Allah.
I bear witness that Muḥammad is the Messenger of Allah.
Come to Prayer! Come to Prayer!
Come to success! Come to success!
Allah is the greatest! Allah is the greatest!
There is no God but Allah.

Sunan Abû Dâwûd, *1:136, #500 and #501. See also* Ṣaḥîḥ Muslim, *1:287, #379.*

What one says while listening to the Adhân

1.5 As the Prophet ﷺ taught, one should repeat all the words of the Call to Prayer after they have been said by the Caller, except when one hears "Come to Prayer! Come to Prayer!" and "Come to success! Come to success!" Then one says after each mention, "There is no strength nor might except with Allah."

The Prophet ﷺ said that whoever says this from his heart shall enter the Garden. Ṣaḥîḥ Muslim, *1:289, #385.*

What one says after hearing the Adhân

1.6 O Allah, Lord of this consummate call and imminent Prayer, grant Muḥammad *al-Wasîla* [the rank of honor in Paradise], and raise him to the Station of Praise [*Maqâm Maḥmûd*] which You have promised him.

The Prophet ﷺ said that whoever says this after hearing the Adhân *shall enjoy my intercession on the Day of Resurrection.* Ṣaḥîḥ al-Bukhârî, *2:94, #614, and* Sunan al-Tirmidhî, *1:413, #211.*

1.7 I bear witness that there is no God but Allah, alone—He has no partner—and that Muḥammad is His servant and messenger. I am well pleased with Allah as the Lord, with Muḥammad as the Messenger, and with Islam as the religion.

The Prophet ﷺ said that whoever says this after hearing the Caller to Prayer (Mu'adhdhin) *shall be forgiven his sins.* Ṣaḥîḥ Muslim, *1:290, #386.*

Ritual Prayer (*Ṣalât*)

Islam prescribes five daily obligatory Prayers (*Ṣalawât*, sing. *Ṣalât*) for every able Muslim male and female who has reached the age of discernment. While "prayer" in popular usage is used to mean supplication, the *Ṣalât* is a glorification of and obeisance to God. The blending of ritual devotion and direct supplication is among the most gratifying features of worship in Islam. The timings of each of the five daily Prayers are set within definite timespans during the day. The time for Dawn Prayer (*Fajr*) begins at dawn and ends at sunrise. The time for Noon Prayer (*Ẓuhr*) begins shortly after the sun has passed its zenith and ends when the sun is about midway between the meridian and setting. The time for Midafternoon Prayer (*ʿAṣr*) begins when Noon Prayer time expires and ends at the commencement of sunset. The Sunset Prayer (*Maghrib*) is performed immediately after the sun has completely set. The time for Nightfall Prayers (*ʿIshâ'*) begins when the night falls and may extend until just before dawn.

The unit by which the *Ṣalât* is measured is called a *rakʿa*, which means "bowing." It begins with the believer, standing upright in the direction of the Kaʿba, saying the words *Allâhu akbar*, or "God is the greatest," followed by a recitation of the opening sura of the Quran and then by the recitation of any other portion of the Quran. Subsequent postures include bending deeply at the waist into a bowing position (*rukûʿ*); rising from this position (*qiyâm*); then bowing down twice with the knees, the forehead, and the palms of the hands to the ground (*sujûd*), with a brief sitting between the first and second motions. This completes one *rakʿa* or cycle of Prayer. Between every two cycles, as well as in the last cycle of a Prayer, one sits (in *jalsâ*) and utters specific and selected supplications. The Prayer is concluded with a greeting of peace, *As-Salâmu ʿalaykum wa raḥmatullâh* ("Peace be upon you, and the mercy of God"), said first to the right and then to the left.

The Noon, Midafternoon, and Nightfall Prayers are comprised of four cycles. The Dawn Prayer is two cycles and the Sunset Prayer three. In addition, it is highly recommended to pray the Odd-Number Prayer (*Witr*) consisting of between one and eleven cycles (but always odd-numbered) after the Nightfall Prayer. In each of the positions of the Prayer described above, glorification of God and, in most postures, supplications are offered. Some that the Prophet ﷺ used to say follow.

What to say while lining up for the Prayer (Ṣalât)

1.8 O Allah, give me the best of what You give to Your righteous servants.

Al-Nasâ'î, ʿAmal al-Yawm wa al-Layla, *p. 180. The text of this supplication was voiced by a*

Companion of the Prophet while he was approaching a congregation for a daily Prayer. The Prophet ﷺ then explained to him that seeking the best of rewards may require readiness to strive for the cause of Allah. The Prophet, peace be upon him, commented, "Your horse may be slain and you may face martyrdom for the sake of Allah."

What one may choose to say after beginning the Prayer with "Allâhu akbar"

1.9 Glory be to You, O Allah, and all praise. Blessed is Your name and exalted is Your grandeur. There is no God other than You.

Ṣaḥîḥ Muslim, *1:299, #399. It was reported that ʿUmar ibn al-Khaṭṭâb used to say this, and others attributed it to the Prophet ﷺ. See* Sunan al-Tirmidhî, *2:11, #243.*

1.10 O Allah, distance me from my sins as You have distanced the East from the West. O Allah, purify me of sins as a white cloth is purified of dirt. O Allah, wash away my sins with water, snow, and sleet.

Ṣaḥîḥ al-Bukhârî, *2:227, #744, and* Ṣaḥîḥ Muslim, *1:419, #598.*

1.11 I turn my face to Him who originated the heavens and the earth, being upright, and I am not of the idolaters. Truly, my Prayer [*Ṣalât*], my worship, my life, and my death are for Allah, Lord of the Worlds, who has no partner. And with this I have been commanded, and I am of the Muslims.

O Allah, You are the King. There is no God but You. You are my Lord, and I am Your servant. I have wronged myself and have admitted my sins; so forgive me all of my sins, for no one forgives sins but You. And guide me to the best of character, for no one guides to the best of it but You. And turn the worst of it away from me, for no one can turn the worst of it away from me but You.

Here I am, O Allah, at Your service. All good is in Your Hand and evil is not of You. I am, because of You! And I will return to You. You are ever blessed and exalted. I seek Your forgiveness and repent to You.

Ṣaḥîḥ Muslim, *1:534–35, #771, and* Sunan Abû Dâwûd, *1:201–2, #760.*

1.12 O Allah, for You is all praise! You are the Light of the heavens and the earth. For You is all praise! You are the Sustainer of the heavens and the earth. For You is all praise! You are the Lord of the heavens and the earth and all therein. You are the Truth. Your promise is the truth. Your word is the truth. The meeting with You is true. The Garden is true. The Fire is true. The Hour is true. O Allah, to You I submit. In You I believe. On You I rely. To You I turn in penitence. For You I oppose. To You I refer in judgment. So forgive me whatever I may have done and whatever I may do; whatever I have concealed and whatever I have revealed. You are my God. There is no God but You.

Ibn ʿAbbâs reported that the Prophet ﷺ used to open his nightly voluntary Prayer (Ṣalât) *with this supplication.* Ṣaḥîḥ Muslim, *1:532–33, #769, and* Sunan Abû Dâwûd, *1:205, #771.*

1.13 O Allah—Lord of Gabriel, Mikâ'îl [Michael], and Isrâfîl—originator of the heavens and the earth, knower of the unseen and the seen, You judge between Your servants regarding that which they dispute. Guide me, by Your permission, to the truth of what is disputed, for You guide whomever You will to the straight way.

Ṣaḥîḥ Muslim, *1:534, #770. ʿÂ'isha reported that whenever the Prophet ﷺ awoke at night for Prayer, he opened it with this supplication.*

1.14 O Allah, put light in my heart, light in my sight, and light in my hearing; light to my right and light to my left; light above me and light beneath me; light before me and light behind me; and grant me great light.

Ṣaḥîḥ Muslim, *1:526, #763, and* Ṣaḥîḥ al-Bukhârî, *11:116, #6316.*

What one says immediately before reciting al-Fâtiḥa

1.15 I seek refuge in Allah, the All-Hearing, the All-Knowing, from Satan, the accursed.

Sunan Abû Dâwûd, *1:206, #775, and* Ṣaḥîḥ al-Bukhârî, *10:518, #6115.*

1.16 I seek refuge in Allah from Satan, the accursed, from his ⌜evil⌝ inspirations, his promptings, and his incantations.

Ṣaḥîḥ Ibn Ḥibbân (al-Iḥsân), *3:135, #1777, and* Sunan Ibn Mâjah, *1:265, #807.*

*What to say after reciting al-*Fâtiḥa *in* Prayer

1.17 The Prophet ﷺ said, "When the *imâm* [one leading a Prayer] says *'Âmîn'* [O God, accept our prayer!], say, *'Âmîn.'* For when one's ⌜utterance of⌝ *'Âmîn'* coincides with that of the angels, his previous sins are forgiven."

Ṣaḥîḥ Muslim, *1:307, #410.*

What one says while in the position of rukûʿ *(bowing)*

1.18 Glory be to my Lord, the Magnificent.

To be said three times. Ṣaḥîḥ Muslim, *1:536–37, #772.*

1.19 Glory be to You, O Allah, our Lord, and all praise. O Allah, forgive me.

Ṣaḥîḥ Muslim, *1:350, #484. The Prophet, peace be upon him, used to repeat this during both* rukûʿ *and* sujûd.

1.20 O Allah, to You I bow, in You I believe, to You I submit. Humbled to You are my hearing, my sight, my marrow, my bones, and my nerves.

Ṣaḥîḥ Muslim, *1:535, #771.*

1.21 The All-Glorious, the All-Holy, Lord of the angels and the spirit.

Ṣaḥîḥ Muslim, *1:353, #487.*

1.22 Glory be to the possessor of irresistible might, of all sovereignty, imperiousness, and magnificence.

Sunan Abû Dâwûd, *1:230–31, #873.*

What one says after rising from bowing in **rukûᶜ**, *upon hearing or saying, "***Indeed, Allah hears whomever praises Him***"*

1.23 O Allah, our Lord, for You is all praise.

Ṣaḥîḥ al-Bukhârî, *2:283, #796.*

1.24 Our Lord, for You is all praise, much praise, wholesome and blessed.

Ṣaḥîḥ al-Bukhârî, *2:284, #799, and* Sunan al-Nasâ'î, *2:196.*

1.25 Our Lord, for You is all praise as much as fills the heavens and the earth and fills anything else You will. You are most worthy of extolment and glory. The truest saying of a servant—and all of us are Your servants—is, "O Allah, none can withhold that which You give, and none can give that which You withhold. And wealth will not avail the wealthy against You."

Ṣaḥîḥ Muslim, *1:347, #477.*

What one says in the position of **sujûd** (*bowing down to the ground*)

1.26 Glory be to my Lord, the Most High.

To be said three times. Ṣaḥîḥ Muslim, *1:536–37, #772.*

1.27 Glory be to You, O Allah, our Lord, and all praise. O Allah, forgive me.

The Prophet ﷺ used to repeat this during both sujûd *and* rukûᶜ. Ṣaḥîḥ Muslim, *1:350, #483.*

1.28 O Allah, to You I bow down, in You I believe, to You I submit. My face is bowed down to Him who created it, fashioned it, and opened within it its hearing and sight. Blessed is Allah, the best of creators.

Ṣaḥîḥ Muslim, *1:535, #771.*

1.29 O Allah, I seek refuge in Your pleasure from Your displeasure and in Your pardon from Your punishment. And I seek refuge in You from You. I am unable to enumerate the extolling of You. You are as You have extolled Yourself.

Ṣaḥîḥ Muslim, *1:352, #486.*

1.30 O Allah, give my soul its Godfearingness and purify it. You are the best to purify it. You are its patron and its Lord.

Ṣaḥîḥ Muslim, *4:2088, #2722.*

1.31 Glory be to the possessor of irresistible might, all sovereignty, imperiousness, and magnificence.

Sunan Abû Dâwûd, *1:230–31, #873.*

1.32 O Allah, forgive me my sins, all of them—minute and enormous, first and last, manifest and hidden.

Ṣaḥîḥ Muslim, *1:350, #483.*

What one says in the interval between the two acts of bowing down

1.33 My Lord, forgive me. My Lord, forgive me.

Sunan Abû Dâwûd, *1:231, #874;* Sunan Ibn Mâjah, *1:282, #897; and* Sunan al-Nasâ'î, *3:226.*

1.34 O Allah, forgive me, have mercy on me, replenish me, exalt me, provide for me, guide me, and grant me well-being.

Sunan al-Bayhaqî, *2:122. There are several similar reports that vary slightly with regard to the order of what is prayed for. See also* Sunan Abû Dâwûd, *1:224, #850.*

1.35 O Allah, forgive me, have mercy on me, guide me, grant me well-being, and provide for me.

Ṣaḥîḥ Muslim, *4:2073, #2697.*

A *special supplication, called* qunût, *that may be said after (or before) the last* rukûᶜ *(bowing) of the* Dawn *or* Witr Prayers

1.36 O Allah, guide me among those You guide and grant me well-being among those You grant well-being. Look after me among those You look after, and bless for me what You have given me, and protect me from the evil of what You have decreed; for it is You who decrees and none decrees against You. And none is abased whom You uphold and none is honored whom You oppose. Blessed are You our Lord, and exalted.

Sunan al-Bayhaqî, *2:209. A similar text is found in* Sunan Abû Dâwûd, *2:63, #1425, and* Sunan al-Tirmidhî, *2:238, #464.*

What to recite during Witr *Prayer and the supplication made after the Prayer*

1.37 The Prophet ﷺ recited during *Witr* Prayers Sûrat al-Aʿlâ (87) in the first *rakʿa*, Sûrat al-Kâfirûn (109) in the second, and Sûrat al-Ikhlâṣ (112) in the third. Then, after finishing the Prayer, he would say three times, "Glory be to the King, the All-Holy."

Sunan al-Nasâ'î, *3:235; al-Nasâ'î,* ʿAmal al-Yawm wa al-Layla, *p. 441, #729; and* Musnad Aḥmad, *3:406.*

What is said in the middle or end of the Prayer (Ṣalât) *known as* al-Tashahhud (*Testification*) *or* al-Taḥiyyât (*Salutations*)

1.38 All salutations are for Allah, and all prayers and goodness. Peace be upon you, O Prophet, and the mercy of Allah and His blessings. Peace be upon us and upon the righteous servants of Allah. I bear witness that there is no God but Allah, and I bear witness that Muḥammad is His servant and messenger.

Ṣaḥîḥ Muslim, *1:301–2, #402, and* Sunan al-Tirmidhî, *2:81, #289.*

Then one adds in the last sitting of al-Tashahhud *the following*:

1.39 O Allah, grace Muḥammad and the family of Muḥammad as You have graced Abraham and the family of Abraham, for truly You are the All-Praised, the Glorious. O Allah, bless Muḥammad and the family of Muḥammad, as You have blessed Abraham and the family of Abraham, for truly You are the All-Praised, the Glorious.

Musnad Aḥmad, *4:241, and* Sunan al-Tirmidhî, *2:352–53.*

What one may say before final salutations (taslîm)

1.40 O Allah, forgive me for whatever I have done and whatever I may do, whatever I have concealed and whatever I have revealed, what I have done in excess and that about which You know better than myself. You are the Forwarder and You are the Delayer. There is no God but You.

Ṣaḥîḥ Muslim, *1:535–36, #771. A similar text is found in* Sunan al-Tirmidhî, *5:453, #3421.*

1.41 O Allah, I seek refuge in You from the torment of Hell and the torment of the grave, and from the trial of life and that of death, and from the evil of the trial of the False Messiah [al-Dajjâl].

Ṣaḥîḥ Muslim *(al-Nawawî's), 5:87. In ʿAbd al-Bâqî's edition, it is* ḥadîth *#588. The last clause is from a similar report in* Ṣaḥîḥ al-Bukhârî, *2:317, #832.*

1.42 O Allah, I seek refuge in You from sin and debt.

Ṣaḥîḥ Muslim *(al-Nawawî's), 5:87.*

1.43 O Allah, truly I have wronged myself with many wrongs, and none forgives sins but You. So forgive me with Your forgiveness and have mercy upon me. Truly, it is You who are the All-Forgiving, the Mercy-Giving.

Ṣaḥîḥ al-Bukhârî, *2:317, #834;* Ṣaḥîḥ Muslim, *4:2078, #2705; and* Sunan al-Nasâʾî, *3:53.*

1.44 O Allah, I ask You for the Garden and I seek refuge in You from the Fire.

Musnad Aḥmad, *3:474.*

1.45 O Allah, I ask You for firmness in my affairs and resolve to do what is right. And I ask You for thankfulness for Your grace and for excellence in Your worship. I ask You for a truthful tongue and a sound heart. I seek refuge in You from the evil of everything that You know ⌜exists⌝. I ask You for the best of everything that You know ⌜exists⌝. And I ask You to forgive me for what You know ⌜of me⌝. Indeed, You are all-knowing of all that is unseen.

Sunan al-Tirmidhî, *5:443–44, #3407. A slightly variant version is found in* Musnad Aḥmad, *4:125.*

1.46 O Allah, by Your knowledge of the unseen and Your omnipotence over creation, let me live as long as You know life to be good for me, and take my soul when You know death to be good for me. O Allah, I ask You that I have reverence for You in private and in public, and I ask You that I say the word of truth in contentment and in anger. I ask You for prudence in poverty and in wealth, and I ask You for delight without end. I ask You for joy without cessation, and I ask You for contentment with Your decree. I ask You for a soothing life after death, and I ask You for the pleasure of looking upon Your Face and for the yearning to meet You, free from suffering distress or from trial that leads ⌜one⌝ astray. O Allah, adorn us with the ornament of faith and make us guides and rightly guided.

Sunan al-Nasâ'î, *3:54–55.*

1.47 O Allah, bind our hearts together. Set aright relations among us. Guide us upon the way of peace. Deliver us from darkness into light. Separate us from vile deeds, whatever may be concealed of them and whatever revealed. Bless us in our hearing and our sight, our hearts and our spouses, and our children. Grant us repentance, for You are the All-Relenting, the Mercy-Giving. And enable us to be thankful for Your grace, and to extol ⌜You⌝ for it, and to be accepting of it. And perfect it for us.

Sunan Abû Dâwûd, *1:254, #969. See also al-Ḥâkim's* al-Mustadrak, *1:265. Dhahabî, in his commentary on this* ḥadîth, *said it is authentic and meets the requirements of Imâm Muslim.*

What one says to end the **Prayer (Ṣalât)**

1.48 Peace be upon you, and the mercy of Allah [*As-salâmu ʿalaykum wa raḥmatullâh*].

Said with one's face turned first to the right and then repeated with the face turned to the left.
Sunan Ibn Mâjah, *1:296, #914, and* Ṣaḥîḥ Muslim *(al-Nawawî's), 5:82.*

Supplications Following Ritual Prayers (*Ṣalât*)

The Prophet ﷺ used to entreat God and repeat His remembrance immediately after completing the daily obligatory Prayers. He did so by freely beseeching God in his own words (which his Companions themselves committed to memory and passed down to us) and by reciting specific passages from the Quran. Certain of his petitions and recitations were especially associated with one or more of the five daily obligatory Prayers. Some of his supplications follow.

1.49 O Allah, You are Peace and from You is peace. Blessed are You, O Lord of Majesty and Generosity.

Ṣaḥîḥ Muslim *(al-Nawawî's), 5:90, and* Sunan Abû Dâwûd, *2:84, #1512.*

1.50 O Allah, help me in the remembrance of You, and thankfulness to You, and excellence in the worship of You.

Sunan Abû Dâwûd, *2:86, #1522;* Sunan al-Nasâ'î, *3:53; and al-Nasâ'î,* ʿAmal al-Yawm wa al-Layla, *p. 181.*

1.51 O Allah, our Lord and Lord of all things, I am a witness that You—and You alone—are the Lord, and that You have no partner. O Allah, our Lord and Lord of all things, I am a witness that Muḥammad is Your servant and messenger. O Allah, our Lord and Lord of all things, I am a witness that all worshippers are brethren.

O Allah, our Lord and Lord of all things, make me and my family sincere to You in every moment of this life and the Hereafter. O Lord of Majesty and Generosity, hear me and answer me. Allah is the greatest, the greatest! Allah is the light of the heavens and the earth. Allah is the greatest, the greatest! Sufficient is Allah for me and an excellent trustee. Allah is the greatest, the greatest!

Musnad Aḥmad, *4:369. A slightly variant version is found in* Sunan Abû Dâwûd, *2:83, #1508. See also al-Nasâ'î,* ʿAmal al-Yawm wa al-Layla, *p. 184.*

1.52 O Allah, I seek refuge in You from feebleness, laziness, cowardliness, miserliness, senility, and from the torment of the grave. O Allah, give my soul its Godfearingness and purify it. You are the best to purify it; You are its patron and Lord. O Allah, I seek refuge in You from knowledge that does not benefit, from a heart that is not humble, from a soul that is never satisfied, and from any prayer that is not answered.

Ṣaḥîḥ Muslim, *4:2088, #2722. A similar version is found in* Sunan al-Nasâ'î, *8:285.*

1.53 O Allah, suffice me with what You have made lawful against what You have made unlawful. And enrich me with Your favor so that I need none but You.

Sunan al-Tirmidhî, *5:523, #3563.*

1.54 There is no God but Allah, alone; He has no partner. To Him belongs all dominion and for Him is all praise, and He is powerful over all things. There is no strength nor might except with Allah. There is no God but Allah, and we do not worship other than Him. His is all grace, and His is all graciousness, and His are the excellent exaltations. There is no God but Allah, making religion sincerely for Him, even if the disbelievers abhor it.

The Companion Ibn Zubayr said, "The Messenger ﷺ used to say this after each Prayer." Ṣaḥîḥ Muslim *(al-Nawawî's), 5:91–92. Al-Nasâ'î,* ʿAmal al-Yawm wa al-Layla, *p. 196.*

1.55 The recitation of the Verse of the Seat ˹of Divinity˺, *Âyat al-Kursî*

Allah! There is no God but Him, the Living, the Self-Subsisting. Slumber does not overtake Him, nor does sleep. To Him belongs whatever is in the heavens and whatever is in the earth. Who is it that shall intercede with Him except by His permission? He knows what is before them and what is behind them, and they do not comprehend anything of His knowledge except that which He wills. His Seat ˹of Divinity˺ encompasses the heavens and the earth, and preserving them does not fatigue Him. And He is the Exalted, the Magnificent (2:255).

The Prophet ﷺ said that whoever recites the Verse of the Seat ˹of Divinity˺ after each obligatory Prayer, nothing will prevent him from entering the Garden except what remains of his life before death. Al-Nasâʾî, ʿAmal al-Yawm wa al-Layla, *pp. 182–83, #100.*

1.56 The recitation of Sûrat al-Ikhlâṣ

Say: He is Allah, One. Allah, the Everlasting Refuge. He does not beget, nor is He begotten. And there is none comparable to Him (112:1–4).

It is recommended to repeat this sura after each Prayer (Ṣalât), *especially the Dawn* (Fajr) *and Sunset* (Maghrib) *Prayers. See al-Mundhirî,* al-Targhîb wa al-Tarhîb, *3:265, who says that repeating this sura after Prayer is based on a sound report by the Companion Abû Umâmah. See also* Musnad Aḥmad, *5:266.*

1.57 The recitation of Sûrat al-Falaq and Sûrat al-Nâs

Say: I seek refuge in the Lord of the daybreak from the evil of that which He created, and from the evil of darkness when it overspreads, and from the evil of those ˹sorcerers˺ who blow upon knots, and from the evil of an envier when he envies (113:1–5).

Say: I seek refuge in the Lord of all people, King of all people, God of all people, from the evil of the sneaking whisperer, who whispers in the chests of people, from the jinn and people (114:1–6).

Sunan al-Nasâʾî, *3:68.*

What one says after the Fajr (Dawn) Prayer

1.58 There is no God but Allah, alone; He has no partner. To Him belongs all dominion and for Him is all praise. He gives life and causes death, and He is powerful over all things.

The Prophet ﷺ said that whoever says this ten times immediately after Dawn Prayer while sitting in the Prayer position, the reward of ten good deeds is inscribed for him or her and ten misdeeds are erased. And he or she shall be raised ten stations and the rest of the day shall be shielded from all abominable things and will be guarded from Satan. See Sunan al-Tirmidhî, *5:481, #3474.*

1.59 O Allah, I ask You for knowledge that is beneficial, deeds that will be accepted, and provision that is wholesome.

Musnad Aḥmad, *6:318, and al-Nasâ'î,* ʿAmal al-Yawm wa al-Layla, *p. 184.*

1.60 O Allah, grant me refuge from the Fire.

To be said seven times after Dawn and Sunset Prayers. Sunan Abû Dâwûd, *4:320, #5079.*

1.61 O Allah, You are my Lord. There is no God but You. You created me, and I am Your servant. I uphold Your covenant and Your promise, as much as I am able. I seek refuge in You from the harm of whatever I may have done. To You do I acknowledge Your grace upon me and to You do I bring my sins. Forgive me, for none forgives sins except You.

The Prophet, peace be upon him, said that this is the master supplication for seeking forgiveness, and that whoever says it during the day with full conviction and then dies before the end of the day shall be among the People of the Garden; and whoever says it during the night with full conviction and then dies before the morning shall be among the People of the Garden. Ṣaḥîḥ al-Bukhârî, *11:97–98, #6306.*

What one says after the Maghrib (Sunset) Prayer

1.62 There is no God but Allah, alone; He has no partner. To Him belongs all dominion and for Him is all praise. He gives life and causes death, and He is powerful over all things.

To be said ten times. Al-Adhkâr, *p. 61, and al-Mundhirî,* al-Targhîb wa al-Tarhîb, *1:239.*

1.63 O Allah, grant me refuge from the Fire.

To be said seven times. Sunan Abû Dâwûd, *4:320 #5079.*

1.64 The recitation of Sûrat al-Ikhlâṣ
Say: He is Allah, One. Allah, the Everlasting Refuge. He does not beget, nor is He begotten. And there is none comparable to Him (112:1–4).

Repeating this sura after Prayer (Ṣalât) *is based on a sound report by the Companion Abû Umâmah. See al-Mundhirî,* al-Targhîb wa al-Tarhîb, *3:265.*

FASTING (*Ṣiyâm*)

Ramadan, the ninth month of the lunar year, is a particularly blessed time for remembrance and supplication. It is the month in which the revelation of the Quran to the Prophet Muḥammad ﷺ began. Fasting throughout Ramadan is one of the five pillars of Islam that every able Muslim is obliged to perform. One fasts by abstaining from all food, all drink (including water), and marital relations from dawn to sunset every day of the month. The Night of Decree *(Laylat'ul-Qadr)* is the most blessed time for prayer in all the year, equal to a thousand months of devotion. It is the night of the first revelation of the Quran, most likely falling on one of the odd-numbered nights of the last ten days of Ramadan.

What one says upon breaking fast at sunset

1.65 O Allah, for You we have fasted, and with Your provision we have broken our fasts. So do accept it from us, for truly You are the All-Hearing, the All-Knowing.

Abû Bakr ibn al-Sunnî, ʿAmal al-Yawm wa al-Layla, *p. 162, #481.*

1.66 Gone is the thirst. Moist are the veins. And, God willing, the reward is assured.

Al-Nasâ'î, ʿAmal al-Yawm wa al-Layla, *pp. 268–69, #299.*

1.67 O Allah, I ask You by Your mercy, which encompasses all things, to forgive me.

The Companion ʿAbdullâh ibn ʿAmr ibn al-ʿÂṣ used to say this at the time of breaking fast.
Sunan Ibn Mâjah, *1:557, #1753, and al-Ḥâkim's* al-Mustadrak, *1:4422.*

What one says upon breaking fast when being hosted

1.68 May those fasting break their fasts with you, and may the virtuous eat of your food, and may the angels pray for you.

Sunan Abû Dâwûd, *3:367, #3854;* Sunan Ibn Mâjah, *1:556, #1747; and al-Nasâ'î,* ʿAmal al-Yawm wa al-Layla, *p. 268, #297.*

What one says during the Night of Decree *(Laylat'ul-Qadr)*

1.69 O Allah, You are all-pardoning and You love to pardon, so pardon me.

Musnad Aḥmad, *6:182, and al-Nasâ'î,* ʿAmal al-Yawm wa al-Layla, *p. 499, #872.*

PILGRIMAGE (Ḥajj)

The time for Ḥajj falls in the twelfth month of the lunar year. It memorializes the acts of Prophet Abraham, his wife Hâjar (Hagar), and their son Ishmael. The Day of the Standing on ʿArafât is one of the specially blessed times of prayer, when supplications may find greater acceptance. Some of the special prayers made by the Prophet ﷺ during the Pilgrimage follow.

What one says when journeying to Ḥajj*, particularly after donning* iḥrâm *(the pilgrim's garb)*

1.70 Ever at Your service, O Allah, ever at Your service. Ever at Your service, for You there is no partner, ever at Your service. Indeed, all praise and grace are Yours—and all dominion. For You there is no partner.

Ṣaḥîḥ Muslim, *2:841, #1184. The Prophet ﷺ used to start this supplication by saying, "There is no God but Allah." See* Ṣaḥîḥ Muslim, *2:886–87, #1218.*

What one says upon seeing the Kaʿba

1.71 Allah is the greatest! O Allah, You are Peace and from You is peace. Greet us, our Lord, with peace. O Allah, increase this House in eminence, magnificence, honor, and reverence. And increase whoever approaches it in Pilgrimage [*Ḥajj*] or the Lesser Pilgrimage [*ʿUmrâ*] in honor, eminence, magnificence, and virtuousness.

Whenever the Prophet ﷺ entered Makkah and saw the Kaʿba, he would raise his hands and say "Allah is the greatest" and then make the above supplication. Sunan al-Bayhaqî, *5:73.*

1.72 When circumambulating the Kaʿba (making *ṭawâf*), the Prophet ﷺ often prayed, *Our Lord, give us good in this world and good in the Hereafter, and save us from the torment of the Fire* (2:201).

The Prophet ﷺ was heard voicing this supplication while between the Yemeni corner and the Black Stone corner of the Kaʿba. Musnad Aḥmad, *3:411. See also al-Ḥâkim's* al-Mustadrak, *1:455.*

1.73a When touching the Black Stone, one may say, "O Allah, ⌜I do this⌝ out of faith in You and to affirm Your Book, and to fulfill Your covenant, and to follow the way of Your Prophet, Muḥammad, God's blessings and peace be upon him."

This statement is attributed to ʿAbdullâh ibn ʿUmar and ʿAlî ibn Abî Ṭâlib. Al-Nawawî's al-Majmûʿ, *8:30–31. See Ibn Ḥajar al-ʿAsqalânî,* Talkhîṣ al-Ḥabîr, *2:247, for a discussion on the authenticity of the report.*

1.73b The Prophet ﷺ after circumambulating the Kaʿba (making *ṭawâf*), proceeded toward the Station of Abraham (Maqâm Ibrâhîm) and faced it in the direction of the Kaʿba and recited: *And take the Station of Abraham as a place of Prayer* (2:125). Then he prayed two *rakʿas* and recited in the first *rakʿa* Sûrat al-Kâfirûn (109) and in the second Sûrat al-Ikhlâṣ (112). After this, he approached Mount al-Ṣafâ, and when he neared it he recited: *Indeed,* ⌈*Mounts*⌉ *al-Ṣafâ and al-Marwa are among the waymarks of Allah* (2:158). Then he said, "I begin with that which Allah has begun." Then he started by ascending Mount al-Ṣafâ, until he saw the Kaʿba. He faced the direction of the Kaʿba and said, "There is no God but Allah, alone; He has no partner. To Him belongs all dominion and for Him is all praise, and He is powerful over all things. There is no God but Allah, alone. He fulfilled His promise, gave victory to His servant, and He alone defeated the confederates." He then descended from al-Ṣafâ and walked to al-Marwa and repeated the same supplication.

For the full text, see Ṣaḥîḥ Muslim, *2:887–88, #1218.*

1.74a Imâm al-Nawawî said that it is traditional to stand near Mount al-Ṣafâ and face the Kaʿba and extol the name of Allah, and then one may say: "Allah is the greatest! Allah is the greatest! Allah is the greatest! And for Allah is all praise. Allah is the greatest for guiding us, and all praise is for Allah for all that He has bestowed upon us. There is no God but Allah, alone; He has no partner. To Him belongs all dominion and for Him is all praise. He gives life and causes death. All good is in His Hand. And He is powerful over all things. There is no God but Allah. He fulfilled His promise, gave victory to His servant, and He alone defeated the confederates. There is no God but Allah. We worship none but Him, making religion sincerely for Him, even if the disbelievers abhor it. O Allah, truly You have said, *Call upon Me; I shall answer you*, and You never fail the promise. And so I ask You, as You guided me to Islam, never to take it from me, so that You take my soul as a Muslim."

Al-Adhkâr, *p. 167.*

What one says on the **Day** *of* ʿ**Arafât** *and the following four days*

1.74b Allah is the greatest! Allah is the greatest! ⌜Allah is the greatest!⌝ There is no God but Allah. Allah is the greatest! Allah is the greatest! And for Allah is all praise.

Imâm al-Shâfiʿî says that it is good to add the following:

Allah is the greatest, the greatest! And all praise is for Allah, much ⌜praise⌝. And glory be to Allah at dawn and in the afternoon. There is no God but Allah. Our religion is sincerely His, even if the disbelievers abhor it. There is no God but Allah, alone. He fulfilled His promise, gave victory to His servant, and He alone defeated the confederates. There is no God but Allah. Allah is the greatest!

Ibn al-Qayyim's Zâd al-Maʿâd, *2:395–96.*

What one says while returning from **Ḥajj** *or* ʿ**Umrâ**

1.74c There is no God but Allah, alone; He has no partner. To Him belongs all dominion and for Him is all praise, and He is powerful over all things. We return repentant, worshipful, bowing down to and praising our Lord. Allah is true to His promise, and granted victory to His servant, and alone defeated the confederates.

The Companion ʿAbdullâh ibn ʿUmar reported that the Prophet ﷺ used to say three times, "Allah is the greatest," when returning from Ḥajj *or traveling over hilly terrain. He then would say the above supplication.* Ṣaḥîḥ Muslim, *2:980, #1344; and* Ṣaḥîḥ al-Bukhârî, *11:188, #6385.*

What one says to a returning pilgrim

1.75 O Allah, grant forgiveness to this pilgrim and to those whom the pilgrim has asked to be forgiven.

Sunan al-Bayhaqî, *5:261.*

What one says upon slaughtering an animal for food

1.76 In the name of Allah, and Allah is the greatest.

Ṣaḥîḥ Muslim, *3:1557, #1966.*

Praying for oneself, one's family, and one's community while making the offering on the Feast of Sacrifice

1.77 The Prophet ﷺ brought a special lamb, laid it on its side, sharpened a knife, and said, "In the name of Allah. O Allah, accept this from Muḥammad, and from the family of Muḥammad, and from the community of Muḥammad." Then he slaughtered it and distributed its meat for the sake of Allah among his family, his neighbors, and the needy.

Ṣaḥîḥ Muslim, *3:1557, #1967.*

2. Remembering God by Day and by Night

THE COMING OF a new day and the waning of the night are occasions for celebrating God's glory, expressing gratitude for the gift of life and seeking God's protection against every disturbance. Some of the Prophet's ﷺ special entreaties and recitations at these times follow.

What one says before going to and after arising from sleep

2.1 The Prophet ﷺ said that when one approaches his bed, an angel and a satan hasten to him. The angel says, "Conclude with goodness." And the satan says, "Conclude with evilness." When one remembers Allah, then sleeps, the angel safeguards him through the night. When one awakens, the angel says, "Commence with goodness." And the satan says, "Commence with evilness." So one should say:

> All praise is for Allah who has returned to me my soul and did not cause it to die in its sleep. All praise is for Allah, who *holds the heavens and the earth from vanishing, and surely if they vanish, no one would hold them after Him. Indeed, He is forbearing, all-forgiving* (35:41). All praise is for Allah, who *holds the heaven so it does not fall upon the earth, except by His permission. Indeed, to all people Allah is all-kind and mercy-giving* (22:65).

According to the Prophet ﷺ, if one says this supplication then falls dead, even at his bedside, he shall enter the Garden. Al-Nasâ'î, ʿAmal al-Yawm wa al-Layla, *pp. 489–90, #854.*

What one says upon awakening

2.2 All praise is for Allah who has given us life after He has taken our souls, and to Him is the resurrection.

Ṣaḥîḥ al-Bukhârî, *11:115, #6314.*

2.3 All praise is for Allah who has given my body well-being and restored my soul to me and has allowed me to remember Him.

Al-Nasâ'î, ʿAmal al-Yawm wa al-Layla, *p. 496, #866.*

What one says after awakening

2.4 O Allah, originator of the heavens and the earth, knower of the unseen and the seen, there is no God but You, Lord and Master of all things. I seek refuge in You from my own wrongdoings, and the evil of Satan and his traps, and from any harm that I may commit against myself or that I may bring to a Muslim.

One may also say this when retiring to sleep. Sunan al-Tirmidhî, *5:506, #3529.*

2.5 O Allah, in whatever blessing I find myself this morning, it is from You and You alone. You have no partner. And for You are all praise and thanks.

The Prophet ﷺ said that whoever says this in the morning will fulfill the due gratitude and thanks to Allah for the day. Sunan Abû Dâwûd, *4:318, #5073.*

2.6 O Allah, I come to the morning having grace and well-being and shelter from You, so complete Your grace upon me, and well-being and shelter in this world and the Hereafter.

To be said three times. Abû Bakr ibn al-Sunnî, ʿAmal al-Yawm wa al-Layla, *p. 29, #55. This report by the Companion Ibn ʿAbbâs is strengthened by a similar report by the Companion Abû Hurayrah. See Ibn Ḥajar's* Natâ'ij al-Afkâr fî Takhrîj Aḥâdîth al-Adhkâr, *2:389, #211.*

2.7 In the name of Allah, with whose name nothing can be harmed in the earth and the heavens. He is the All-Hearing, the All-Knowing.

To be said three times. Sunan al-Tirmidhî, *5:434, #3388.*

2.8 I am well pleased with Allah as the Lord, with Islam as the religion, and with Muḥammad as the Prophet.

The Prophet ﷺ said whoever says this in the morning or the evening, it is incumbent upon Allah to please such a person on the Day of Judgment. Al-Nasâ'î, ʿAmal al-Yawm wa al-Layla, *p. 135, #4. See also* Sunan Abû Dâwûd, *4:318, #5072, and* Sunan al-Tirmidhî, *5:434, #3389.*

What one says in the morning

2.9 The Prophet ﷺ said, "Whoever says in the morning three times, 'I seek refuge in Allah, the All-Hearing, the All-Knowing, from Satan, the accursed,' and recites the last three verses of Sûrat al-Ḥashr (59:22–24), Allah entrusts such a person to seventy thousand angels who pray for him until the evening. And if one dies on that day, one dies a martyr. And if a person says this in the evening, such a person shall be at the same rank."

Musnad Aḥmad, *5:26, and* Sunan al-Tirmidhî, *5:167, #2922.*

2.10 O Allah, by Your ⌜leave⌝ we have come to the morning and by Your ⌜leave⌝ we have come to the evening and by Your ⌜leave⌝ we live, and by Your ⌜leave⌝ we die. And to You is the ⌜ultimate⌝ resurrection.

Sunan Abû Dâwûd, *4:317, #5068, and* Sunan al-Tirmidhî, *5:435, #3391.*

2.11 O Allah, I ask You for pardon and well-being in this life and in the Hereafter. O Allah, I ask You for pardon and well-being in my religion, my life, my family, and my wealth. O Allah, cover my faults and soothe my fears. O Allah, protect me from before me and from behind me, and from my right and from my left, and from above me, and I seek refuge in You from being seized from beneath me.

Sunan Ibn Mâjah, *2:1273, #3871.*

2.12 O Allah, I come to this morning calling upon You to bear witness—as I call upon Your Throne Bearers, Your angels, and all of Your creation to bear witness—that indeed You are Allah, there is no God but You, and Muḥammad is Your servant and Your messenger.

The Prophet ﷺ said whoever says this in the morning and the evening four times shall be saved from Hellfire. Sunan Abû Dâwûd, *4:317, #5069, and* Sunan al-Tirmidhî, *5:493, #3501.*

2.13 We come to the morning in conformity with ˹the way of˺ Islam and with the sincere word of faith and with the religion of our Prophet Muḥammad ﷺ and with the way of our father Abraham, who was upright and was not of the idolaters.

Al-Nasâ'î, ʿAmal al-Yawm wa al-Layla, *p. 290, #343. See a similar text in* Musnad Aḥmad, *3:406, and* Sunan al-Dârimî, *2:292, which excludes the last clause.*

What one says at the approach of evening

2.14 *The Messenger believes in what has been sent down to him from his Lord, as do the believers. All believe in Allah and His angels and His Books and His messengers: "We do not distinguish between any of His messengers." And they say, "We hear and we obey. Your forgiveness, our Lord! For to You is the ultimate destiny." Allah does not task a soul beyond its capacity. For it is ˹the good˺ it has earned, and against it is ˹the evil˺ it sought to earn. "Our Lord, hold us not accountable if we forget or err. Our Lord, lay not upon us a burden like that which You have laid upon those before us. Our Lord, lay not upon us that which we do not have the strength to bear. And pardon us, and forgive us, and have mercy upon us. You are our Patron. So help us against the disbelieving people"* (2:285–86).

The Prophet ﷺ said that whoever reads these verses during the night, they will be sufficient for him. Ṣaḥîḥ Muslim, *1:55, #808.*

2.15 O Allah, in whatever blessing I find myself this evening, it is from You and You alone. You have no partner. And for You are all praise and thanks.

The Prophet ﷺ said that whoever says this in the evening will fulfill the gratitude and thanks due to Allah for the night. Sunan Abû Dâwûd, *4:318, #5073.*

2.16 We come to this evening, as does all of Allah's dominion. And all praise is for Allah. There is no God but Allah, alone; He has no partner. To Him belongs all dominion and for Him is all praise, and He is powerful over all things. My Lord, I ask You for the good of what is in this night and the good of what comes after it. And I seek refuge in You from the harm of what is in this night and the harm of what comes after it. My Lord, I seek refuge in You from laziness and the ills of old age. My Lord, I seek refuge in You from torment in the Fire and torment in the grave.

Ṣaḥîḥ Muslim, *4:2088–89, #2723; and* Sunan al-Tirmidhî, *5:435, #3390. This is repeated in the morning, as well, with the word "evening" replaced by "morning" and the word "night" by "day."*

2.17 I am well pleased with Allah as the Lord, with Islam as the religion, and with Muḥammad as the Prophet.

The Prophet ﷺ said that whoever says this in the evening, it is incumbent upon Allah to please such a person on the Day of Judgment. Sunan al-Tirmidhî, *5:434, #3389.*

What one says when retiring to sleep

2.18 O Allah, by Your ⌜leave⌝ we have come to the evening. And by Your ⌜leave⌝ we live, and by Your ⌜leave⌝ we die. And to You is the ⌜ultimate⌝ resurrection.

Sunan Abû Dâwûd, *4:317, #5068, and* Sunan al-Tirmidhî, *5:435, #3391.*

2.19 My Lord, save me from Your torment on the day You resurrect Your servants.

To be said three times. Sunan al-Tirmidhî, *5:439, #3399.*

2.20 All praise is for Allah who has fed us and has given us drink, who has sufficed us and has given us shelter. For how many are there who have neither sufficient provision nor shelter!

Ṣaḥîḥ Muslim, *4:2085, #2715.*

2.21 All praise is for Allah who has sufficed me, and has given me shelter, and has given me food and drink. And it is He who has bestowed upon me much favor, and it is He who has given me abundance. All praise is for Allah in every condition. O Allah, Lord of all things and their sovereign, and the God of all things, I seek refuge in You from the Fire.

Sunan Abû Dâwûd, *4:313–14, #5058.*

2.22 In Your name, my Lord, I lay my side down, and in Your [name] I raise it. If You keep hold of my soul, then have mercy on it. If You send it back, then protect it as You protect Your righteous servants.

Ṣaḥîḥ al-Bukhârî, *11:126–27, #6320.*

2.23 In the name of Allah, I lay my side down. O Allah, forgive me my sins and impel away my devil and release my debts and place me among the highest assembly.

Sunan Abû Dâwûd, *4:313, #5054.*

2.24 O Allah, Lord of the heavens and Lord of the earth and Lord of the magnificent Throne, our Lord and the Lord of all things. O You who cleave grain and pit, who sent down the Torah, the Gospel, and the Quran [the Criterion], I seek refuge in You from the evil of every evil one whose forelock You take hold of.

O Allah, You are the First; there is nothing before You. You are the Last; there is nothing after You. You are the Manifest; there is nothing more exalted than You. You are the Hidden; there is nothing beyond You. Satisfy our debts for us and suffice us against poverty.

Ṣaḥîḥ Muslim, *4:2084, #2713.*

2.25 According to ʿÂ'isha, every night before the Prophet ﷺ went to sleep, he used to cup his hands and recite softly into them suras 112, 113, and 114 of the Quran. He then would pass his hands over what he could of his body, starting with his head and face and then the front of his body. He would do this three times.

Sunan al-Tirmidhî, *5:441, #3402, and* Ṣaḥîḥ al-Bukhârî, *11:125, #6319.*

2.26 O Allah, in Your name I die and I live.

Ṣaḥîḥ al-Bukhârî, *11:115, #6314.*

2.27 O Allah, I submit myself to You and I turn my face toward You and I entrust You with my affairs, and I fall back upon You, hopeful yet fearful of You. There is no haven nor deliverance from You except in You. I have believed in Your Book which You have sent down and in Your Prophet whom You have sent.

The Prophet ﷺ said that before going to bed one should make ablution as one does for Prayer (Ṣalât). *Then lie on your right side and say the above-cited prayer. He added, "Then if you die on this night, you will do so upon the natural state of purity. And make these words the last with which you speak."* Ṣaḥîḥ al-Bukhârî, *11:115, #6315; a slightly variant version is found in* Ṣaḥîḥ Muslim, *4:2081–82, #2710.*

2.28 **The recitation of the Verse of the Seat ⌜of Divinity⌝, *Âyat al-Kursî***

Allah, there is no God but Him, the Living, the Self-Subsisting. Slumber does not overtake Him, nor does sleep. To Him belongs whatever is in the heavens and whatever is in the earth. Who is it that shall intercede before Him, except by His permission? He knows what is before them and what is behind them, and they do not comprehend anything of His knowledge except as He wills. His Seat ⌜of Divinity⌝ encompasses the heavens and the earth, and preserving them does not fatigue Him. And He is the Exalted, the Magnificent (2:255).

Al-Nasâ'î, ʿAmal al-Yawm wa al-Layla, *p. 532, #959.*

2.29 **The recitation of Sûrat al-Kâfirûn**

Say: O you disbelievers, I do not worship what you worship. And you are not worshipping what I worship. Nor shall I worship what you worship. And you are not worshipping what I worship. For you is your religion. And for me is my religion (109:1–6).

See Sunan al-Tirmidhî, *5:442, #3403.*

What one says after pleasant or unpleasant dreams

2.30 The Messenger of God ﷺ said, "When one of you sees a dream that he likes, it is from Allah; so let one praise Allah for it, and one may speak of it. But if one sees other than this, of what he finds repugnant, it is from Satan, so let one seek refuge in Allah from its evil and not mention it to anyone, for it shall not harm him."

Al-Nasâ'î, ʿAmal al-Yawm wa al-Layla, *p. 505, #893.*

What one says after a nightmare or an unpleasant dream

2.31 I seek refuge in the perfect words of Allah from His wrath, from His punishment, from the evil of His servants, and from the promptings of satans and from them coming near me.

The Prophet ﷺ said that when one wakes up fearful and utters this supplication, such a person shall not be harmed. Sunan al-Tirmidhî, *5:506, #3528.*

What one says after waking up during the night

2.32 There is no God but Allah, alone; He has no partner. To Him belongs all dominion and for Him is all praise, and He is powerful over all things. All praise is for Allah, and glory be to Allah, and there is no God but Allah, and Allah is the greatest. There is no strength nor might except with Allah. O Allah, forgive me.

The Prophet ﷺ said that one's supplication after repeating the above will be answered. If one rises from bed, makes ablution, and then prays, his Prayer (Ṣalât) *is accepted.* Ṣaḥîḥ al-Bukhârî, *3:39, #1154, and* Sunan al-Tirmidhî, *5:447, #3414. A slightly differing version is found in* Sunan Abû Dâwûd, *4:314, #5060.*

2.33 There is no God but You. Glory be to You, O Allah. I seek Your forgiveness for my sins. And I ask You for Your mercy. O Allah, increase me in knowledge and let not my heart swerve, after You have guided me, and grant me mercy from Your own ⌜bounty⌝. Indeed, it is You who are the All-Granting.

Sunan Abû Dâwûd, *4:314, #5061, and al-Nasâ'î,* ʿAmal al-Yawm wa al-Layla, *p. 495, #865.*

3. Prayers for Anxiety, Worry, and Sadness

AT TIMES, ONE may experience fear, distress, or other unpleasant feelings. But to allow oneself to be overcome by these states is to forfeit one's composure and open oneself up to demoralization and regret. The model for humanity, Prophet Muḥammad ﷺ showed us that especially at times of concern or sorrow one should rush to God in prayer, for He is the Comforter (*al-Mu'min*) and the Everlasting Refuge (*al-Ṣamad*).

What one says in moments of fear

3.1 When fearing that harm may touch someone or something dear, one should say, "O Allah, bless him [*or* her *or* it] and do not let him be harmed."

Ibn al-Sunnî, ʿAmal al-Yawm wa al-Layla, *p. 81, #208. This report is strengthened by several other reports. The meaning of this* ḥadîth *is found in* Musnad Aḥmad, *3:447.*

3.2 *Sufficient is Allah for us and a most excellent trustee* (3:173).

Prophet Abraham ﷺ said this invocation when his people cast him into the fire because of his stand for faith in the one and true God. Prophet Muḥammad ﷺ said the same when he learned that his enemies were gathering forces against him and the believers. Ṣaḥîḥ al-Bukhârî, *8:229, #4563 and #4564, and al-Nasâ'î,* ʿAmal al-Yawm wa al-Layla, *p. 393, #603.*

3.3 When fearing harm from someone, one should say, "O Allah, we set You at their throats, and we seek refuge in You from their evil."

Sunan Abû Dâwûd, *2:89, #1537.*

What one says in moments of distress, concern, or sorrow

3.4 The Prophet ﷺ said that whenever a Muslim says the prayer uttered by Prophet Jonah when he was in the belly of the whale—*There is no God but You, glory be to You. Truly I was among the wrong-doing* (21:87)—the prayer will be answered.

Sunan al-Tirmidhî, *5:495, #3505, and al-Ḥâkim's* al-Mustadrak, *2:583.*

3.5 Allah! Allah is my Lord. I associate nothing with Him.

Sunan Abû Dâwûd, *2:87, #1525, and* Sunan Ibn Mâjah, *2:1277, #3882.*

3.6 O Allah, Your mercy do I request. So do not leave me to myself even for the blink of an eye. And set aright for me all of my affairs. There is no God but You.

Sunan Abû Dâwûd, *4:324, #5090, and* Ṣaḥîḥ Ibn Ḥibbân (al-Iḥsân), *2:158, #966.*

3.7 O All-Living, O Self-Subsisting, Your mercy do I invoke for help.

Sunan al-Tirmidhî, *5:504, #3524, and al-Ḥâkim's* al-Mustadrak, *1:509.*

3.8 There is no God but Allah, the Magnificent, the Forbearer. There is no God but Allah, Lord of the magnificent Throne. There is no God but Allah, Lord of the heavens and Lord of the earth, and Lord of the Throne, the All-Generous.

Ṣaḥîḥ al-Bukhârî, *11:145, #6346, and* Ṣaḥîḥ Muslim, *4:2093, #2730.*

3.9 Allah is sufficient for me and a most excellent trustee is He.

Two people presented their dispute before the Prophet, peace be upon him. The person against whom the Prophet ﷺ judged said despondently, "Allah is sufficient for me and a most excellent trustee is He." The Prophet ﷺ advised him to have resolve. He said, "Yet if you are overwhelmed by something or someone, then say, 'Allah reproaches one for slothfulness. Instead, employ your skill.'" Sunan Abû Dâwûd, *3:313, #3627.*

3.10 O Allah, nothing is easy except what You make easy. And, if You will, You make what is difficult easy.

Ṣaḥîḥ Ibn Ḥibbân (al-Iḥsân), *2:160–61, #970.*

3.11 O Allah, to You I complain of my weakness, my lack of facility, my helplessness before people. O most merciful of the merciful, You are the Lord of the weak, and You are my Lord. To whom will You entrust me? To strangers who will ill-treat me or to foes whom You have given authority over me? So long as You are not angry with me, I do not care. Yet the well-being You give is ever enough for me. I seek refuge in the light of Your Face, by which all darkness is illuminated and the affairs of this world and the next are set aright, lest You make Your wrath descend upon me or Your anger beset me. Still it is Yours to reproach until You are well pleased. There is no strength nor might except with You.

Ibn Hishâm, al-Sîra al-Nabawiyya, *2:61–62. Ibn Isḥâq reported this without disclosing the chain of reporters to the Prophet, peace be upon him. See also al-Haythamî,* Majmaᶜ al-Zawâ'id wa Manbaᶜ al-Fawâ'id, *6:35.*

3.12 O Allah, I am indeed Your servant, the son of Your servant, the son of Your maidservant. My forelock is in Your Hand. Your decree upon me is done, and Your judgment upon me is just. I beseech You by every one of Your names—with which You have named Yourself, or have taught to any one of Your creation, or have sent down in Your Book, or have kept to Yourself within the knowledge of the unseen—to make the Quran the springtime of my heart, the light within my chest, the departure of my sadness, and the vanishing of my worries.

The Prophet ﷺ said that whenever one struck by worry or grief says the above supplication, Allah removes his worry and substitutes it with relief. Musnad Aḥmad, *1:391.*

What one says in moments of anger

3.13 At the time of anger, one should say, "I seek refuge in Allah from Satan, the accursed."

Ṣaḥîḥ al-Bukhârî, *10:518, #6115, and* Ṣaḥîḥ Muslim, *4:2015, #2610. Performing ablution is also recommended as is changing one's position; namely to sit if standing and to lay down if sitting. See* Sunan Abû Dâwûd, *4:249 #4782 and #4784.*

What one says when experiencing distracting thoughts, especially during worship

3.14 One should seek refuge in Allah and blow (as if spitting) three times to his left.

A Companion complained to the Prophet ﷺ of intervening thoughts during Prayer (Ṣalât) *and the Prophet ﷺ attributed this to a particular devil named "Khinzab," who tries to pollute and divert thoughts while one is in Prayer.* Ṣaḥîḥ Muslim, *4:1728–29, #2203.*

What one says when burdened with debt

3.15 O Allah, suffice me with what You have made lawful against what You have made unlawful. And enrich me with Your favor so that I need none but You.

Sunan al-Tirmidhî, *5:523, #3563.*

What one says when repaying a loan

3.16 May Allah bless for you your family and your wealth. Indeed, the ⌜due⌝ recompense for a loan is commendation and repayment.

The Prophet ﷺ once borrowed 40,000 dirhams from the Companion ʿAbdullâh ibn Abî Rabîʿa for community needs after the Conquest of Makkah, 8 H./629 C.E. It is reported that he made this prayer upon repaying the full amount to the lender. Al-Nasâ'î, ʿAmal al-Yawm wa al-Layla, *p. 300, #372.*

What one says when faced with a decision or choice: **The prayer** *for making the best choice or decision* **(istikhâra)**

3.17 O Allah, enable me through Your knowledge to choose what is best, and empower me through Your power. I ask You ⌜to grant me⌝ from Your vast bounty, for truly You have power, and I have no power, and You know, and I do not know. You are truly the Supreme Knower of the Unseen. O Allah, if You know this matter to be best for me regarding my religion, livelihood, and ultimate end, then decree it for me. And if You know this matter to be evil for me regarding my religion, livelihood, and ultimate end, then turn it away from me and turn me away from it, and decree for me what is best, wherever it may be, then make me pleased with it.

Ṣaḥîḥ al-Bukhârî, *11:183, #6382. Another version includes "...to be best in my immediate affair or in the life to come."*

4. *Prayers when Faced with Sickness or Death*

FEAR AND GRIEF may grip one when faced with serious injury or illness or with the passing of a loved one, for at such times we become acutely aware of human frailty and mortality. The Prophet ﷺ taught us that though we are limited, hope in God's help—for recovery, forgiveness, and eternal delight in the Afterlife—is unlimited and that one should turn to Him for healing, patience, relief, and well-being. Prayers that the Prophet ﷺ made at such times follow.

What one says when ill

4.1 When feeling bodily aches, one places his or her hand over the aching part and says, "In the name of Allah" three times and then the following seven times, "I seek refuge in Allah and His might from the harm of which I suffer and fear."

Ṣaḥîḥ Muslim *4:1728, #2202, and al-Nasâ'î,* ʿAmal al-Yawm wa al-Layla, *p. 551, #1000.*

What one says for those who are ill

4.2 Remove the affliction, Lord of all people. Heal him ⌜or her⌝, for You are the Healer. There is no healing but Your healing, for it is a healing that leaves no ailment.

ʿÂ'isha said that whenever a person complained of an ailment, the Prophet ﷺ would wipe over the ailing part with his right hand and say this supplication. Ṣaḥîḥ Muslim, *4:1721–22, #2191.*

4.3 I ask Allah, the Magnificent, the Lord of the magnificent Throne, to heal you.

The Companion Ibn ʿAbbâs said that whoever visits an ill person, whose decreed time has not yet come, and says this supplication seven times in the presence of the ill person, Allah will relieve him of the ailment. Sunan Abû Dâwûd, *3:187, #3106, and* Sunan al-Tirmidhî, *4:357, #2083.*

4.4 May there be no harm. It is, God willing, a purification.

Whenever the Prophet ﷺ visited a sick person, he would say this supplication. Ṣaḥîḥ al-Bukhârî, *10:624, #3616.*

4.5 In the name of Allah, who shall cure you and shall heal you from every illness and shall protect you from the evil of an envier when he envies and from the evil of everyone with an evil eye.

Whenever the Prophet ﷺ complained of an illness, Angel Gabriel ﷺ made this supplication for him. Ṣaḥîḥ Muslim, *4:1718, #2185.*

What one says when receiving inquiry about the condition of one who is ill

4.6 When one receives inquiry about the condition of one who is suffering from sickness, an encouraging response is offered, such as, "All praise is for Allah, he or she is approaching recovery and has a full life ahead of him or her," and the like.

Sunan Ibn Mâjah, *1:462, #1438.*

What one says to oneself when seeing another afflicted with illness

4.7 All praise is for Allah who has preserved my well-being against what He has tested you with and has truly favored me over many of those He created.

This is an expression of gratitude to Allah for good health. Sunan al-Tirmidhî, *5:459, #3431. It is noted that one should say this to himself so that the afflicted person does not hear it.* Sunan al-Tirmidhî, *5:460.*

What one says when death is imminent

4.8 O Allah, forgive me. Have mercy upon me, and join me with the Highest Companion.

Ṣaḥîḥ Muslim, *4:1893–94, #2444.*

4.9 O Allah, help me against the dazedness of death.

Sunan al-Tirmidhî, *3:308, #978.*

What one says after the passing of loved ones

4.10 To Allah we belong and to Him we return. O Allah, recompense me for my calamity and replace for me better than that which I have lost.

The Prophet ﷺ said that whenever a calamity strikes a Muslim who then says this supplication, Allah will substitute his or her loss with something better. Ṣaḥîḥ Muslim, *2:631–32, #918, and al-Nasâ'î,* ʿAmal al-Yawm wa al-Layla, *p. 580, #1072.*

4.11 O Allah, forgive me and forgive him [*or* her] and let this be succeeded by a good outcome.

The Prophet ﷺ advised Umm Salama to say this when her first husband died. Ṣaḥîḥ Muslim, *2:633, #919.*

What one says to those near death

4.12 The Prophet ﷺ instructed us to say to one approaching death, "There is no God but Allah."

Ṣaḥîḥ Muslim, *2:631, #916.*

What one says for the deceased immediately after death

4.13 O Allah, forgive [name of the deceased] and raise his rank among the rightly guided. And be with his surviving posterity. And forgive us and him, O Lord of the Worlds. And widen for him his grave and give him light in it.

Ṣaḥîḥ Muslim, *2:634, #920. The Prophet ﷺ entered upon Abû Salama who was on his deathbed with his eyes transfixed. The Prophet ﷺ then closed them and said, "When the spirit is taken away, the eyes follow it." When a number of Abû Salama's family members bewailed him, the Prophet ﷺ said, "Never pray for yourselves anything except what is good. For angels say 'Amen' to what you say." The Prophet ﷺ then repeated the above prayer for Abû Salama.*

What one says to console the relatives of the deceased

4.14 Indeed, what Allah has taken belongs to Him, as does what He has given. And everything has a stated term with Him. Let ˹the bereaved˺ be patient and seek God's reward.

Ṣaḥîḥ Muslim, *2:635–36, #923. Usâma ibn Zayd reported, "While we were with the Messenger of Allah ﷺ one of his daughters sent for him when her child was facing death." The Prophet ﷺ asked the messenger to relate to her the above statement. When she urged him to come, he went to her along with three of his Companions; and they handed the boy to him at the moment of his death. The Prophet's eyes filled with tears. Saʿad ibn ʿUbâda then asked, "What is this, O Messenger of Allah!" The Prophet ﷺ said, "This is mercy which Allah puts in the hearts of His servants. And indeed, Allah has mercy upon the merciful among His servants." See also* Ṣaḥîḥ al-Bukhârî, *3:151, #1284.*

What one says when seeking protection against disease

4.15 O Allah, I seek refuge in You from leprosy, insanity, vitiligo, and from the worst of ailments.

Sunan Abû Dâwûd, *2:93, #1554.*

What one says during a funeral

4.16 O Allah, this is Your servant, the son of Your maidservant. He has need of Your mercy, and You have no need to torment him. O Allah, if he has excelled in doing good, then increase his goodness. And if he did wrong, then absolve him.

Al-Ḥâkim's al-Mustadrak, *1:359.*

4.17 ***Imâm al-Nawawî cited the following supplication compiled by Imâm al-Shâfiʿî from various traditions and sayings of Companions and Successors with regard to funerals:***
O Allah, this is Your servant and the son of Your servant. He has departed the breeze of this world and its spaciousness—wherein

were the things he loved and his loved ones—for the darkness of the grave and whatever he will meet. He testified that there is no God but You, and that Muḥammad is Your servant and Your messenger, and You know best about him.

O Allah, he has indeed arrived to You, and You are the best of hosts; he has become more in need of Your mercy, and You have no need to torment him. We come to You as Your worshippers, with hope in You, pleading for him.

O Allah, if he has excelled in doing good, then increase his goodness. And if he did wrong, then absolve him. And give him, by Your mercy, Your pleasure. And protect him from the trial of the grave and its torment. And widen for him his grave and keep away the earth from his sides. And bring to him, by Your mercy, security from Your torment until You send him to Your Garden, O most merciful of the merciful.

Al-Adhkâr, *p. 134. See also al-Shâfiʿî's work* al-Umm, *1:309;* Sunan al-Bayhaqî, *4:42; and* al-Majmûʿ Sharḥ al-Muhadhdhab, *5:238.*

4.18 O Allah, forgive him and have mercy on him. Grant him well-being and pardon him. Make gracious his place of rest and make spacious his entrance ⌜into the grave⌝. Cleanse him with water, snow, and coolness. And purify him of sins as You purify white cloth of dirt. Grant him a home finer than his home ⌜in this world⌝, and a household finer than his household, and a spouse finer than his spouse. And enter him into the Garden and protect him from the torment of the grave [*or* from the torment of the Fire].

Ṣaḥîḥ Muslim, *2:662–63, #963, and al-Nasâ'î,* ʿAmal al-Yawm wa al-Layla, *p. 586, #1087.*

4.19 O Allah, forgive those of us who are alive and those of us who are dead, those who are young and those who are old, those who are male and those who are female, those who are present and those who are absent. O Allah, let those of us You keep alive live with faith. And those of us whose souls You take, take them while they are in Islam. O Allah, do not deprive us of his reward and do not leave us to stray after him.

Sunan Abû Dâwûd, *3:211, #3201.*

4.20 O Allah, indeed "So-and-so" [name of the deceased], the son [*or* daughter] of "So-and-so" [the name of the parents], is under Your protection. So save him from the trials of the grave and the torment of the Fire. And You are worthy of fulfilling ˹Your promise˺ and worthy of all praise. O Allah, forgive him and have mercy upon him, for You are the All-Forgiving, the Mercy-Giving.

Sunan Abû Dâwûd, *3:211, #3202.*

What one says while awaiting the preparation of the deceased's grave

4.21 O Allah, I seek refuge in You from the torment of the grave.

To be said three times. Al-Ḥâkim's al-Mustadrak, *1:37.*

What one says when lowering the body into the grave

4.22 In the name of Allah and ˹following˺ the way of the Messenger of Allah.

This should be repeated as the body of the deceased is being lowered into the grave. Al-Nasâ'î, ʿAmal al-Yawm wa al-Layla, *p. 586, #1088.*

What one says after burial is complete

4.23 O Allah, forgive him ˹or her˺ and make him ˹or her˺ steadfast in the face of questioning in the grave.

This supplication is based on what the Companion ʿUthmân ibn ʿAffân reported, stating that the Prophet ﷺ used to instruct those attending the burial "to seek forgiveness for your brother and ask for steadfastness for him. For he is now being questioned." See Sunan Abû Dâwûd, *3:215, #3221.*

4.24 O Allah, You are the Lord of this ˹deceased soul˺. You have created it and You have guided it to Islam. And You have drawn forth its spirit and You know best its secret and open deeds. We have come as its intercessors, so forgive him.

Sunan Abû Dâwûd, *3:210, #3200, and al-Nasâ'î,* ʿAmal al-Yawm wa al-Layla, *pp. 582–83, #1076, #1077, and #1078.*

What one says when visiting the cemetery

4.25 Peace be upon you, dwellers of this abode of the believers and Muslims. God willing, we shall certainly join ˹you˺. I ask Allah for well-being—for us and for you.

Ṣaḥîḥ Muslim, *2:671, #975.*

5. *Prayers* Occasioned *by* Natural *Phenomena*

NATURAL EVENTS DISPLAY the splendor and power of God. A gust of wind, a dawning day, and a rain shower are but a few signs of God's magnificence, awakening humankind to fall into harmony with creation by raising God's praise or expressing our dependence upon Him for sustenance and protection. The Quran calls us to observe both the slight and the momentous happenings in creation, and the Prophet ﷺ taught us to treat them as occasions for remembering and entreating the Lord of Majesty and Honor.

What one says at dawn and sunrise

5.1 Upon seeing the break of dawn, the Prophet ﷺ would say, "Let those who hear us convey ˹the fact˺ that we enjoy praising Allah and enjoy His great favor upon us. Our Lord, be with us, and be most favorable to us. I seek refuge in Allah from the Fire."

Ṣaḥīḥ Muslim, *4:2086, #2718.*

What one says during storms

• *With regard to a windstorm:*

5.2 One day when the wind gusted strongly, a man cursed it. So the Prophet ﷺ said to him, "Do not curse it. Rather, ask Allah for its good and the good of what is in it and the good that was sent along with it. And seek refuge in Allah from its harm and the harm of what is in it and the harm that was sent along with it."

Al-Nasâ'î, ʿAmal al-Yawm wa al-Layla, *p. 522, #937.*

5.3 O Allah, I ask You for the good ˹of this wind˺ and the good of what is in it and the good that was sent along with it. And I seek refuge in You from its harm and the harm of what is in it and the harm that was sent along with it.

Ṣaḥîḥ Muslim, *2:616, #899, and al-Nasâ'î,* ʿAmal al-Yawm wa al-Layla, *p. 522, #940.*

5.4 The recitation of the last two suras of the Quran (113 and 114).

Once while the Prophet ﷺ was journeying, a strong windstorm came and the sky became severely overcast. He recited Sûrat al-Falaq (113) and Sûrat al-Nâs (114). He taught this to his Companion ʿUqba ibn ʿÂmir, who was traveling with the Prophet ﷺ. Sunan Abû Dâwûd, *2:73, #1463. Al-Mundhirî,* al-Targhîb wa al-Tarhîb, *3:200.*

• *With regard to rainstorms:*

5.5 O Allah, let it come around us and not upon us! O Allah, let it come upon the hillocks, upon the knolls, in the midst of the valleys, and wherever trees grow.

When a torrential rainstorm caused property damage and closed the roads, a bedouin approached the Prophet ﷺ while he was delivering the Friday sermon and said, "O Messenger of Allah, ask Allah to withhold ˹the rain˺ from us." The Prophet then raised his hands and said this supplication. Ṣaḥîḥ Muslim, *2:612–14, #897.*

What one says when asking for rain

5.6 O Allah, give us rainfall! O Allah, give us rainfall! O Allah, give us rainfall!

When lack of rain threatened pastures and livestock, some Companions appealed to the Prophet ﷺ to ask God for rain. He then made the above supplication. The phrase, "Allâhumma aghithnâ," *may also mean, "O Allah, help us." For the background of this prayer, see* Ṣaḥîḥ Muslim, *2:612–14, #897.*

5.7 All praise is for Allah, Lord of the Worlds, the All-Merciful, the

Mercy-Giving, Master of the Day of Judgment. There is no God but Allah. He does what He wills. O Allah, You are the only God, there is no God but You, the Self-Sufficient. And truly we are in need, so bring down to us rainfall. And let what You have brought down for us be a ˹source of˺ strength and means for a time.

Sunan Abû Dâwûd, *1:304, #1173. See* Sunan Abû Dâwûd *for the background of this* ḥadîth.

5.8 O Allah, provide water to Your servants and Your beasts, and spread Your mercy. And give life to this lifeless land of Yours.

Sunan Abû Dâwûd, *1:305, #1176.*

5.9 *Seek forgiveness from your Lord. Indeed, He is most forgiving. He sends the heaven's ˹rain˺ upon you in abundance* (71:10–11).

Seek forgiveness from your Lord, then repent to Him. He shall send the heaven's ˹rain˺ upon you in abundance. And He will increase you in strength, adding to your strength. And do not turn away as trespassers (11:52).

During the caliphate of ʿUmar ibn al-Khaṭṭâb there was a drought, during which ʿUmar prayed to Allah for rain by asking Allah for forgiveness and kept reciting these verses (71:10–11 and 11:52). Tafsîr al-Ṭabarî, *12:249, #34998, and* Tafsîr Ibn Kathîr, *4:665.*

5.10 Upon seeing the approach of rain clouds, the Prophet ﷺ prayed, "O Allah, make it a salubrious rain cloud."

Al-Nasâʾî, ʿAmal al-Yawm wa al-Layla, *p. 514, #918.*

What one says on hearing lightning and thunder

5.11 O Allah, let us not be slain by Your wrath nor destroyed by Your torment, and grant us well-being above all.

Musnad Aḥmad, *2:100–101, and* Sunan al-Tirmidhî, *5:469, #3450. Upon hearing thunder and seeing lightning, the Prophet ﷺ said this supplication, glorified Allah, and recited the verses of the Quran (13:12–13).* Tafsîr al-Ṭabarî, *7:360, #20260 and #20265.*

It is He who shows you lightning that you may have fear and hope (13:12). *Thunder glorifies His praise, as do the angels out of fear of Him* (13:13).

What one says upon sighting a new moon

5.12 Allah is the greatest! O Allah, bring it forth upon us with security, faith, peace, Islam, and success to that which is beloved and pleasing to our Lord. Our Lord and your Lord is Allah.

The Prophet ﷺ addressed the moon itself with the statement, "Our Lord and your Lord is Allah."
Sunan al-Dârimî, *2:3–4.*

5.13 O Allah, bring it forth upon us with security, faith, peace, and Islam. My Lord and your Lord is Allah.

Sunan al-Tirmidhî, *5:470, #3451.*

5.14 May this be a crescent of goodness and guidance. [*Repeat three times.*] I have believed in Him who created you. [*Repeat three times.*] All praise is for Allah, who has taken away the month of ˹name of month˺ and brought forth the month of ˹name of new month˺.

Sunan Abû Dâwûd, *4:324, #5092.*

What one says at the time of an eclipse

5.15 The Prophet ﷺ said, "The sun and the moon are two of Allah's signs. They do not eclipse because of anyone's death or life. So whenever you observe them, glorify Allah by saying, *Allâhu akbar* [Allah is the greatest]. And call upon Allah and Pray [*Ṣalât*] and give charity, until it is removed."

Ṣaḥîḥ Muslim, *2:618, #901. The phrase "until it is removed" is an addition from another report in* Ṣaḥîḥ Muslim, *2:630, #915. There is a special Prayer to be performed during eclipses. For details about the Prayer consult a* fiqhî *source.*

What one says upon observing the yield of crops or fruits

5.16 O Allah, bless for us our town and our fruits and our scales and our bushel measures—blessings upon blessings.

Ṣaḥîḥ Muslim, *2:1000, #1373.*

6. *Prayers for* Traveling *and for* Entering *and* Exiting

THE PROPHET ﷺ REMINDED believers that one should be "as a traveler" in this life, journeying to the final assembly before God in the Afterlife. From birth to death, we proceed through a labyrinth of passages that make up the tapestry of our lives. The relationships we choose, the places we frequent, and the knowledge we seek—such are the way-stations of our journey. Truly, much of what we seek to accomplish entails movement from one place to another, leaving loved ones and home for a time. Yet the best compass is a sound heart filled with a yearning for God, and the best provision is remembrance of God and prayer to Him.

What one says when departing one's residence for everyday affairs

6.1 In the name of Allah, I rely on Allah. There is no strength nor might except with Allah.

The Prophet ﷺ said that when one says this, it is said to him or her, "You are guided, sufficed, and protected," and satans are turned away from him or her. Sunan Abû Dâwûd, *4:325, #5095.*

6.2 O Allah, I seek refuge in You from straying or being led astray, from erring or slipping into error, from oppressing or being oppressed, from ignorance or from the ignorance of others against me.

Sunan Abû Dâwûd, *4:325, #5094.*

What one says when departing on a journey

6.3 When the Prophet ﷺ mounted his ride for traveling, he would say, "Allah is the greatest," three times. Then he would recite verses of the Quran: *Glory be to Him who has subjugated this to us, and we were not capable of doing it. And truly to our Lord we shall return* (43:13–14). Then he would say: "O Allah, we ask You, in this journey of ours, for righteousness and Godfearingness, and for deeds that well-please You. O Allah, make this, our journey, easy for us, and shorten its distance for us. O Allah, You are our Companion in travel and the Overseer of our families. O Allah, I seek refuge in You from the rigors of travel, from distressing sights, and from harm that may unsettle wealth and families." [And upon his return, the Prophet ﷺ would say the same, adding, "We return repentant, worshipful—praising our Lord."]

The phrase "sû' al-munqalab" *(harm that may upset) may also mean "harm" that disappoints one "upon returning" to one's family and property.* Ṣaḥîḥ Muslim, *2:978, #1342.*

What one says to those one leaves behind when departing on a journey

6.4 To Allah I entrust ˹preserving˺ your religion, your covenants, and the outcome of your deeds, and I say, "Peace be with you."

The Prophet ﷺ stated that Loqman the Wise said, "Whenever something is entrusted to God, He preserves it." The Prophet ﷺ then said the above supplication. This can also be said to one embarking on a journey. Al-Nasâ'î, ʿAmal al-Yawm wa al-Layla, *p. 355, #516. See also a variant report in* Sunan al-Tirmidhî, *5:466, #3439.*

6.5 I entrust you to Allah, who never neglects His trusts.

The Prophet ﷺ said this to his Companion Abû Hurayrah, who taught it to his students. Musnad Aḥmad, *2:403.*

6.6 May Allah provide you with Godfearingness, and may He forgive your sins, and may He facilitate good for you wherever you may be.

The Prophet ﷺ said this to a Companion about to go on a journey. Sunan al-Tirmidhî, *5:466, #3444.*

What one says during travels

6.7 The Prophet ﷺ taught his Companion ʿUqba ibn ʿÂmir that during a journey one should recite the last two suras of the Quran (113 and 114).

Sunan al-Nasâ'î, *8:251–54.*

What one says when camping or making a rest stop in an open area while traveling

6.8 O land, my Lord and your Lord is Allah. I seek refuge in Allah from your harm and whatever harm is in you and the harm of what was created in you and from the harm of whatever treads upon you. And I seek refuge in Allah from lions and cobras and from serpents and scorpions, and from the dwellers of the area, and from whatever begets and whatever is begotten.

Sunan Abû Dâwûd, *3:34–5, #2603, and* Musnad Aḥmad, *3:124.*

What one says before entering a town or city

6.9 O Allah, Lord of the seven heavens and of that upon which they cast their shadows! O Lord of the seven earths and of that which they bear! O Lord of the devils and of whomever they send astray! O Lord of the winds and of that which they scatter! We ask You for the good of this town and the good of its people. And we seek refuge in You from its harm and the harm of its people and the harm of whatever is in it.

Al-Ḥâkim's al-Mustadrak, *2:100, based on sound authority.*

What one says while returning from traveling (such as Pilgrimage)

6.10 There is no God but Allah, alone; He has no partner. To Him belongs all dominion and for Him is all praise, and He is powerful over all things. We return repentant, worshipful—bowing down to and praising our Lord. Allah is true to His promise, and has granted victory to His servant, and has alone defeated the confederates.

The Companion ʿAbdullâh ibn ʿUmar reported that the Prophet ﷺ used to say three times when traveling over hilly terrain, "Allah is the greatest," followed by the above supplication. Ṣaḥîḥ al-Bukhârî, *11:188, #6385, and* Ṣaḥîḥ Muslim, *2:980, #1394.*

What one says when entering the rest room

6.11 In the name of Allah, I seek refuge in Allah from every demon and demoness.

For a shorter version see Ṣaḥîḥ al-Bukhârî, *1:242–44, #142. However, Ibn Ḥajar endorses the soundness of the above report and says it meets* Ṣaḥîḥ Muslim*'s criteria for authenticity. See Ibn Ḥajar's discussion of this report in* Ṣaḥîḥ al-Bukhârî, *1:244.*

What one says when exiting the rest room

6.12 All praise is for Allah, who removed harm from me and gave me well-being.

Abû Bakr ibn al-Sunnî, ʿAmal al-Yawm wa al-Layla, *p. 18, #22.*

6.13 I ask for Your forgiveness!

Sunan al-Tirmidhî, *1:12, #7, and* Musnad Aḥmad, *6:155.*

What one says when entering a mosque

6.14 O Allah, open for me the gates of Your mercy.

Ṣaḥîḥ Muslim, *1:494, #713, and* Sunan Abû Dâwûd, *1:126–27, #465.*

6.15 In the name of Allah, O Allah, bless Muḥammad.

Abû Bakr ibn al-Sunnî, ʿAmal al-Yawm wa al-Layla, *p. 41, #88.*

6.16 Peace and blessings be upon the Messenger of Allah. O Allah, forgive us our sins.

Abû Bakr ibn al-Sunnî, ʿAmal al-Yawm wa al-Layla, *p. 41, #89.*

What one says when exiting from the mosque

6.17 O Allah, truly I ask You for Your bounty.

Ṣaḥîḥ Muslim *1:494, #713;* Sunan Abû Dâwûd, *1:126–27, #465; and* Sunan al-Nasâ'î, *2:53.*

6.18 In the name of Allah, O Allah, bless Muḥammad.

Abû Bakr ibn al-Sunnî, ʿAmal al-Yawm wa al-Layla, *p. 41, #88 and #89.*

6.19 Peace and blessings be upon the Messenger of Allah. O Allah, forgive us our sins and open for us the gates of Your bounty.

Abû Bakr ibn al-Sunnî, ʿAmal al-Yawm wa al-Layla, *p. 41, #89.*

6.20 Peace and blessings be upon the Messenger of Allah. O Allah, distance me from Satan.

Al-Nasâ'î, ʿAmal al-Yawm wa al-Layla, *p. 178, #90.*

What one says when entering the marketplace

6.21 There is no God but Allah, alone; He has no partner. To Him belongs all dominion and for Him is all praise. He gives life and causes death. He is ever-living and never dies. All good is in His Hand, and He is powerful over all things.

Sunan al-Tirmidhî, *5:457, #3428.*

What one says upon entering a house

6.22 O Allah, I ask You for the best entrance and the best exit. In the name of Allah we enter. In the name of Allah we exit. And upon our Lord, Allah, we rely. [Then greet the family with, "*As-salâmu ʿalaykum*" or "Peace be with you."]

Sunan Abû Dâwûd, *4:325, #5096.*

What one says after entering one's own home

6.23 O Allah, truly I have wronged myself with many wrongs, and none forgives sins but You. So forgive me with Your forgiveness and have mercy upon me. Truly, it is You who are the All-Forgiving, the Mercy-Giving.

Al-Nasâ'î reported in his work, ʿAmal al-Yawm wa al-Layla, *p. 221, #179, that Abû Bakr al-Ṣiddîq asked the Prophet ﷺ to teach him a prayer that he could say both in his* Ṣalât *and when entering his home. The Prophet ﷺ then taught him the above prayer. See also* Ṣaḥîḥ al-Bukhârî, *2:317, #834;* Ṣaḥîḥ Muslim, *4:2078, #2705; and* Sunan al-Nasâ'î, *3:53.*

7. Prayers for Sustenance and Grooming

WHOLESOME NOURISHMENT AND the beauty of our physical creation are among the blessings that should send one rushing to express gratitude to God. The Prophet ﷺ taught us as well that we should be eager to show our gratitude by feeding the hungry from what we have been provided with and by praying for those who share food with us. Our cleanliness, appearance, and moral bearing are expressions of thankfulness to God for fashioning us in the most excellent form and clothing us through the resources of His creation.

What one says before and after eating and drinking

• *Before*

7.1 In the name of Allah. (Then one eats with the right hand.)

The young Companion ʿUmar ibn Abî Salama was eating with the Prophet ﷺ and taking from all parts of the main dish. The Prophet ﷺ told him, "Young man, say the name of Allah, and eat with your right hand, and take food from the portion nearest you." See Ṣaḥîḥ Muslim, *3:1599, #2022.*

7.2 If one forgets to begin a meal "in the name of Allah," one should say, "In the name of Allah, in its beginning and in its end."

ʿÂ'isha reported that the Prophet ﷺ was sharing food with six of his Companions, when a bedouin joined them and devoured the food in two scoops. The Prophet ﷺ said, "Had he mentioned the name of Allah before eating, the food would have been sufficient for all of you." Sunan al-Tirmidhî, *4:254, #1858.*

• *After*

7.3 All praise is for Allah who has fed us and given us drink, and has made us Muslims.

Sunan al-Tirmidhî, *5:474, #3457.*

7.4 All praise is for Allah who has fed me this and provided me with it without any might or power from myself.

The Prophet ﷺ said that when one says this after a meal, his or her past sins will be forgiven.
Sunan al-Tirmidhî, *5:474, #3458.*

7.5 All praise is for Allah, much praise, wholesome and blessed. ⌜Though our praising⌝ is not sufficient, it shall be unceasing and is indispensable, our Lord!

Ṣaḥîḥ al-Bukhârî, *9:580, #5458, and* Sunan al-Tirmidhî, *5:473, #3456, with slight variation.*

7.6 O Allah, You have given food and drink, and You have enriched and satisfied, and guided and given life. For You is all praise for what You have given.

Sunan al-Nasâ'î al-Kubrâ, *as cited by Ibn Ḥajar in* Fatḥ al-Bârî, *9:581.*

7.7 All praise is for Allah who has provided food and drink, then made it palatable, and then caused it to be disposed of.

Sunan Abû Dâwûd, *3:366, #3851.*

What one says in appreciation of those hosting a meal

7.8 O Allah, bless for them what You have provided them. Forgive them and have mercy upon them.

The Prophet ﷺ shared a meal with the Companion ʿAbdullâh ibn Busr. Before the Prophet ﷺ left, ʿAbdullâh said to him, "Pray for us." The Prophet ﷺ then made this supplication. Ṣaḥîḥ Muslim, *3:1615–16, #2042, and al-Nasâ'î,* ʿAmal al-Yawm wa al-Layla, *p. 266, #291.*

7.9 O Allah, feed those who have fed me and give drink to those who have given drink to me.

Ṣaḥîḥ Muslim, *3:1625–26, #2055.*

7.10 May those fasting break their fasts with you, and may the virtuous eat of your food, and may the angels pray for you.

The Prophet, peace and blessings of God be upon him, was invited to a meal by Saʿad ibn ʿUbâda and was served bread and oil. After completing the meal, the Prophet ﷺ prayed this supplication. Sunan Abû Dâwûd, *3:367, #3854;* Sunan Ibn Mâjah, *1:556, #1747; and al-Nasâ'î,* ʿAmal al-Yawm wa al-Layla, *p. 268, #297.*

What one says to thank God for providing sustenance

7.11 All praise is for Allah, who feeds and is never fed. He has been gracious to us, and guided us, and fed us, and given us drink; and every good favor has He conferred upon us. All praise is for Allah, who is not to be forsaken, nor is it possible to recompense Him, nor is it befitting to be ungrateful to Him, nor ˹is it possible˺ to be sufficed without Him.

All praise is for Allah, who has fed us from this food and has given us to drink from this beverage, and has provided clothing to cover nakedness, and given guidance instead of misguidance, and He has given us vision instead of blindness, and granted abundant favor over much of His creation. All praise is for Allah, Lord of the Worlds.

Al-Nasâ'î, ʿAmal al-Yawm wa al-Layla, *pp. 269–70, #301.*

What one says after putting on a new garment

7.12 All praise is for Allah who has clothed me with this ˹garment˺ and provided me with it, without any might or power from myself.

The Prophet ﷺ said that when one says this after putting on a new garment, his or her past sins will be forgiven. Sunan Abû Dâwûd, *4:42, #4023.*

7.13 O Allah, for You is all praise. As You have clothed me with this ˹garment˺, I ask You for the good of it and the good it has been made for. And I seek refuge in You from its evil and the evil it has been made for.

Whenever the Prophet ﷺ received a new article of clothing, he would name it, and then say this supplication. Sunan al-Tirmidhî, *4:210, #1767;* Sunan Abû Dâwûd, *4:41, #4020; and al-Nasâ'î,* ʿAmal al-Yawm wa al-Layla, *p. 274, #309.*

What one says to another who puts on a new garment

7.14 May you always wear new clothing, live praisefully, and die a martyr.

This prayer may also be said to one wearing a freshly washed article of clothing. The Prophet ﷺ saw a bright white shirt on ʿUmar and asked him, "Is this shirt new or washed?" ʿUmar answered that it was washed. Then the Prophet ﷺ offered him this supplication. Sunan Ibn Mâjah, *2:1178, #3558, and al-Nasâ'î,* ʿAmal al-Yawm wa al-Layla, *p. 275, #311.*

What one says when looking in the mirror

7.15 All praise is for Allah. O Allah, as You have made excellent my physical creation, make excellent my character.

Abû Bakr ibn al-Sunnî, ʿAmal al-Yawm wa al-Layla, *pp. 65–66;* Ṣaḥîḥ Ibn Ḥibbân (al-Iḥsân), *2:154, #955; and al-Nawawî's* al-Adhkâr, *p. 260. Another report is found in* Musnad Aḥmad, *6:155, with slight variation.*

8. *Prayers for* Forgiveness, Pardon, *and* Protection Against Satan

AN IMPORTANT AIM of prayer is petitioning God for mercy and forgiveness. While human beings are moral creatures imbued with qualities of natural goodness, they are still susceptible to sin, error, and the beguilement of Satan, the avowed enemy. Prayer, moreover, attests to one's recognition that he or she has a Lord who punishes as well as forgives, and that God is indeed the All-Forgiving, the All-Pardoning. The Prophet ﷺ reported that God, the Exalted, has said:

> O Son of Adam, so long as you call upon Me and ask of Me, I shall forgive you for what you have done, and I shall not be concerned ⌜about your sins⌝. O Son of Adam, were your sins to reach the clouds of the sky and were you then to ask forgiveness of Me, I would forgive you, and I shall not be concerned ⌜about your sins⌝. O Son of Adam, were you to come to Me with sins nearly as great as the earth and were you then to face Me—not associating anything with Me—I would bring you forgiveness nearly as great as the earth.[90]

Asking God for forgiveness

8.1 *Our Lord, hold us not accountable if we forget or err. Our Lord, lay not upon us a burden like that which You have laid upon those before us. Our Lord, lay not upon us that which we do not have the strength to bear. And pardon us, and forgive us, and have mercy upon us. You are our Patron. So help us against the disbelieving people* (2:286).

8.2 *Our Lord, let not our hearts swerve after You have guided us, and grant us mercy from Your own ˹bounty˺. Indeed, it is You who are the All-Granting* (3:8).

8.3 *Our Lord, indeed we have believed. So forgive us our sins and save us from the torment of the Fire* (3:16).

8.4 *Our Lord, forgive us our sins and our excesses in our affairs, and set firm our feet, and help us against the disbelieving people* (3:147).

8.5 *Our Lord, we have heard a caller calling to faith, 'Believe in your Lord!' So we have believed. Our Lord, do forgive us our sins, and absolve us of our misdeeds, and take our souls ˹while being˺ among the virtuous.* (3:193).

8.6 *Our Lord, we have wronged ourselves, and if You do not forgive us and have mercy upon us, we shall surely be of the losers* (7:23).

8.7 *My Lord, forgive me and my brother and enter us into Your mercy—for You are the most merciful of the merciful* (7:151).

8.8 *You are our Patron, so forgive us and have mercy upon us, for You are the best of those who forgive. And inscribe for us good in this life and in the Hereafter. Indeed, we have turned to You* (7:155–56).

8.9 *My Lord, I seek refuge in You from asking You of what I have no knowledge. And if You do not forgive me and have mercy upon me, I shall be of the losers* (11:47).

8.10 *Our Lord, forgive me and my parents and the believers on the day the reckoning takes place* (14:41).

8.11 *Our Lord, we have believed; so forgive us and have mercy upon us—for You are the best of the merciful* (23:109).

8.12 *My Lord, forgive and have mercy, for You are the best of the merciful* (23:118).

8.13 *My Lord, I have indeed wronged myself; so forgive me* (28:16).

8.14 *Our Lord, You have encompassed everything with mercy and knowledge, so forgive those who have repented and followed Your way. And save them from the torment of Hellfire. Our Lord, and enter them into the Gardens of Eden that You have promised them, and whoever is righteous among their fathers, and their spouses, and their children. Indeed, You are the Overpowering, the All-Wise. And save them from misdeeds, for whomever You save from misdeeds on that day, then surely You have shown him mercy. And this is surely the great success* (40:7–9).

8.15 *Our Lord, forgive us and our brethren who preceded us in faith, and let not into our hearts malice for those who believe. Our Lord, indeed You are all-kind and mercy-giving* (59:10).

8.16 *My Lord, forgive me and my parents, and whoever enters my house as a believer, and the believing men and the believing women. And do not increase the wrongdoers except in ruin* (71:28).

8.17 My Lord, forgive me my misdeeds, my ignorance, any excesses in all my affairs, and that which You know better of than I do. O Allah, forgive me my sins, my deliberate actions, my mistakes, and my ˹imprudent˺ jesting—and all this is with me. So forgive me whatever I may have done and whatever I may do, whatever I have concealed and whatever I have revealed. You are the Forwarder and You are the Delayer. And You are powerful over all things.

Ṣaḥîḥ al-Bukhârî, *11:196, #6398, and* Ṣaḥîḥ Muslim, *4:2087, #2719.*

8.18 Glory be to You, O Allah, and all praise. I seek Your forgiveness and repent to You.

Ṣaḥîḥ Muslim, *1:351, #484.*

8.19 O Lord, forgive me and grant me repentance, for truly You are the All-Relenting, the All-Forgiving.

Sunan al-Tirmidhî, *5:461, #3434. In* Sunan Abû Dâwûd, *2:85, #1516, the report reads, "For truly You are the All-Relenting, the Mercy-Giving."*

8.20 O Allah, forgive me for whatever I have done and whatever I may do, whatever I have concealed and whatever I have revealed, what I have done in excess and that of which You know better than me. You are the Forwarder and You are the Delayer. There is no God but You.

The Prophet ﷺ used to make this supplication before the end of Prayer. Ṣaḥîḥ Muslim, *1:536, #771. A similar text is found in* Sunan al-Tirmidhî, *5:453, #3421.*

8.21 O Allah, truly I have wronged myself with many wrongs, and none forgives sins but You. So forgive me with Your forgiveness and have mercy upon me. Truly, it is You who are the All-Forgiving, the Mercy-Giving.

Ṣaḥîḥ al-Bukhârî, *2:317, #834;* Ṣaḥîḥ Muslim, *4:2078, #2705; and* Sunan al-Nasâ'î, *3:53.*

8.22 O Allah, I ask You for the Garden and I seek refuge in You from the Fire.

Musnad Aḥmad, *3:474.*

8.23 O Allah, forgive me my sins, all of them—minute and enormous, first and last, manifest and hidden.

Ṣaḥîḥ Muslim, *1:350, #483.*

8.24 There is no God but Allah, alone; He has no partner. Allah is the greatest, immensely great! All praise is for Allah, plentifully! Glory be to Allah, Lord of the Worlds. There is no strength nor might except with Allah, the Overpowering, the All-Wise. O Allah, forgive me, have mercy upon me, guide me, and provide for me.

Ṣaḥîḥ Muslim, *4:2072, #2696.*

Seeking refuge in God from Satan and his accomplices

8.25 The *adhân* said at any time drives Satan away.

For the exact text and background, see Ṣaḥîḥ Muslim, *1:290, #388.*

8.26 O Allah, I seek refuge in You from Satan, the accursed, from his promptings, his inspirations, and his incantations.

Sunan Ibn Mâjah, *1:265, #807. See also a similar report in* Sunan Abû Dâwûd, *1:203, which has a slight variation.*

- *Reciting Quran*

8.27 *Allah, there is no God but Him, the Living, the Self-Subsisting. Slumber does not overtake Him, nor does sleep. To Him belongs whatever is in the heavens and whatever is in the earth. Who is it that shall intercede before Him, except by His permission? He knows what is before them and what is behind them, and they do not comprehend anything of His knowledge except as He wills. His Seat ˹of Divinity˺ encompasses the heavens and the earth, and preserving them does not fatigue Him. And He is the Exalted, the Magnificent* (2:255).

The Prophet ﷺ said to his Companion Ubay ibn Kaʿb, "Do you know which verse of the Book of Allah that you have ˹learned˺ is the greatest?" Ubay said that it is the Verse of the Seat ˹of Divinity˺ (2:255). The Prophet ﷺ then praised him for his knowledge. Ṣaḥîḥ Muslim, *1:556, #810.*

8.28 *The Messenger believes in what has been sent down to him from his Lord, as do the believers. All believe in Allah and His angels and His Books and His messengers: "We do not distinguish between any of His messengers." And they say, "We hear and we obey. Your forgiveness, our Lord! For to You is the ultimate destiny." Allah does not task a soul beyond its capacity. For it is ˹the good˺ it has earned, and against it is ˹the evil˺ it sought to earn. "Our*

Lord, hold us not accountable if we forget or err. Our Lord, lay not upon us a burden like that which You have laid upon those before us. Our Lord, lay not upon us that which we do not have the strength to bear. And pardon us, and forgive us, and have mercy upon us. You are our Patron. So help us against the disbelieving people" (2:285–86).

Musnad Aḥmad, *4:118, and* Ṣaḥîḥ Muslim, *1:554, #806.*

8.29 *Say: I seek refuge in the Lord of the daybreak from the evil of that which He created, and from the evil of darkness when it overspreads, and from the evil of sorcerers who blow on knots, and from the evil of an envier when he envies* (113:1–5).

8.30 *Say: I seek refuge in the Lord of all people, King of all people, God of all people, from the evil of the sneaking whisperer, who whispers in the chests of people, from the jinn and people* (114:1–6).

8.31 *My Lord, I seek refuge in You from the urgings of the satans. And I seek refuge in You, my Lord, from their presence* (23:97–98).

8.32 The Prophet said that anyone who memorizes (or recites) the first ten verses (or the last ten) of Sûrat al-Kahf (18) will be immune from the deception of the False Messiah (*al-Dajjâl*).

Ṣaḥîḥ Muslim, *1:555, #809. Al-Nasâ'î, in* ʿAmal al-Yawm wa al-Layla, *p. 527, #949, says "recites" instead of "memorizes." In another report, both Muslim (1:556) and al-Nasâ'î (p. 527, #950) add to this the recitation or memorization of the last ten verses of the same sura (al-Kahf).*

8.33 The Messenger of Allah ﷺ said, "Satan may come to anyone of you and say, 'Who created the heaven? And who created the earth?' One says, 'Allah.' Then ⌜Satan⌝ says, 'Who created your Lord?' When he reaches this point, one should seek refuge in Allah and should stop ⌜such a thought⌝." Or, according to another report, one should say, "I have believed in Allah and His messengers."

Ṣaḥîḥ Muslim *(al-Nawawî's), 2:153–54.*

8.34 O Allah, I seek refuge in You from feebleness, laziness, cowardliness, miserliness, senility, ruthlessness, heedlessness, dependency, humiliation, and indigence. And I seek refuge in You from poverty, disbelief, unrighteousness, schism, hypocrisy, ignominy, and showing off. And I seek refuge in You from deafness, dumbness, insanity, vitiligo, leprosy, and the worst of ailments.

Al-Ḥâkim's al-Mustadrak, *1:712, #1944.*

9. Prayers for Personal Aspirations

GUIDANCE AND KNOWLEDGE are two of God's greatest gifts to humanity. Guidance eases one along the straight way in the company of the blessed; it is the deliverer from error. Knowledge frees a person from fear and superstition and from submitting to anything other than God. The Prophet ﷺ continuously prayed for knowledge and guidance. His words unveil the premier status of the learned and the pursuit of knowledge. He said:

> Whoever treads a path in search of knowledge, Allah shall ease a way for him to the Garden. And angels spread their wings for the seeker of knowledge, pleased with what he is doing. And all who are in the heavens and all who are in the earth—even the great fish in the water—ask forgiveness for the learned. And the excellence of the learned over any other worshipper is like the excellence of the moon over all the planets. Indeed, the learned are the heirs of the prophets; yet the prophets did not bequeath dinars nor dirhams. But surely they have bequeathed knowledge. So whoever acquires it acquires an ample share.[91]

Prayers for seeking guidance

9.1 O Allah, I ask You for guidance and direction.

The Prophet ﷺ advised ʿAlî ibn Abî Ṭâlib to say this prayer and to be conscious of the way of God and to be tenacious in seeking what pleases Him. Ṣaḥîḥ Muslim, *4:2090, #2725.*

9.2 O Allah, to You I submit, in You I believe, on You I rely, to You I turn, and for You I oppose. O Allah, I seek refuge in Your majesty—there is no God but You!—from letting me go astray. You are the All-Living, who never dies, while all jinn and human beings die.

Ṣaḥîḥ Muslim, *4:2086, #2717.*

Prayers for seeking knowledge

9.3 O Allah, benefit me in what You have taught me and teach me what benefits me. Increase me in knowledge. All praise is for Allah in every condition. And I seek refuge in Allah from the condition of the People of the Fire.

Sunan al-Tirmidhî, *5:540, #3599.*

9.4 O Allah, I seek refuge in You from knowledge that does not benefit, from a heart that is not humble, from a soul that is never satisfied, and from any prayer that is not answered.

Ṣaḥîḥ Muslim, *4:2088, #2722; a similar version in found in* Sunan al-Nasâ'î, *8:285.*

What one says when seeking protection

9.5 O Allah, I ask You for pardon and well-being in this life and in the Hereafter. O Allah, I ask You for pardon and well-being in my religion, my life, my family, and my wealth. O Allah, cover my faults and soothe my fears. O Allah, protect me from ˹whatever is˺ before me and from ˹whatever is˺ behind me, and from my right and from my left, and from above me, and I seek refuge in You from being seized from beneath me.

Sunan Ibn Mâjah, *2:1273, #3871.*

What one may say when asking God for children

9.6 *My Lord, grant me ˹a child˺ of the righteous* (37:100).

God answered Abraham ﷺ when he made the above prayer, bestowing upon him his son Ishmael.

9.7 *My Lord, leave me not alone* [*childless*], *though You are the best of inheritors* (21:89).

God answered Zechariah ﵇ and gave him his son Yaḥyâ (John) ﵇ when he made the above prayer.

9.8 *My Lord, grant me from Your bounty wholesome children. Indeed, You are the hearer of prayer* (3:38).

What one may say when asking God to protect one's family and children from straying and to grant them guidance

9.9 *My Lord, make this land secure and keep me and my children away from worshipping idols* (14:35).

9.10 *My Lord, make me steadfast in Prayer—and also my children. Our Lord, and do accept my prayer* (14:40).

9.11 *Our Lord, and make us obedient to You, and, from our children, a community obedient to You. And show us our ˹religious˺ rites, and grant us repentance. Indeed, it is You who are the All-Relenting, the Mercy-Giving* (2:128).

9.12 *Our Lord, grant us, in our spouses and children, comfort to our eyes. And make us exemplary to the God-fearing* (25:74).

What one may say when seeking forgiveness for oneself and the believers, in general

9.13 *Our Lord, forgive us and our brethren who preceded us in faith, and let not into our hearts malice for those who believe. Our Lord, indeed You are kind and mercy-giving* (59:10).

Praying for one's parents

9.14 *Our Lord, forgive me and my parents and all the believers on the day the reckoning takes place* (14:41).

9.15 *My Lord, have mercy upon both of them just as they have raised me as a small child* (17:24).

9.16 *My Lord, forgive me and my parents, and whoever enters my house as a believer, and the believing men and the believing women. And do not increase the wrongdoers except in ruin* (71:28).

10. *Prayers* Expressed *in* Social *Interaction*

ONE OF THE joys of life is pleasant interaction. We crave companionship, meaningful exchange, and esteem. Though often underestimated, our greetings to one another, our polite discourse, and the sincerity of our communication all form the bedrock of civility. The degeneration of such social formulas eats away at the fabric and adhesion of brotherhood and of a refined society. Elevated interchange develops admiration and love, and brings about appropriate honor and reverence for oneself and one's fellows in creation. One of the keys to sincere human relations is praying for those whom we accompany throughout life's experiences. The Prophet ﷺ was peerless in the eminence of his discourse with others.

What one says to greet another

10.1 The universal Muslim greeting "*As-salâmu ʿalaykum*" ("Peace be upon you!") should be said upon meeting others. If one wishes, one may also say, "Peace be upon you, and the mercy of Allah and His blessings."

The Prophet ﷺ said that one gets ten rewards for saying "Peace be upon you!" and twenty rewards for saying "Peace be upon you and the mercy of Allah," and thirty rewards for saying, "Peace be upon you, and the mercy of Allah and His blessings." Sunan Abû Dâwûd, *4:350, #5195, and al-Nasâ'î,* ʿAmal al-Yawm wa al-Layla, *p. 287, #337.*

Other occasions when one says, "As-salâmu ʿalaykum"

10.2 When entering one's home or seeking permission to enter the home of another.

Sunan Abû Dâwûd, *4:325, #5096. See also the Quran, 24:27.*

10.3 When joining with or parting from a gathering.

When one joins a gathering say, "Peace be upon you," and when one leaves the gathering say, "Peace be upon you." The Prophet added that the former is not worthier than the latter. Sunan Abû Dâwûd, *4:353, #5208.*

What one says after sneezing

10.4 When one sneezes, he or she should say, "All praise is for Allah." Then any present observer should respond, "May Allah have mercy upon you." Then the person who sneezed answers, "May Allah guide you and set aright your affairs."

Ṣaḥîḥ al-Bukhârî, *10:608, #6224.*

What one says to the newlywed

10.5 May Allah bless you and bestow His blessings upon you and unite both of you in goodness.

Sunan Abû Dâwûd, *2:241, #2130, and* Sunan Ibn Mâjah, *1:614, #1905.*

10.6 May you live with goodness, blessings, and the best of happiness.

This is what the ladies of Madinah said to ʿÂ'isha, the Prophet's wife, right before her wedding. Ṣaḥîḥ al-Bukhârî, *7:223, #3894.*

A prayer a bridegroom says for his bride

10.7 O Allah, I ask You for the best of her and the best of what You have endowed her with. And I seek refuge in You from the worst of her and the worst of what You have endowed her with.

The bride may also make the same prayer with respect to the bridegroom. Sunan Abû Dâwûd, *2:248, #2160.*

What one says prior to marital intimacy

10.8 In the name of Allah. O Allah, keep us away from Satan and keep Satan away from whatever ⌜offspring⌝ You grant us.

The Prophet ﷺ said that if a child is to be conceived on that occasion, Satan will not harm it.
Ṣaḥîḥ al-Bukhârî, *11:191, #6388.*

What one says to a newborn

10.9 *First, the* **Adhân** *is said in the right ear of the newborn.*
Allah is the greatest! Allah is the greatest!
Allah is the greatest! Allah is the greatest!
I bear witness that there is no God but Allah.
I bear witness that there is no God but Allah.
I bear witness that Muḥammad is the Messenger of Allah.
I bear witness that Muḥammad is the Messenger of Allah.
Come to Prayer! Come to Prayer!
Come to success! Come to success!
Allah is the greatest! Allah is the greatest!
There is no God but Allah.

Sunan Abû Dâwûd, *4:328, #5105;* Musnad Aḥmad, *6:9; and* Sunan al-Tirmidhî, *4:82, #1514.*

Then, the **Iqâma** *is said in the left ear*
Allah is the greatest! Allah is the greatest!
I bear witness that there is no God but Allah.
I bear witness that Muḥammad is the Messenger of Allah.
Come to Prayer! Come to success!
Prayer has commenced! Prayer has commenced!
Allah is the greatest! Allah is the greatest!
There is no God but Allah.

See Ibn al-Qayyim, Zâd al-Maʿâd, *2:333.*

What one says when beginning or concluding a meeting

10.10 O Allah, grant us as much reverence for You as will be a deterrent between us and sinning against You, and as much obedience to You as will deliver us to Your Garden, and as much certainty of faith as will ease for us the misfortunes of this world. And let us enjoy our hearing, our sight, and our strength for so long as You extend our lives, and make them endure after us. And set our vengeance against those who have wronged us. And give us victory over those waging animosity against us. And let not our loss be in our religion, nor let this world be the greatest of our concerns, nor the extent of our knowledge, and do not give authority over us to any who will not have mercy on us.

Sunan al-Tirmidhî, *5:493–94, #3502.*

10.11 Glory be to You, O Allah, and all praise. I bear witness that there is no God but You, and I seek Your forgiveness and repent to You.

The Prophet ﷺ used to make this prayer after a meeting. Sunan Abû Dâwûd, *4:265, #4859.*

Prayer for those expressing their love for the sake of God

10.12 Anas ibn Mâlik reported that a man was sitting with the Prophet, God's blessings and peace be upon him. Another man passed by them. The first said, "O Messenger of Allah, indeed I love this man." The Prophet ﷺ said to him, "Did you make this known to him?" He said, "No." The Prophet ﷺ said, "Then make it known to him." Then the man caught up with him and said, "Indeed, I love you for the sake of Allah." Then he said, "May He, for whose sake you love me, love you."

Sunan Abû Dâwûd, *4:333, #5125.*

What to say to someone who removes an undesirable object from your person

10.13 May Allah wipe away from you whatever you dislike.

Abû Bakr ibn al-Sunnî, ʿAmal al-Yawm wa al-Layla, *p. 104, #282, and* al-Wâbil al-Sayyib, *Ibn al-Qayyim, p. 183.*

10.14 May no harm come to you. May no harm come to you.

Abû Bakr ibn al-Sunnî, ʿAmal al-Yawm wa al-Layla, *p. 104, #283.*

What one says upon embracing Islam

10.15 O Allah, forgive me, have mercy on me, guide me, grant me well-being, and provide for me.

Whenever a person embraced Islam, the Prophet ﷺ taught him the Muslim Prayer (Ṣalât) *and asked him to say the above supplication.* Ṣaḥîḥ Muslim, *4:2073, #2697 (35).*

Prayers for one's companions and their relatives

10.16 O Allah, make him steadfast, and make him guided and a source of guidance.

The Prophet ﷺ offered this prayer to his Companion Jarîr ibn ʿAbdullâh when he proceeded to dismantle a pagan shrine known as Dhû 'l-Khalaṣa. Ṣaḥîḥ Muslim, *4:1925–26, #2475 and #2476.*

10.17 O Allah, make him knowledgeable in Islam and teach him interpretation.

The Prophet ﷺ said this prayer for the young Companion ʿAbdullâh ibn ʿAbbâs. Ṣaḥîḥ Ibn Ḥibbân (al-Iḥsân), *9:98, #7015.*

10.18 O Allah, teach him wisdom, or, O Allah, teach him the Book [the Quran].

The Prophet ﷺ embraced ʿAbdullâh ibn ʿAbbâs and said this prayer. Ṣaḥîḥ al-Bukhârî, *7:100, #3756.*

10.19 O Allah, answer Saʿd whenever he prays to You.

The Prophet ﷺ said this prayer for the Companion Saʿd ibn Abî Waqqâs. One may make a similar prayer for a loved one. Sunan al-Tirmidhî, *5:607, #3751.*

10.20 O Allah, increase him in wealth and children and bless for him whatever You give him.

The Prophet ﷺ said this prayer for the Companion Anas ibn Mâlik. Ṣaḥîḥ Muslim, *4:1928, #2480.*

10.21 The Companion Abû Hurayrah asked the Prophet ﷺ to say a prayer for his non-Muslim mother. The Prophet ﷺ said, "O Allah, guide Abû Hurayrah's mother." After she accepted Islam, Abû Hurayrah requested the Prophet ﷺ to say a prayer that both of them (Abû Hurayrah and his mother) would be loved by the believers. The Prophet ﷺ then said: "O Allah, make this servant of Yours and his mother beloved to Your believing servants, and grant them love for the believers."

Ṣaḥîḥ Muslim, *4:1938–39, #2491.*

10.22 O Allah, forgive ʿUbayd Abû ʿÂmir. O Allah, rank him on the Day of Resurrection high above many of the people. O Allah, forgive ʿAbdullâh ibn Qays his sins and let him enter ˹the Garden˺ on the Day of Resurrection with a gracious entrance.

This prayer, originally said for ʿUbayd Abû ʿÂmir and ʿAbdullâh ibn Qays, may be said for any believing loved one. Ṣaḥîḥ Muslim, *4:1943–44, #2498.*

Offering prayer for children

10.23 O Allah, truly I love him, so do love him and love those who love him.

The Prophet, peace be upon him, said this upon seeing his grandson Ḥasan. Ṣaḥîḥ Muslim, *4:1882–83, #2421.*

What one says in times of war or when facing an enemy

10.24 *Our Lord, pour forth upon us patience, and set firm our feet, and help us against the disbelieving people* (2:250).

10.25 O Allah, revealer of the Book, mover of the clouds, and defeater of the confederates, defeat them and give us victory over them!

The Prophet ﷺ said, "O people, do not yearn to confront the enemy, and ask Allah for safety and well-being. Yet if you face them, be patient and know that the Garden is under the shade of the sword." Then he said the above supplication. Ṣaḥîḥ Muslim, *3:1362, #1742.*

10.26 By Allah, were it not for You, we would not have been guided nor would we have given charity nor would we have performed Prayer [*Ṣalât*]. So send down tranquility upon us and set firm our feet if we come to confront ˹the enemy˺. Indeed, those idolaters have transgressed against us. And if they desire to put us to trial, we shall resist.

Salamah ibn al-Akwaʿ sought permission from the Prophet ﷺ to say these lines in preparing for the Battle of the Confederates. The Prophet ﷺ agreed and in fact said these lines along with him. Ṣaḥîḥ Muslim, *3:1430–31, #1802 and #1803.*

What one says upon receiving a favor from another

10.27 May Allah reward you with goodness [*Jazâka Allahu khayran*].

Sunan al-Tirmidhî, *4:333, #2035. The Prophet ﷺ said that whenever one receives a favor and says to its doer, "May Allah reward you with goodness," such a person has offered the best of commendations.*

11. Prayers for Refuge

SEEKING REFUGE IN God in moments of fear and trial was the practice of all the prophets and great believers. Noah prayed, *"My Lord, I seek refuge in You from asking You of what I have no knowledge"* (11:47). Joseph implored God to preserve him from the moral depravity of the ladies of Egyptian high society: *"My Lord, prison is more beloved to me than that to which they call me. For if You do not turn their cunning away from me, I may incline toward them and become of the ignorant"* (12:33). Moses sought God's protection from Pharaoh when fleeing Egypt: *"My Lord, deliver me from the wrongdoing people"* (28:21). Mary invoked God's safekeeping from the angel that came to her in human form to give glad tidings of the conception of Jesus: *"I seek refuge in the All-Merciful from you, if you are God-fearing!"* (19:18). And the Prophet Muḥammad ﷺ besought God's refuge in countless prayers. In a well-known supplication, he prayed:

> O Allah, I seek refuge in You from knowledge that does not benefit, from a heart that is not humble, from a soul that is never satisfied, and from any prayer that is not answered.[92]

What one says in seeking refuge from poverty

11.1 O Allah, I seek refuge in You from disbelief, from poverty, and from the torment of the grave.

Sunan al-Nasâ'î, *8:262.*

11.2 O Allah, I seek refuge in You from being overpowered by debt and being overpowered by an enemy and from the malice of enemies.

Sunan al-Nasâ'î, *8:265 and 8:268.*

What one says in seeking refuge from hunger

11.3 O Allah, I seek refuge in You from hunger, for it is a miserable bedfellow. And I seek refuge in You from betrayal, for it is miserable company.

Sunan al-Nasâ'î, *8:263.*

What one says in seeking refuge from personal calamity

11.4 O Allah, I seek refuge in You from ruin, and I seek refuge in You from downfall, and I seek refuge in You from drowning and burning, and I seek refuge in You from being battered by Satan at the moment of death. And I seek refuge in You from dying while in retreat from Your path, and I seek refuge in You from dying from a poisonous sting.

Sunan al-Nasâ'î, *8:283.*

What one says in seeking refuge from base character and contemptible qualities

11.5 O Allah, I seek refuge in You from abhorrent character, actions, and inclinations.

Sunan al-Tirmidhî, *5:536, #3591.*

11.6 O Allah, I seek refuge in You from the harm of my hearing, the harm of my sight, the harm of my tongue, the harm of my heart, and the harm of my seed.

Sunan al-Nasâ'î, *8:259, and* Sunan al-Tirmidhî, *5:489, #3492.*

11.7 O Allah, I seek refuge in You from the removal of Your grace, the reversal of the well-being You have bestowed, the suddenness of Your vengeance, and all Your displeasure.

Ṣaḥîḥ Muslim, *4:2097, #2739, and* Sunan Abû Dâwûd, *2:91, #1545.*

11.8 O Allah, I seek refuge in You from schism, hypocrisy, and bad character.

Sunan al-Nasâ'î, *8:264.*

11.9 O Allah, I seek refuge in You from any desire that leads to vice and from any desire that leads to what is undesirable and from any desire for which there is no fulfillment.

Musnad Aḥmad, *5:232, and al-Ḥâkim's* al-Mustadrak, *1:716, #1956.*

What one says in seeking refuge from misdeeds

11.10 O Allah, I seek refuge in You from the harm of what I have done and from the harm of what I have not done.

Ṣaḥîḥ Muslim, *4:2085, #2716, and* Sunan al-Nasâ'î, *8:280–81.*

What one says in seeking refuge from trials

11.11 O Allah, I seek refuge in You from the misfortunes of fate, the malice of enemies, the depths of misery, and the distress of trials.

Sunan al-Nasâ'î, *8:270. See also* Ṣaḥîḥ Muslim, *4:2080, #2707, and* Ṣaḥîḥ al-Bukhârî, *11:148, #6347.*

11.12 O Allah, I seek refuge in You from insanity, vitiligo, leprosy, and from the worst of ailments.

Sunan al-Nasâ'î, *8:270.*

11.13 O Allah, I seek refuge in You from the trial of the Fire, the torment of the Fire, and from any evil of wealth and poverty.

Sunan Abû Dâwûd, *2:91, #1543.*

11.14 O Allah, I seek refuge in You from insufficiency, poverty, and humiliation. And I seek refuge in You from doing wrong or being wronged.

Sunan al-Nasâ'î, *8:261, and* Sunan Ibn Mâjah, *2:1263, #3842.*

12. *Prayers to Glorify God and Beseech His Blessings and Love*

TO BE EVER-MINDFUL of God is an important goal of worship, for the Quran warns: *And be not like those who had forgotten Allah, so He caused them to forget their own souls* (59:19). To remember God is to be impelled to proclaim His praises and to glorify and extol Him. What does the worshipper hope to gain thereby? The best of this life and of the Hereafter. In a word, the Muslim strives for no less than the love of God and the company of those whom He loves. In the recesses of the human soul each one of us knows that the path to God's love begins with obedience to Him and is sustained by His sincere remembrance. The Prophet ﷺ said, "All the hearts of the Children of Adam are between two fingers of the All-Merciful like one heart. He changes them as He wills." Then the Prophet ﷺ said, "O Allah, You change hearts, so change our hearts to be obedient to You."[93]

Glorifying God

12.1 The Prophet ﷺ said, "*Glory be to Allah and all praise!* equaling the numerousness of His creation, and as much as it pleases Him, and as great as the weight of His Throne, and as much as the ink His words require."

Said three times. Ṣaḥîḥ Muslim, *4:2090, #2726, and* Sunan al-Tirmidhî, *5:519, #3555.*

12.2 *Glory be to Allah!* equaling the numerousness of what He has created in the heavens. And *Glory be to Allah!* equaling the numerousness of what He has created in the earth. And *Glory be to Allah!* as abundant as what is between them. And *Glory be to Allah!* equaling the numerousness of what He will create. And *Allah is the greatest!* as much as all of this. And *All praise is for Allah!* as much as all of this. And *There is no strength nor might except with Allah* as much as all of this.

Sunan al-Tirmidhî, *5:525–26, #3568.*

What one says seeking God's blessings

12.3 O Allah, I ask You for the best of requests, the best of prayers, the best of success, the best of deeds, the best of rewards, the best in life, and the best in death. And make me steadfast; make ˹my righteous deeds˺ weighty ˹in˺ my balance; make true my faith; exalt my rank; accept my Prayer [*Ṣalât*]; and forgive my misdeeds. And I ask You for the highest stations of the Garden.

O Allah, I ask You for the best in whatever I advance, the best of whatever I do, the best of what is hidden, the best of what is disclosed, and the highest stations of the Garden.

O Allah, I ask You to raise my renown, to alleviate my burden, to set aright my affairs, to purify my heart, and to guard my chastity. And illuminate my heart for me and forgive my sins. And I ask You for the highest stations of the Garden.

O Allah, I ask You to bless for me my whole self—my hearing, my sight, my spirit, my physical being, my character, my family, my life, my death, and my deeds. So accept my good deeds. And I ask You for the highest stations of the Garden.

Al-Dhahabî endorsed al-Ḥâkim's judgment that this ḥadîth *has been attributed to the Prophet ﷺ by his wife Umm Salama on good authority. See al-Ḥâkim's* al-Mustadrak, *1:520. See also al-Haythamî,* Majmaʿ al-Zawâ'id wa Manbaʿ al-Fawâ'id, *10:278, #17380.*

What one says seeking God's love

12.4 O Allah, endow me with Your love and the love of all whose love benefits me with You. O Allah, with whatever You have endowed me of that which I love, let it strengthen me in what You love. O Allah, whatever You have kept from me of that which I love, let it strengthen me in what You love.

Sunan al-Tirmidhî, *5:488–89, #3491.*

The Address of Need (Khuṭbah al-Ḥâja) *said before expressing a specific need to Allah*

12.5 Indeed, all praise is for Allah. We praise Him and we seek His help and we seek His forgiveness. And we seek refuge in Allah from the evils of our selves and from the harm of our actions. Whomever Allah guides, there is none to lead him astray. And whomever He leads astray, there is none to guide him. And I bear witness that there is no God but Allah, alone; He has no partner. And I bear witness that Muḥammad is His servant and His Messenger.

(*Then one joins to this statement these passages from the Quran.*)

O you people, fear your Lord, who created you from a single soul; and from it, He created its spouse. And from both of them, He spread ˹about˺ many men and women. And fear Allah—by whom you ask of one another—and ˹fear for your˺ kindred. Indeed, Allah is all-vigilant over you. (4:1)

O you who believe, fear Allah His rightful fear, and do not die except while you are Muslims. (3:102)

O you who believe, fear Allah and say forthright words. He shall make righteous for you your deeds and forgive you your sins. And whoever obeys Allah and His Messenger has then truly succeeded with a great success. (33:70–71)

This report is from Sunan Ibn Mâjah, *1:609–10, #1892. Variant reports are found in* Sunan Abû Dâwûd, *2:238, #2118, and al-Nasâ'î,* ʿAmal al-Yawm wa al-Layla, *p. 343, #488.*

12.6 O Allah, I seek refuge in You from any deed that disgraces me. And I seek refuge in You from any companion that brings me down. And I seek refuge in You from any hope that diverts me. And I seek refuge in You from any impoverishment that causes me to forget ⌜my duties⌝. And I seek refuge in You from wealth that causes me to transgress.

Abû Bakr ibn al-Sunnî, ʿAmal al-Yawm wa al-Layla, *p. 51, #119. Ibn Ḥajar,* Natâʾij al-Afkâr fî Takhrîj al-Aḥâdîth al-Adhkâr, *2:299. Ibn Ḥajar stated that this* ḥadîth *is eligible for use in encouraging excellent deeds because of its variant channels of report.*

12.7 O Allah, I ask You to enable me to do what is good and to leave what is bad, and to have love for the needy, and ⌜I ask You⌝ to forgive me and have mercy on me. And if it is Your will that some people are put to trial, take my soul without me falling into temptation. I ask You for Your love and the love of those who love You and the love of deeds that draw ⌜me⌝ near to Your love.

The Prophet, God's blessings and peace be upon him, said, "This ⌜supplication⌝ is true, so study it and learn it." Sunan al-Tirmidhî, *5:343–44, #3235. See also Ibn Ḥajar,* Natâʾij al-Afkâr fî Takhrîj al-Aḥâdîth al-Adhkâr, *2:299.*

12.8 O Allah, You change hearts, so change our hearts to be obedient to You.

Ṣaḥîḥ Muslim, *4:2045, #2654.*

What one says seeking stability and serenity in the land

12.9 O Allah, establish for us in our land its own blessings, its own beauty, and its own serenity.

According to al-Haythamî, this ḥadîth *is reported by Ṭabarânî on good authority. See al-Haythamî,* Majmaʿ al-Zawâʾid wa Manbaʿ al-Fawâʾid, *10:292, #17425.*

What one says seeking provision for old age

12.10 O Allah, bestow upon me the most bounteous of Your provision when I reach old age and near the end of my life.

Al-Haythamî, Majmaᶜ al-Zawâ'id wa Manbaᶜ al-Fawâ'id, *10:291, #17420.*

Appendix

Form & Substance Quranic Calligraphy

A Word on Arabic Script and Quranic Calligraphy

THE PERIOD OF Arab life before Islam is known as the Age of Ignorance, and, indeed, the Quran refers to the Arabs of that era as *ummiyyûn,* or illiterate (62:2). This description, however, does not dispossess them of *all* knowledge nor does it negate in absolute terms their awareness of the mechanics and apparatus of writing. Rather, it points out the prevalence of their religious illiteracy; for prior to the revelation of the Quran, the Arabs possessed no divine writ, unlike the People of the Book (that is, the Jews and the Christians) who had the Torah and the Gospel. While current scholarship lacks detailed knowledge about the origin of the Arabic script and its early development, it is historically well established that the Arabs used writing for various purposes as early as three centuries before Islam.[94]

The Quran and the Ascension of Writing

From the very outset of its revelation, the Quran exalted knowledge and its expression in reading and writing, and it specified them as blessings of God upon people, which He taught through "the pen." *Read! For your Lord is the Most Generous, who taught by the pen. He taught man what he did not know* (96:4–5). In the second episode of revelation (in which the opening verses of sura 68 were revealed), the Quran honored "the pen" (from which sura 68 takes its name) as a tool for recording knowledge. Indeed, in this sura God makes both the pen and writing the objects of a divine oath, by which He asserts the excellence of the Prophet's character and the soundness of his mind (68:1–4). Moreover, the Prophet ﷺ himself instructed some of his early Companions to commit the revealed verses to writing; they wrote on paper (when available), as well as leather, fabric, wood, bones, and stones. Notable among the foremost scribes of the Quran were the four "Rightly Guided" Caliphs: Abû Bakr, ʿUmar ibn al-Khaṭṭâb, ʿUthmân ibn ʿAffân, and ʿAlî ibn Abî Ṭâlib, as well as Zayd ibn Thâbit, Arkam ibn Abî Arkam, and Jaʿfar ibn Abî Ṭâlib.[95]

Regard for writing and transcribing the Quran accompanied the spread of Islam into Asia, Africa, and Europe, and particularly in certain cities of these lands that grew into cultural hearths of Islam. It is also of interest that the Arabic alphabet ultimately became the script of several languages, including Persian, Malay, Turkish, Urdu, and a number of African languages. These peoples in turn contributed their particular genius to the artistic development of Arabic script, especially in the form of specialized calligraphy. The first milestone in this regard occurred in the newly established city of Kûfa in the year 17 H./638 C.E., where a new style of Arabic script was developed that bore the city's name. The *kûfic* script quickly supplanted the earlier styles used in the western Arabian Ḥijâz, especially in Makkah and Madinah.

Soon thereafter, the rise of the use of paper fueled rapid refinement of Arabic orthography. This coincided with the increased spread of writing in society, in keeping the records of state and court, in financial transactions, and in the burgeoning scholarship of university classrooms and mosque courtyards. It is at this juncture of history that we see the emergence of master scribes adept in the art of calligraphy.

In the fourth Islamic century, Abû Alî Muḥammad ibn Muqla (338 H./948 C.E.),[96] a minister of state in the ʿAbbâsid government and renowned man of letters and calligraphic art, pushed beyond the dominance of *kûfic* script by developing a new style, opening the way for important innovations in Arabic orthography, including the development of *naskh* and *thuluth* styles. More importantly, his *Treatise on Orthography and the Science of the Stylus* became the definitive text for scribes until the seventh Islamic century. It was then that Yaʿqût Ibn ʿAbdullâh al-Musta'simiy (d. 689 H./1299 C.E.)[97] perfected Arabic orthography. His style remains the basis for contemporary calligraphy and writing—especially in the *naskh* and *thuluth* scripts—as well as in the transcription of the Quran.

The Calligraphy of This Book

More than fourteen hundred years since their revelation, the Quran's verses remain the focus of the preeminent visual art of Islamic civilization, calligraphy, the mastery of which is still passed from teacher to student. The modern calligrapher Aḥmad ʿIffat ʿAfîfî penned an original selection of Quranic verses and several *ḥadîth* (which have not, until now, ever been published) using various calligraphic styles. Many of the plates premiering in this volume were drawn by him. (Years ago I acquired from him personally the original plates of his calligraphy in Cairo.)

Born in Cairo, Egypt, March 3, 1908, Aḥmad ʿIffat ʿAfîfî graduated from the School of Arabic Script in Cairo, studying under several masters of calligraphy and ornamentation. He learned *farsî* script under Najîb Ḥawânî, *diwân* with Muḥammad Raḍwân, *thuluth* under Ibrâhîm al-Jandî, *kûfî* with Yûsuf Aḥmad, and *naskh* under both Muḥammad Gharîb and Muḥammad al-Makkâwî. Finally, he studied the art of illumination at the hand of Yûsuf Kâmil. ʿAfîfî went on to become the director general of the Bureau of Citations in the presidential palace, from which he retired in 1967. He has himself been cited for distinguished service as a calligrapher in Egypt and recognized internationally for his compositions.

The calligraphic plates of the Quran's verses (and several supplications of the Prophet, God's blessings and peace be upon him) that appear in this book have been written in the various scripts mentioned above, each within its own context of illumination. They have been interpreted into English to accurately convey the power of their meanings as expressed by the prophets and believers who originally uttered them, for the believers of every generation and land shall find these supplications speaking the language of their hearts.

The eminence of the prayers of the Quran and the Prophet ﷺ are such that they inspire the artistic impulse in Islamic civilization and have been a dear subject matter of master reciters, scribes, and calligraphers since the dawn of Islam—not only among native Arabic speakers, but wherever in the world God's Revelation has illuminated the hearts and lives of people.[98]

Notes
Bibliography
and
Indices

Text Notes

1. Al-Ghazâlî, *Iḥyâ’ ʿUlûm al-Dîn*, 1:293.

2. Al-Ḥâkim’s *al-Mustadrak*, 2:98–99 (on sound authority).

3. Jinn, angels, and human beings are intelligent creatures. God created angels from light, jinn from fire, and human beings from earth. Angels are obedient creatures who unfailingly carry out God’s commands. Jinn, like human beings, have choice and free will. They are, therefore, subject to obligation by God and answerable to Him for their deeds, and God shall assemble them on the Day of Resurrection and recompense them with reward or punishment. Jinn, like angels, are invisible to human beings, yet they see us from where we do not see them (7:27). While their creation predates that of humankind’s, several verses of the Quran and a substantial number of verified statements of the Prophet ﷺ confirm that they too live on earth—eating, drinking, procreating, and dying—and that, like humans, they agree and disagree, choose belief or disbelief, and are charged with adhering to the religion of Islam. As the formation of jinn differs from that of humans, differences of nature arise, the pertinent consequences of which are several. In addition to normally being invisible to humans, jinn have the ability to travel vast distances in moments (39:40); to pierce the earth’s atmosphere and penetrate high into the heavens (72:8–9); to assume, at times, animal or human forms; and to access human thought and introduce suggestions to it. The Quran states emphatically, however, that jinn—Satan being the chief of the disbelieving ones—possess no authority whatever over human beings. Their “power” is merely one of suggestion. Thus, whoever so elects may follow their evil suggestions, and he or she shall bear full responsibility for this. Jinn may attempt to scare human beings (though they themselves may be frightened of some human believers). In any case, the Quran stresses the importance of seeking refuge in God from them and seeking protection against their evil doings (Quran, suras 113 and 114). See al-Ṭabarî, *Jâmiʿ al-Bayân*, 7:514, 8:236, and 12:258–77.

4. *Ṣaḥîḥ Muslim*, 4:1994–95, #2577.

5. *Sunan al-Tirmidhî*, 5:483, #3479.

6. *Ṣaḥîḥ Muslim*, 2:703, #1015.

7. *Ṣaḥîḥ Muslim*, 4:2096, #2735.

8. *Sunan al-Tirmidhî*, 5:431, #3381.

9. *Ṣaḥîḥ Muslim*, 4:2304, #3009. In a similar report (*Ṣaḥîḥ Muslim*, 2:634, #920), the Prophet Muḥammad ﷺ said, "Do not pray for yourselves except with what is good. For the angels say '*Âmin*.'"

10. *Ṣaḥîḥ al-Bukhârî*, 11:150, #6351.

11. *Sunan Abû Dâwûd*, 2:77, #1482.

12. *Sunan Ibn Mâjah*, 2:1264, #3846.

13. *Ṣaḥîḥ Muslim*, 4:2076, # 2704.

14. *Sunan al-Tirmidhî*, 5:431, #3382.

15. *Ṣaḥîḥ Muslim*, 1:350, #482.

16. Al-Nawawî, *al-Adhkâr*, p. 341.

17. See Abû Ḥayyân al-Tawḥîdî, *al-Baḥr al-Muḥîṭ*, 2:131, for his commentary on this verse.

18. The statement, "O Allah, I seek refuge in You from detestable characteristics, actions, and longings," is from *Sunan al-Tirmidhî*, 5:536, #3591. "O Allah, I seek refuge in You from leprosy, insanity, and malignant illnesses," is from *Sunan Abû Dâwûd*, 2:93, #1554.

19. Al-Haythamî, *Majmaᶜ al-Zawâ'id wa Manbaᶜ al-Fawâ'id*, 10:146, #16977–78.

20. *Sunan al-Tirmidhî*, 5:493–94, #3502.

21. *Ṣaḥîḥ Muslim*, 5:2094, #2732 and #2733.

22. *Sunan Abû Dâwûd*, 1:210, #792.

23. *Sunan al-Tirmidhî*, 5:169, #2926.

24. *Ṣaḥîḥ Muslim*, 4:2068, #2675. A similar *ḥadîth* is found in *Ṣaḥîḥ Muslim*, 4:2061, #2675.

25. *Ṣaḥîḥ Muslim*, 1:296, #395.

26. The Prophet's ﷺ instruction to say "*Âmîn*" after reciting al-Fâtiḥa is reported in *Ṣaḥîḥ Muslim*, 1:310, #415.

27. Ibn Kathîr, *Tafsîr* (Shaᶜb ed.), 2:422–28. See also Ibn Ḥajr in *Fatḥ al-Bârî*, 6:361, who cites an authentic *ḥadîth* on the authority of Abû Dharr and endorsed by Ibn Ḥibbân, stating that the Prophet ﷺ said that the number of prophets is 124,000 and the number of messengers is 313. Prophethood is realized when God communicates in a special manner to a prophet, but when God commissions a prophet to convey the message to others, this prophet becomes also a messenger. Thus, every messenger is a prophet, though not all prophets are messengers.

28. See *Note 3* regarding the jinn.

29. See the Quran, 11:25–48. Details of Prophet Noah's life, family, and the response of his people to his call appear in many other suras, namely suras 7, 10, 19, 23, 26, 29, 37, and 66.

30. *Ṣaḥîḥ Muslim*, 4:2076, #2704.

31. The Quran names twenty-five prophets, twenty-one of whom are referred to in the Bible. The Prophet Shuʿayb, commissioned by God to warn and guide the Arabs of Midian, of the northwestern region of the Arabian peninsula, is among the four prophets of whom the Bible does not make explicit mention. He most likely lived after Joseph and before Aaron and Moses.

32. *Sunan al-Tirmidhî*, 4:575–76, #2516.

33. *Musnad Aḥmad*, 1:307–8.

34. *Ṣaḥîḥ al-Bukhârî*, 8:294, #4630.

35. *Musnad Aḥmad*, 1:170 [Ḥalabî]; and *Sunan al-Tirmidhî*, 5:495, #3505.

36. The suras and verses that give an account of Moses' life and mission include: 2:51–74; 5:20–26; 7:103–61; 10:75–92; 11:96–99; 14:5–8; 17:101–3; 18:60–82; 19:51–53; 20:9–79; 23:45–49; 25:35–36; 26:10–68; 27:7–14; 28:3–43; 29:39–40; 37:114–22; 40:23–46; 43:46–56; 44:17–29; 51:38–40; 54:41–42; 61:5; 73:15–16; and 79:15–26.

37. *Ṣaḥîḥ Muslim*, 4:2295, #2999.

38. *Ṣaḥîḥ Muslim*, 4:1991–93, #2571–74.

39. *Ṣaḥîḥ Muslim*, 4:2064, #2680.

40. Sayyid Quṭb, *Fî Ẓilâl al-Qur'ân*, 5:26–37.

41. *Sunan Abû Dâwûd*, 4:317, #5069; and *Sunan al-Tirmidhî*, 5:493, #3501.

42. Or he said, "in my immediate affair or in the life to come."

43. Or he said, "in my immediate affair or in the life to come."

44. *Ṣaḥîḥ al-Bukhârî*, 11:183, #6382.

45. *Ṣaḥîḥ Muslim*, 4:2088, #2722.

46. *Sunan al-Tirmidhî*, 5:506, #3528.

47. *Sunan Abû Dâwûd*, 3:34–35, #2603; and *Musnad Aḥmad*, 3:124.

48. *Sunan al-Tirmidhî*, 5:470, #3451.

49. *Sunan Ibn Mâjah*, 2:1273, #3871.

50. *Sunan al-Nasâ'î*, 8:259; and *Sunan al-Tirmidhî*, 5:489, #3492.

51. *Sunan al-Tirmidhî*, 5:434, #3407. A slightly variant version is found in *Musnad Aḥmad*, 4:125.

52. Al-Nasâ'î, *ʿAmal al-Yawm wa al-Layla*, pp. 367–68, 543–44.

53. Al-Nasâ'î, *ʿAmal al-Yawm wa al-Layla*, pp. 172–73. Al-Nawawî endorsed the authenticity of this *ḥadîth*. See *al-Adhkâr*, p. 24. A variant report is found in *Sunan al-Tirmidhî*, 5:492–93, #3500.

54. *Ṣaḥîḥ Muslim*, 4:2087, #2719. This *ḥadîth* is somewhat different than what is found in the "Prayers for All Times" section.

55. Ibn ʿAbbâs reported that the Prophet ﷺ used to open his nightly voluntary Prayer

(*Ṣalât*) with this supplication. *Ṣaḥîḥ Muslim*, 1:532–33, #769; and *Sunan Abû Dâwûd*, 1:205, #771.

56. *Ṣaḥîḥ Muslim*, 4:2078, #2705; and *Sunan al-Nasâ'î*, 3:53.

57. *Ṣaḥîḥ al-Bukhârî*, 11:116, #6316.

58. *Sunan al-Tirmidhî*, 1:77–78, #55.

59. *Sunan al-Bayhaqî*, 2:209. A similar text is found in *Sunan Abû Dâwûd*, 2:63, #1425; and *Sunan al-Tirmidhî*, 2:238, #464.

60. *Ṣaḥîḥ Muslim*, 4:2088, #2722.

61. *Ṣaḥîḥ Muslim*, 1:352, #486.

62. *Ṣaḥîḥ Muslim*, 4:2069, #2688.

63. *Sunan al-Nasâ'î*, 2:138.

64. Al-Haythamî, *Majmaᶜ al-Zawâ'id wa Manbaᶜ al-Fawâ'id*, 6:379, #10502–6.

65. *Sunan al-Tirmidhî*, 5:493–94, #3502.

66. *Sunan Abû Dâwûd*, 4:314, #5061, and al-Nasâ'î, *ᶜAmal al-Yawm wa al-Layla*, p. 495, #865.

67. *Ṣaḥîḥ Muslim*, 4:2045, #2654.

68. *Sunan al-Tirmidhî*, 5:512, #3540.

69. *Ṣaḥîḥ Muslim*, 4:1986, #2564.

70. *Ṣaḥîḥ al-Bukhârî*, 1:56, #13.

71. *Musnad Aḥmad*, 3:166.

72. *Sunan al-Tirmidhî*, 4:572, #2509.

73. Uḥud is a mountain one mile north of Madinah where the battle that bears its name took place on Friday, the 6th of Shawwâl, of the year 3 H./624 C.E.

74. *Ṣaḥîḥ Ibn Ḥibbân (al-Iḥsân)*, 2:9, #619.

75. *Ṣaḥîḥ Muslim*, 1:530, #763 (version 189).

76. *Sunan Abû Dâwûd*, 1:254; and al-Ḥâkim's *al-Mustadrak*, 1:265. Dhahabî said that it is authentic and meets Muslim's requirements.

77. For this and other supplications of refuge see *Sunan al-Nasâ'î*, 8:250–85; and *Ṣaḥîḥ Muslim*, 4:2086, #2097.

78. Ibn Ḥajar makes an excellent comparison of various versions of this authentic report in *Fatḥ al-Bârî*, 6:505–11. Authenticated variations are included in this English text for clarity. For details concerning this narrative, see *Ṣaḥîḥ Muslim*, 4:2099, #2743; and *Ṣaḥîḥ al-Bukhârî*, 4:408–9, #2215. Other versions of the same report are in *Ṣaḥîḥ al-Bukhârî*, #2272, #2333, #3465, and #5974.

79. Ibn Hishâm, *al-Sîra al-Nabawiyya*, 1:344.

80. Ibn Hishâm, *al-Sîra al-Nabawiyya*, 1:359–60.

81. *Ṣaḥîḥ Muslim*, 1:459, #649.

82. *Ṣaḥîḥ Bukhârî*, 11:208–9, #6408.

83. *Ṣaḥîḥ Muslim*, 4:2275–77, #2964; and *Ṣaḥîḥ al-Bukhârî*, 6:500–503, #3464.

84. *Ṣaḥîḥ Muslim*, 1:39, #9.

85. *Ṣaḥîḥ Muslim*, 2:700, #1010.

86. *Sunan al-Tirmidhî*, 5:425, #3371.

87. Al-Ḥâkim's *al-Mustadrak*, 1:669, #1812.

88. *Sunan Abû Dâwûd*, 2:76-77, #1476.

89. *Ṣaḥîḥ Muslim*, 1:39, #9.

90. *Sunan al-Tirmidhî*, 5:512, #3540.

91. *Sunan al-Tirmidhî*, 5:4748, #2682.

92. *Ṣaḥîḥ Muslim*, 4:2088, #2722. A similar version in found in *Sunan al-Nasâ'î*, 8:285.

93. *Ṣaḥîḥ Muslim*, 4:2045, #2654.

94. Nâṣiruddîn al-Asad, *Maṣâdir al-Shiʿr al-Jâhilî*, p. 46.

95. Dr. Muṣṭafâ Aẓamî has counted sixty-one Companions who served as scribes for the Prophet ﷺ. See Aẓamî's work, *Kuttâb al-Nabî*, 3d ed. (Beirut: al-Maktab al-Islâmî, 1981), pp. 37–176.

96. Al-Dhahabî, *Siyar Aʿlâm al-Nubulâ'*, 15:229.

97. Al-Dhahabî, *Siyar Aʿlâm al-Nubulâ'*, 8:131–32.

98. For a more elaborate treatment of the art, history, and illustrations of Arabic calligraphy, see the excellent and succinct introduction of *Fann al-Khaṭ Târîkhuhu wa Namâdhij min Rawâ'iʿihi ʿalâ Marr al-ʿUṣûr* by the Research Centre for Islamic History, Art, and Culture. See also two works by Nâjî Zaynuddîn, *Badâ'iʿ al-Khaṭ al-ʿArabî* and *Manẓûr al-Khaṭ al-ʿArabî*.

Margin Notes

(Sources of quotes, other than those of Quranic verses, that appear in the margins)

Page 4 MARGIN
Al-Ḥâkim's *al-Mustadrak*, 1:496, #1824

Page 6 MARGIN
Sunan al-Tirmidhî, 5:428–29, #3377

Page 8 MARGIN
Ṣaḥîḥ Muslim, 2:697–98, #1006

Page 10 MARGIN
Ṣaḥîḥ Muslim, 3:1458, #1828

Page 11 MARGIN
Ṣaḥîḥ al-Bukhârî, 11:206, #6406

Page 12 MARGIN
Sunan Abû Dâwûd, 1:144, #521

Page 13 MARGIN
Ṣaḥîḥ Muslim, 4:2093, #2731

Page 14 MARGIN
Ṣaḥîḥ Muslim, 1:203, #223

Page 16 MARGIN
Ṣaḥîḥ Muslim, 4:2113, #2759

Page 17 MARGIN
Ṣaḥîḥ al-Bukhârî, 11:208, #6407

Page 18 MARGIN
Al-Nasâ'î, *ʿAmal al-Yawm wa al-Layla*, p. 151, #30

Page 20 MARGIN
Abû Ḥâmid al-Ghazâlî, *Iḥyâ' ʿUlûm al-Dîn*, 1:301

Page 21 MARGIN
Thâbit ibn Aslam al-Bunânî (d. 127/743), as quoted in al-Ghazâlî's *Iḥyâ' ʿUlûm al-Dîn*, 1:294

Page 29 MARGIN
Sunan al-Tirmidhî, 5:144, #2876

Page 40 MARGIN
Ṣaḥîḥ al-Bukhârî, 6:287, #3194

Page 90 MARGIN
Ṣaḥîḥ Muslim, 3:1517, #1909

Page 107 MARGIN
Al-Nasâ'î, *ʿAmal al-Yawm wa al-Layla*, p. 330, #456; and *Sunan Ibn Mâjah*, 2:1254–55, #3819

Page 108 MARGIN
Ṣaḥîḥ al-Bukhârî, 11:116, #6316. See also *Ṣaḥîḥ Muslim*, 1:530, #763

Page 113 MARGIN
Sunan al-Tirmidhî, 5:470, #3451

Page 114 MARGIN
Al-Haythamî attributed this report to the collection of al-Ṭabarânî and commented that the chain of reporters includes Mûsâ ibn Maṭayr who is abandoned as a reliable source by *ḥadîth* authorities. See al-Haythamî's *al-Majmaʿ al-Zawâ'id*, 10:272, #17360.

Page 115 MARGIN
Ṣaḥîḥ Muslim, 1:327, #442 (136)

Page 118 MARGIN
Ṣaḥîḥ al-Bukhârî, 11:196, #6398; and *Ṣaḥîḥ Muslim*, 4:2087, #2719

Page 119 MARGIN
Al-Nasâ'î, *ʿAmal al-Yawm wa al-Layla*, p. 163, #55

Page 120 MARGIN
The text of this *ḥadîth* varies with supplication 1.14 in the "Prayers for All Times and Occasions" section, by the inclusion of "... And grant me light the day of meeting You." Ibn Ḥajar cites al-Ṭabarânî's report that ends with "... give me light on the Day of Resurrection," *Ṣaḥîḥ al-Bukhârî*, 11:117. See also *Ṣaḥîḥ Muslim*, 1:530, #763.

Page 121 MARGIN
Ṣaḥîḥ Muslim, 1:50, #19

Page 129 MARGIN
Sunan Abû Dâwûd, 1:254, #969; and al-Ḥâkim's *al-Mustadrak*, 1:265

Page 132 MARGIN
Ṣaḥîḥ Muslim, 4:2073, #2698

Page 136 MARGIN
Musnad Aḥmad, 2:509

Page 137 MARGIN
Ṣaḥîḥ Muslim, 4:2078, #2704 (47)

Page 140 MARGIN
Ṣaḥîḥ Muslim, 1:65, #38

Page 144 MARGIN
Ṣaḥîḥ Muslim, 4:1980, #2553

Page 147 MARGIN
Ṣaḥîḥ Muslim, 1:69, #48

Page 148 MARGIN
Ṣaḥîḥ Muslim, 1:67, #45

Page 151 MARGIN
Ṣaḥîḥ Muslim, 4:2001, #2589

Page 153 MARGIN
Ṣaḥîḥ Muslim, 4:2109, #2754

Page 155 MARGIN
Sunan Abû Dâwûd, 1:125, #456; and *Musnad Aḥmad*, 5:371

Page 158 MARGIN
Ṣaḥîḥ Muslim, 4:2174, #2824

Page 160 MARGIN
Ṣaḥîḥ Muslim, 4:1997, #2581

Page 162 MARGIN
Musnad Aḥmad, 4:188. Al-Haythamî, commenting on Aḥmad's report, stated that this *ḥadîth* is

on good authority. See al-Haythamî, *Majmaᶜ al-Zawâ'id*, 7:542, #12178.

Page 173 MARGIN
Al-Ḥâkim's *al-Mustadrak*, 1:406–7

Page 174 MARGIN
Al-Haythamî, *Majmaᶜ al-Zawâ'id*, 4:126; and Yûsuf al-Qaraḍâwî, *al-Muntaqâ*, 1:290

Page 176 MARGIN
Ṣaḥîḥ al-Bukhârî, 3:33; and *Ṣaḥîḥ Muslim*, 1:509, #738

Page 182 MARGIN
Sunan Abû Dâwûd, 4:336, #5139

Page 189 MARGIN
Ṣaḥîḥ Muslim, 4:2092, #2730

Page 194 MARGIN
Ṣaḥîḥ al-Bukhârî, 3:1273

Bibliography

ʿAbd al-Bâqî, Muḥammad Fu'âd. *Al-Muʿjam al-Mufahras li Alfâẓ al-Qur'ân al-Karîm.* Dâr al-Ḥadîth: Cairo, 1407/1987.

Abû Dâwûd, Sulaymân ibn al-Ashʿath. *Sunan Abû Dâwûd.* 4 parts (in 2 vols.). Damascus: Dâr al-Fikr, n.d. (First printed in 1934).

Abû Ḥayyân, Abû ʿAbdullâh Muḥammad ibn Yûsuf. *Al-Tafsîr al-Kabîr al-Musammâ bi al-Baḥr al-Muḥîṭ.* 8 vols. Riyâḍ: Maktabat wa Maṭâbiʿ al-Naṣr al-Ḥadîtha, n.d.

Abû al-Saʿûd, Muḥammad ibn Muḥammad al-ʿImâdî. *Tafsîr Abî al-Saʿûd* [or *Irshâd al-ʿAql al-Salîm ilâ Mazâyâ al-Qur'ân al-Karîm*]. 9 vols. (in 5). Beirut: Dâr Iḥyâ' al-Turâth al-ʿArabî, n.d.

al-ʿAjlûnî, Ismâʿîl. *Kashf al-Khafâ' wa Muzîl al-Ilbâs ʿamma Ashtahara min al-Aḥâdîth ʿalâ Alsinat al-Nâs.* Edited by Aḥmad al-Qallâsh. 2 vols. Beirut: Mu'assasat al-Risâla, 1979.

al-Alûsî, Shihâbuddîn al-Sayyid Maḥmûd. *Rûḥ al-Maʿânî fî Tafsîr al-Qur'ân al-Aẓîm wa Sabʿ al-Mathânî.* 30 vols. (in 15). Beirut: Dâr Iḥyâ' al-Turâth al-ʿArabî, n.d.

ʿAmâyra, Ismâʿîl Aḥmad, and ʿAbd al-Ḥamîd Muṣṭafâ al-Sayyid. *Muʿjam al-Adawât wa al-Ḍamâ'ir fî al-Qur'ân al-Karîm.* Beirut: Mu'assasat al-Risâla, 1988.

al-Aṣfahânî, al-Râghib. *Al-Mufradât.* Beirut: Dâr al-Fikr, 1972.

al-Ashqar, Muḥammad Sulaymân ʿAbdullâh. *Zubdat al-Tafsîr min Fatḥ al-Qadîr.* Kuwait: Wazârat al-Awqâf, 1406/1985.

al-ʿAẓamî, Muḥammad Muṣṭafâ. *Kuttâb al-Nabî.* Beirut: Al-Maktab al-Islâmî, 1981.

al-Banna, Ḥasan. *Al-Ma'thurât*. Cairo: Dâr al-Shihâb, n.d.

al-Bayḍâwî, Nâṣiruddîn ʿAbdullâh ibn ʿUmar. *Anwâr al-Tanzîl wa Asrâr al-Ta'wîl* (or *Tafsîr al-Bayḍâwî*). 5 vols. (in 2). Beirut: Mu'assasat Shaʿbân, n.d.

al-Bayhaqî, Abû Bakr Aḥmad ibn al-Ḥusayn ibn ʿAlî. *Al-Sunan al-Kubrâ* (or *Sunan al-Bayhaqî*). 10 vols. Beirut: Dâr al-Maʿrifa, n.d.

al-Bilâdî, ʿÂtiq ibn Ghayth. *Faḍâ'il al-Qur'ân*. Edited by Fârûq Ḥamâda. Makkah: Dâr Makkah, 1410/1990.

al-Biqâʿî [or al-Buqâʿî], Burhânuddîn Abû al-Ḥasan Ibrâhîm ibn ʿUmar. *Maṣâʿid al-Naẓar li al-Ishrâf ʿalâ Maqâṣid al-Suwar*. Edited by ʿAbd al-Samîʿ Muḥammad Aḥmad Ḥasanayn. 3 vols. Riyâḍ: Maktabat al-Maʿârif, 1987.

____. *Naẓm al-Durur fî Tanâsub al-Ayât wa al-Suwar*. 22 vols. Hyderabad: Maṭbûʿât Dâ'ira al-Maʿârif ʿUthmâniyya (Osmania Oriental Publications Bureau), 1404/1984.

Al-Dârimî, Abû Muḥammad ʿAbdullâh ibn ʿAbd al-Raḥmân. *Sunan al-Dârimî*. Cairo: Dâr al-Fikr, 1978.

Darwaza, Muḥammad ʿAzzat. *Al-Tafsîr al-Ḥadîth*. 12 vols. (in 6). Cairo: ʿÎsâ al-Bâbî al-Ḥalabî, n.d.

____. *Al-Dustûr al-Qur'ânî wa al-Sunna al-Nabawiyya*. 1966.

Encyclopaedia of Islam. 1st ed. 9 vols. Leiden: E. J. Brill, 1913–1936.

Encyclopaedia of Islam. New Edition. 8 vols. to date. Leiden: E. J. Brill, 1954–.

al-Faryâbî, Abû Bakr Jaʿfar ibn Muḥammad ibn al-Ḥasan. *Kitâb Faḍâ'il al-Qur'ân wa Mâ Jâ'a fîhi min al-Faḍl wa fî Kam Yuqra' wa al-Sunna fî Dhâlik*. Edited by Yûsuf ʿUthmân Faḍl Allâh Jibrîl. Riyâḍ: Maktabat al-Rushd, 1989.

al-Fayrûzabâdî, Majduddîn Muḥammad ibn Yaʿqûb. *Baṣâ'ir Dhawî al-Tamyîz fî Laṭâ'if al-Kitâb al-ʿAzîz*. Edited by Muḥammad ʿAlî al-Najjâr. 8 vols. Beirut: Maktaba al-ʿIlmiyya, n.d.

al-Ghazâlî, Abû Ḥâmid Muḥammad al-Ṭûsî. *Iḥyâ' ʿUlûm al-Dîn*. 5 vols. Beirut: Dâr al-Maʿrifa, n.d.

____. *Invocations and Supplications (Kitâb al-Adhkâr wa al-Daʿawât)*. Translated by Kojiro Nakamura. Cambridge: Islamic Texts Society, 1990.

____. *Jawâhir al-Qur'ân*. Edited by Muḥammad Rashîd Riḍa al-Qabbânî. Beirut: Dâr Iḥyâ' ʿUlûm, 1985.

____. *The Ninety-Nine Beautiful Names of God*. Translated by David B. Burrell and Nazih Daher. Cambridge: Islamic Texts Society, 1992.

al-Ghazâlî, Muḥammad. *Fann al-Dhikr wa al-Duʿâ' ʿInd Khâtim al-Anbiyyâ'*. Cairo: Dâr al-Iʿtiṣâm, n.d.

Ḥaddâd, Muḥammad. *Nuqaṭ Fawq al-Ḥurûf*. Cairo: Maktabat Miṣr, n.d.

al-Ḥâkim, Abû ʿAbdullâh Muḥammad ibn ʿAbdullâh al-Nîsâbûrî. *Al-Mustadrak ʿalâ al-Ṣaḥîḥayn fî al-Ḥadîth*. 4 vols. Makkah: Dâr al-Bâz, n.d.

____. *Al-Mustadrak*. 4 vols. Beirut: Dâr al-Kutub al-ʿÂlamiyya, 1990. [References made to *al-Mustadrak* that include a *ḥadîth* number are from this edition.]

____. *Al-Mustadrak*. 4 vols. Hyderabad: n.p., 1334/1915.

Hammad, Ahmad Zaki. *Islamic Law: Understanding Juristic Differences*. Indianapolis: American Trust Publications, 1992.

____. *The Opening to the Quran: Commentary and Vocabulary Reference of al-Fâtiḥa*. Oak Lawn, IL: Quranic Literacy Institute, 1996.

Ḥawwa, Saʿîd. *Al-Asâs al-Tafsîr*. Cairo: Dâr al-Salâm, 1985.

al-Haythamî, Nûruddîn ʿAlî ibn Abî Bakr. *Majmaʿ al-Zawâ'id wa Manbaʿ al-Fawâ'id*. 10 vols. Edited by ʿAbdullâh Muḥammad al-Darwîsh. Beirut: Dâr al-Fikr, 1992.

____. *Majmaʿ al-Zawâ'id wa Manbaʿ al-Fawâ'id*. 10 vols. (in five parts). Beirut: Dâr al-Kitâb al-ʿArabî, 1982.

al-Hilâlî, Salîm ibn ʿÎd. *Ṣaḥîḥ Kitâb al-Adhkâr wa Ḍaʿîfuhu*. 1st ed. Madina: Maktabat al-Ghurubâ' al-Atharîya, 1413/1992.

____. *Ṣaḥîḥ al-Wâbil al-Ṣayyib min al-Kalim al-Ṭayyib li ShamsuddînAbû ʿAbdullâh Ibn al-Qayyim al-Jawziyya*. 2nd ed. Riyad: Dâr Ibn al-Jawzî, 1993.

al-Hindî, ʿAlâ'uddîn ʿAlî al-Muttaqqî ibn Ḥusâmuddîn. *Kanz al-ʿUmmâl fî Sunan al-Aqwâl wa al-Afʿâl*. 15 vols. Beirut: Mu'assasat al-Risâla, 1979.

al-Ḥumûd, Muḥammad ibn Ḥamad. *Al-Nahj al-Asmâ' fî Sharḥ Asmâ' Allâh al-Ḥusnâ*. 2 vols. Kuwait: Maktabat al-Imâm al-Dhahabî, 1413/1992.

Ibn Ḥajar al-ʿAsqalânî, Aḥmad. *Fatḥ al-Bârî bi Sharḥ Ṣaḥîḥ al-Bukhârî*. 13 vols. Riyâḍ: Maktabat al-Riyâḍ al-Ḥadîtha, n.d.

____. *Natâji'u al-Afkâr fî Takhrîj Aḥâdîth al-Adhkâr*. Edited by Ḥamdî ʿAbdul Majîd al-Salafî. 2 vols. Baghdâd: Irshâd Press, 1986–1991.

____. *Talkhîṣ al-Ḥabîr*. 4 vols. (in 2 parts). Beirut: Dâr al-Maʿrifa, 1964.

Ibn Ḥanbal, Aḥmad. *Marwiyyât al-Imâm Aḥmad Ibn Ḥanbal fî al-Tafsîr*. Compiled and edited by Aḥmad al-Bazra, Muḥammad ibn Rizq ibn al-Ṭarhûnî, and Ḥikmat Bashîr Yâsîn. 4 vols. Riyâḍ: Maktabat al-Mu'ayyad, 1994.

____. *Musnad*. 6 vols. Beirut: Al-Maktab al-Islâmî, 1969.

Ibn Ḥibbân, ʿAlâ'uddîn ʿAlî al-Fârisî. *Al-Iḥsân bi Tartîb Ṣaḥîḥ Ibn Ḥibbân*. 6 vols. (in 9 parts). Beirut: Dâr al-Kutub al-ʿÂlamiyya (originally published by Dâr al-Bâz, Makkah), 1987.

Ibn Hisham, Abû Muḥammad ʿAbd al-Malik. *Al-Sîra al-Nabawiyya li Ibn Hishâm*. 4 vols. Edited by Muṣṭafâ al-Saqâ, Ibrâhîm al-Ibyârî, and ʿAbd al-Ḥafîẓ Shalabî. Beirut: Dâr al-Qalam, n.d.

Ibn ʿIllân, Muḥammad ʿAlî ibn Muḥammad ibn ʿIllân al-Ṣiddîqî. *Al-Futuḥât al-Rabbâniyya ʿalâ al-Adhkâr al-Nawâwiyya*. 4 vols. (in 7 parts). Beirut: Iḥyâ' al-Turâth al-ʿArabîy (originally published by Jamʿîyat al-Nashr wa al-Ta'lîf al-Azhariyya), n.d.

Ibn al-Jawzî, Jamâluddîn Abû al-Faraj ʿAbd al-Raḥmân ibn ʿAlî. *Zâd al-Masîr fî ʿIlm al-Tafsîr*. 9 vols. Damascus: Al-Maktab al-Islâmî, 1384/1964.

Ibn Juzayy, Muḥammad ibn Aḥmad al-Kalbî. *Kitâb al-Tashîl li ʿUlûm al-Tanzîl*. 4 parts (in 1 vol.). Beirut: Dâr al-Kitâb al-ʿArabî, n.d.

Ibn Kathîr, Imâduddîn Abû al-Fidâ' Ismâʿîl. *Al-Mukhtaṣar Tafsîr Ibn Kathîr*. Edited by Muḥammad ʿAlî al-Ṣâbûnî. 3 vols. Beirut: Dâr al-Qur'ân al-Karîm, n.d.

____. *Tafsîr al-Qur'ân al-ʿAẓîm*. 4 vols. Beirut: Dâr al-Fikr. n.d.

Ibn Khâlawayh, Abû ʿAbdullâh al-Ḥusayn ibn Aḥmad. *Kitâb Iʿrâb Thalâthîn Sûra min al-Qur'ân al-Karîm*. Cairo: Maktabat al-Mutanabbî, n.d.

Ibn Mâjah, Abû ʿAbdullâh Muḥammad ibn Yazîd. *Sunan Ibn Mâjah*. Edited by Muḥammad Fu'âd ʿAbd al-Bâqî. 2 vols. Cairo: Dâr al-Ḥadîth, n.d.

Ibn Manẓûr, Abû al-Faḍl Jamâluddîn ibn Mukarram. *Lisân al-ʿArab*. 15 vols. Cairo: Dâr Ṣâdir, n.d.

Ibn al-Qayyim, Shamsuddîn Muḥammad ibn Abû Bakr ibn Ayyûb ibn Saʿd ibn Ḥarîz al-Zuraʿî ibn Qayyim al-Jawziyya. *Al-Tafsîr al-Qayyim li al-Imâm Ibn al-Qayyim*. Compiled by Muḥammad Uways al-Nadwî. Edited by Muḥammad Ḥâmid al-Fiqî. Beirut: Dâr al-Fikr, 1408/1988.

____. *Al-Wâbil al-Ṣayyib min al-Kalim al-Ṭayyib*. Beirut: Dâr al-Kutub al-ʿIlmiyya, 1978.

____. *Zâd al-Maʿâd*. 5 vols. Beirut: Mu'assasat al-Risâla, 1986.

Ibn al-Sunnî, al-Dinawrî Abû Bakr Aḥmad ibn Muḥammad al-Dînawrî. *ʿAmal al-Yawm wa al-Layla*. 1st ed. Damascus: Maktabat Dâr al-Bayân, 1987.

Ibn Ṭarhûnî, Muḥammad ibn Rizq. *Mawsûʿat Faḍâ'il Suwar wa Âyât al-Qur'ân*. 2 vols. Dammâm: Dâr Ibn al-Qayyim, 1409/1988.

Ibn Taymiyya, Aḥmad ibn ʿAbd al-Ḥalîm. *Daqâ'iq al-Tafsîr*. Edited by Muḥammad al-Sayyid. 3d ed. 6 vols. (in 3). Beirut: Mu'assasat ʿUlûm al-Qur'ân, 1406/1986.

____. *Al-Kalim al-Ṭayyib min Adhkâr al-Nabîy*. Edited by ʿAbd al-Qâdir al-Arnâ'ûṭ. Saudi Arabia: Ri'âsat Idârât al-Buḥûth al-ʿIlmiyya, n.d.

____. *Majmuʿ al-Fatâwâ*. 39 vols. Rabat: Maktabat al-Maʿârif, n.d.

ʿIlaywî, Ibn Khalîfa. *Jâmiʿ al-Nuqûl fî Asbâb al-Nuzûl wa Sharḥ Âyâtihâ*. 2 vols. Riyâḍ: Maṭâbiʿ al-Shuʿâʿ, 1404/1984.

ʿInâyat, Ghâzî. *Asbâb al-Nuzûl al-Qur'ânî*. Beirut: Dâr al-Jîl, 1991.

al-Istânbûlî, Maḥmûd Mahdî. *Al-Awrâd al-Ma'thûr min al-Qur'ân al-ʿAẓîm wa al-Sunna al-Ṣaḥîḥa*. 2nd ed. Beirut: Al-Maktab al-Islâmî, 1986.

al-Jazâ'irî, Abû Bakr Jâbir. *Aysar al-Tafâsîr li Kalâm al-ʿAliyy al-Kabîr*. 3d ed. 5 vols. Jidda: Râsim, 1410/1990.

Lane, Edward William. *An Arabic-English Lexicon*. 8 parts (Parts 6–8 edited by Stanley Lane-Poole). 1872. Reprint. Beirut: Librairie du Liban, 1980.

Majmaʿ al-Lughat al-ʿArabiyya (Academy of Arabic Language, Egypt). *Muʿjam Alfâẓ al-Qur'ân al-Karîm*. Cairo: Dâr al-Shurûq, 1981.

Mâlik ibn Anas. *Al-Muwaṭṭa'*. Edited by Muḥammad Fu'âd ʿAbd al-Bâqî. 2 vols. n.p.: Dâr al-Turâth al-ʿArabî, n.d.

al-Manâwî, Zaynuddîn ʿAbd al-Ra'ûf. *Al-Fatḥ al-Samâwî bi Takhrîj Aḥâdîth Tafsîr al-Qâḍî al-Bayḍâwî*. 3 vols. Edited by Aḥmad Mujtabâ ibn Nadhîr ʿÂlim al-Salafî. Riyâḍ: Dâr al-ʿÂṣima, 1409/1989.

al-Mâwardî, Abû al-Ḥasan ʿAlî ibn Ḥabîb. *Tafsîr al-Mâwardî*. 4 vols. Kuwait: Maqhawî Press, 1402/1982.

Mu'assasat al-Kutub al-Thaqâfiyya. *Al-Aḥâdîth al-Qudsiyya*. 2 vols. (in one part). Beirut: Mu'assasat al-Kutub al-Thaqâfiyya, 1983.

al-Muḥâmilî, al-Qaḍi Abû ʿAbdullâh al-Ḥusayn ibn Ismâʿîl. *Kitâb al-Duʿâ'*. Edited by Saʿîd ibn ʿAbd al-Raḥmân ibn Mûsâ al-Quzqî. 1st ed. Beirut: Dâr al-Gharb al-Islâmî, 1992.

al-Munajjid, Ṣalâḥuddîn. *Dirâsât fî Târîkh al-Khaṭ al-ʿArabî.* Beirut: Dâr al-Jadîd, 1972.

al-Mundhirî, Abû Muḥammad Zakiyyuddîn ʿAbd al-ʿAẓîm ʿAbd al-Qawîy. *Al-Targhîb wa al-Tarhîb min al-Ḥadîth al-Sharîf.* Edited by Muḥammad Muḥiyyuddîn ʿAbd al-Ḥamîd. 3d ed. 6 vols. n.p.: Dâr al-Fikr, 1979.

Muslim ibn al-Ḥajjâj, al-Qushayrî. *Ṣaḥîḥ Muslim.* Edited by Muḥammad Fu'âd ʿAbd al-Bâqî. 5 vols. Cairo: Dâr Iḥyâ' al-Turâth al-ʿArabî, 1955–56. Reprint. Beirut: Dâr al-Fikr, 1978.

al-Nasâ'î, Abû ʿAbd al-Raḥmân Aḥmad ibn Shuʿayb ibn ʿAlî. *Faḍâ'il al-Qur'ân.* Edited by Fârûq Ḥamâda. Beirut: Dâr Iḥyâ' al-ʿUlûm; Al-Dâr al-Bayḍâ' [Casablanca]: Dâr al-Thaqâfa, 1413/1992.

____. *Sunan al-Nasâ'î.* 4 vols. (in 8 parts). Beirut: Dâr al-Kitâb al-ʿArabî, n.d.

____. *Tafsîr al-Nasâ'î.* Edited by Ṣabrî ibn ʿAbd al-Khâliq al-Shâfiʿî and Sayyid ibn ʿAbbâs al-Jalîmîy. 2 vols. Cairo: Maktabat al-Sunna, 1990.

al-Nawawî, Muḥîyuddîn Abû Zakariyya Yaḥyâ ibn Sharaf. *Kitâb al-Adhkâr.* Edited by Bashîr Muḥammad ʿUyûn. 2nd ed. Damascus: Maktabat Dâr al-Bayân, 1993.

____. *Al-Majmûʿ.* 19 vols. Madina: Maktabat al-Salafiyya, n.d.

____. *Riyâḍ al-Ṣaliḥîn* (With a commentary: *Dalîl al-Râghibîn ilâ Riyâḍ al-Ṣaliḥîn*). Edited by Farûq Ḥamâda. 1st ed. Casablanca: Dâr al-Thaqâfa, 1988.

____. *Ṣaḥîḥ Muslim bi Sharḥ al-Nawawî.* 9 vols. (in 18 parts). Beirut: Dâr Iḥyâ' al-Turâth al-ʿArabî, 1972.

al-Qaraḍâwî, Yûsuf. *Al-Muntaqâ min Kitâb al-Targhîb wa al-Tarhîb al-Mundhirî.* 2 vols. Al-Manṣûra, Egypt: Dâr al-Wafâ', 1994.

al-Qâsimî, Muḥammad Jamâluddin. *Tafsîr al-Qur'ân.* 17 vols. (in 10). Beirut: Dâr al-Fikr, 1978.

al-Qurṭubî, Abû ᶜAbdullâh Muḥammad ibn Aḥmad al-Anṣârî. *Al-Jâmiᶜ li Aḥkâm al-Qur'ân*. 20 vols. Cairo: Dâr al-Kutub al-Miṣriyya, 1952–67.

____. *Al-Tadhkâr fî Afḍal al-Adhkâr min al-Qur'ân al-Karîm*. 1st ed. Beirut: Dâr al-Kutub al-ᶜIlmiyya, 1986.

Quṭb, Muḥammad. *Dirâsât Qur'âniyya*. 3d ed. Beirut (and Cairo): Dâr al-Shurûq, 1402/1982.

Quṭb, Sayyid. *Fî Ẓilâl al-Qur'ân*. 6 vols. Beirut: Dâr al-Shurûq, 1393/1973.

al-Râfiᶜî, Muḥammad ibn Shuᶜayb. *Ṣaḥîḥ al-Duᶜâ' al-Mustajâb*. Cairo: Dâr al-Faḍîla, n.d.

al-Râzî, Fakhruddîn. *Al-Tafsîr al-Kabîr*. 3d ed. 32 vols. (in 15). Beirut: Dâr Iḥyâ' al-Turâth al-ᶜArabî, n.d.

Research Centre for Islamic History, Art, and Culture. *Fann al-Khaṭ Târîkhuhu wa Namâdhij min Rawâ'iᶜihi ᶜalâ Marr al-ᶜUṣûr*. (Introduction by Ekmeleddin Ihsanoglu and compiled by Muṣṭafâ A. Darmân, Nihâd Chatîn, and Ṣâliḥ Saᶜdâwî.) Istanbul: Research Centre for Islamic History, Art, and Culture, 1990.

Riḍâ, Muḥammad Rashîd. *Tafsîr al-Qur'an al-Ḥakîm* (known as *Tafsîr al-Manâr*). 2d ed. 12 vols. Beirut: Dâr al-Maᶜrifa, n.d.

al-Ṣabbâgh, Maḥmûd. *Al-Dhikr fî al-Qur'ân al-Karîm wa al-Sunna al-Muṭahhara*. Cairo: Dâr al-Iᶜtiṣâm, n.d.

al-Ṣâbûnî, Muḥammad ᶜAlî, ed. *Ṣafwat al-Tafâsîr*. 4th ed. 3 vols. Beirut: Dâr al-Qur'ân al-Karîm, 1402/1981.

Sâlim, ᶜAbd al-Razzâq Muḥammad. *Duᶜâ' al-Qur'ân*. Cairo: Al-Sharika al-Miṣriyya li al-Ṭabâᶜa wa al-Nashr, n.d.

Shâhîn, ᶜAbd al-Ṣabûr. *Mafṣal Ayât al-Qur'ân*. 10 vols. Cairo: n.p., 1989.

Shaltût, Maḥmûd. *Tafsîr al-Qur'ân al-Karîm*. 6th ed. Beirut: Dâr al-Shurûq, 1394/1974.

al-Shawkânî, Muḥammad ibn ʿAlî ibn Muḥammad. *Fatḥ al-Qadîr*. 5 vols. Beirut: Dâr Iḥyâ' al-Turâth al-ʿArabî, n.d.

____. *Nayl al-Awṭâr*. 9 vols. Beirut: Dâr al-Jîl, 1973.

____. *Ṭuḥfat al-Dhâkirîn bi ʿIddat al-Ḥiṣn al-Ḥaṣîn min Kalâm Sayyid al-Mursilîn*. 1st ed. Beirut: Dâr al-Maʿrifa, 1988.

Shorter Encyclopaedia of Islam. Edited by H. A. R. Gibb and J. H. Kramers. Leiden: E. J. Brill, 1953.

al-Suyûṭî, ʿAbd al-Raḥmân ibn al-Kamâl Jamâluddin. *ʿAmal al-Yawm wa al-Layla*. Edited by Muṣṭafâ ʿAshûr. Cairo: Maktabat al-Qur'ân, n.d.

____. *Lubâb al-Nuqûl fî Asbâb al-Nuzûl*. Beirut: Dâr Iḥyâ' al-ʿUlûm, 1978.

____. *Tafsîr al-Durr al-Manthûr fî al-Tafsîr al-Ma'thûr*. 8 vols. Beirut: Dâr al-Fikr, 1403/1983.

____. *Tafsîr al-Imâmayn al-Jalâlayn* (from Sûrat al-Kahf to Sûrat al-Nâs by Jalâluddîn al-Maḥallî. From Sûrat al-Baqara to Sûrat al-Isrâ' by al-Suyûṭî). Beirut: Dâr al-Fikr, n.d.

____. *Waṭâ'if al-Yawm wa al-Layla*. Edited by Muṣṭafâ ʿAbd al-Qâdir ʿAṭâ. 1st ed. Beirut: Dâr al-Kutub al-ʿIlmiyya, 1987.

al-Ṭabarî, Abû Jaʿfar Muḥammad ibn Jarîr. *Jâmiʿ al-Bayân fî Tafsîr al-Qur'ân*. 12 vols. Beirut: Dâr al-Kutub al-ʿIlmiyya, 1412/1992.

____. *Mukhtaṣar Tafsîr al-Ṭabarî*. Edited by Muḥammad ʿAlî al-Ṣâbûnî and Ṣâliḥ Aḥmad Riḍâ. 2 vols. Beirut: Dâr al-Qur'ân al-Karîm, 1403/1983.

al-Tirmidhî, Muḥammad ibn ʿÎsâ. *Sunan al-Tirmidhî*. 10 vols. Cairo: Al-Ḥalabî Press, 1965–68.

al-Wâdiʿî, Abû ʿAbd al-Raḥmân Muqbil ibn Hâdî. *Al-Ṣaḥîḥ al-Musnad min Asbâb al-Nuzûl*. 4th ed. Cairo: Maktabat Ibn Taymiyya, 1408/1987.

Wensinck, A. J. *Concordance et Indices de la Traditione Musulmane.* 7 vols. Leiden: E. J. Brill, 1936–1969.

al-Zabîdî, Muḥammad Murtaḍa al-Ḥusaynî. *Tâj al-ʿArûs min Jawâhir al-Qamûs.* 10 vols. Cairo: Khayriyya Press, 1306/1888.

al-Zajjâjî, Abû al-Qâsim ʿAbd al-Raḥmân ibn Isḥâq. *Ishtiqâq Asmâ' Allâh.* 2d ed. Beirut: Mu'assasat al-Risâla, 1986.

al-Zamakhsharî, Muḥammad ibn ʿUmar. *Al-Kashshâf ʿan Ḥaqâ'iq al-Tanzîl wa ʿUyûn al-Aqâwîl fî Wujûh al-Ta'wîl.* 4 vols. Beirut: Dâr al-Maʿrifa, n.d.

al-Zarkashî, Muḥammad ibn Bahâdir. *Kitâb al-Azhiyya fî Aḥkâm al-Adʿiyya.* Edited by Umm ʿAbdullâh bint Maḥrûs al-ʿAsalî. 1st ed. Cairo: Dâr al-Furqân, 1988.

Zâyid, Aḥmad Ṣabrî. *Kunûz al-Duʿâ' fî al-Qur'ân al-Karîm.* Cairo: Dâr al-Faḍîla, n.d.

Zaynuddîn, Nâjî. *Badâ'iʿ al-Khaṭ al-ʿArabî.* Baghdâd: Maktabat al-Nahḍa, 1981.

____. *Manẓûr al-Khaṭ al-ʿArabî.* Baghdâd: Maktabat al-Nahḍa, 1968.

al-Zuḥaylî, Wahba. *Al-Tafsîr al-Munîr fî al-ʿAqîda wa al-Sharîʿa wa al-Manhaj.* 32 parts (in 16 vols.). Beirut: Dâr al-Fikr al-Muʿâṣir; Damascus: Dâr al-Fikr, 1411/1991.

Supplication Index

PRAYERS REGARDING ...

ACCEPTANCE OF WORSHIP

AFFIRMATIONS (OF CREED, FAITH, ETC.)

Self-Subsisting. Slumber does not overtake Him, nor sleep (2:255)

1.58 There is no God but Allah,...He gives life and causes death, and He is powerful over all things

1.61 O Allah, You are my Lord. There is no God but You. You created me, and I am Your servant

1.69 O Allah, You are all-pardoning and You love to pardon

1.70 Ever at Your service, O Allah, ever at Your service. Ever at Your service, there is no partner with You

1.71 Allah is the greatest! O Allah, You are the Peace and from You is peace

1.74a There is no God but Allah. He fulfilled His promise, gave victory to His servant, and He alone defeated the confederates....We worship none but Him, with all sincerity, even if the disbelievers abhor it

2.4 O Allah, originator of the heavens and the earth, knower of the unseen and the seen, there is no God but You, Lord and Master of all things

2.5 O Allah,...You have no partner. And for You are all praise and thanks

2.6 O Allah, I come to the morning with grace and well-being and shelter from You

2.8 I am well pleased with Allah as the Lord, with Islam as the religion, and with Muḥammad as the Prophet *(See also 2.17)*

2.12 O Allah, I come to this morning, calling upon You to bear witness...that indeed You are Allah, there is no God but You, and Muḥammad is Your servant and Your Messenger

2.13 We come to the morning in conformity with Islam and with the sincere word of faith and the religion of our Prophet Muḥammad

2.15 O Allah, in whatever blessing I find myself this evening, it is from You and You alone

2.16 We come to this evening, as does all of Allah's dominion....There is no God but Allah, alone

2.21 O Allah, Lord of all things and their sovereign, and the God of all things

2.22 In Your name, my Lord, I lay my side down, and in Your name I raise it

2.23 In the name of Allah, I lay my side down

2.24 O Allah, Lord of the heavens and Lord of the earth and Lord of the magnificent Throne, our Lord and the Lord of all things

2.26 O Allah, in Your name I die and I live

2.27 O Allah, I submit myself to You and I turn my face toward You and I entrust You with my affairs, and I fall back upon You, hopeful and fearful of You.

2.32 There is no God but Allah, alone; He has no partner. His is all dominion and His is all praise. And He is powerful over all things

2.33 There is no God but You. Glory be to You, O Allah

3.2 *Sufficient is Allah for us and a most excellent trustee* (3:173)

3.4 *There is no God but You, glory be to You. Truly I was among the wrongdoing* (21:87)

3.5 Allah! Allah is my Lord. I associate nothing with Him

3.8 There is no God but Allah, the Magnificent, the Forbearer. There is no

God but Allah, Lord of the magnificent Throne

3.9 Allah is sufficient for me and a most excellent trustee

3.11 O Allah,…O most merciful of the merciful, You are the Lord of the weak, and You are my Lord

3.12 O Allah, I am indeed Your servant, the son of Your servant, the son of Your maidservant. My forelock is in Your Hand

4.10 To Allah we belong and to Him we return

4.14 Indeed, what Allah has taken belongs to Him, as is what He has given

4.24 O Allah, You are the Lord of this [deceased soul]. You have created it and You have guided it to Islam. And You have drawn forth its spirit and You know best its secret and open deeds

5.7 O Allah, You are Allah, there is no God but You, the Self-Sufficient

6.1 In the name of Allah, I rely on Allah. There is no strength nor might except with Allah

6.9 O Allah, Lord of the seven heavens and of that upon which they cast their shadows! O Lord of the seven earths and of that which they bear!

8.24 There is no God but Allah, alone; He has no partner. Allah is the greatest, immensely great! All praise is for Allah, plentifully!

9.2 O Allah,…You are the All-Living, who never dies, while all jinn and human beings die

10.26 By Allah, were it not for You, we would not have been guided nor would we have given charity nor would we have performed Prayer [*Ṣalât*]

BELIEVERS

1.51 O Allah, our Lord and Lord of all things, I am a witness that…all worshippers are brethren

8.10 *Our Lord, forgive me and my parents and the believers on the day the reckoning takes place* (14:41)

8.15 *Our Lord, forgive us and our brethren who preceded us in faith, and let not into our hearts malice for those who believe* (59:10) *(See also 9.13)*

8.16 *My Lord, forgive me and my parents, and whoever enters my house as a believer, and the believing men and the believing women. And do not increase the wrongdoers except in ruin* (71:28)

BLESSINGS, GOODNESS, AND FAVOR

1.2 O Allah,…bless me in my provision

1.8 O Allah, give me the best of what You give to Your righteous servants

1.36 O Allah,…bless for me what You have given me

1.47 Bless us in our hearing and sight, our hearts and spouses, and our children

2.5 O Allah, in whatever blessing I find myself this morning, it is from You and You alone.

2.15 O Allah, in whatever blessing I find myself this evening, it is from You and You alone

3.1 O Allah, bless him [*or* her *or* it]

3.16 May Allah bless for you your family and your wealth

3.17 O Allah,…I ask You of Your vast bounty

CHARACTER

CHILDREN AND FAMILY

DELIVERANCE

EXALTEDNESS

EXCELLENCE IN WORSHIP

EXCELLENT RELATIONS

FAITH AND GODFEARINGNESS

FORGIVENESS, MERCY, AND PARDON

GARDEN

GLORIFICATION AND EXTOLLING

Greatness

Praise and Glorification

GUIDANCE

HELP AND VICTORY

10.25 O Allah, revealer of the Book, mover of the clouds, and defeater of the confederates, defeat them and give us victory over them!

12.5 Indeed, all praise is for Allah. We praise Him and we seek His help

KNOWLEDGE

1.52 O Allah, I seek refuge in You from…knowledge that does not benefit

1.59 O Allah, I ask You for knowledge that is beneficial

2.33 O Allah, increase me in knowledge and let not my heart swerve after You have guided me

6.2 O Allah, I seek refuge in You…from ignorance

8.9 *My Lord, I seek refuge in You from asking You of what I have no knowledge* (11:47)

9.3 O Allah, benefit me in what You have taught me and teach me what benefits me. Increase me in knowledge

9.4 O Allah, I seek refuge in You from knowledge that does not benefit, from a heart that is not humble

10.10 O Allah, do not make this world the greatest of our concerns, nor the extent of our knowledge

10.17 O Allah, make him knowledgeable in Islam and teach him interpretation

10.18 O Allah, teach him wisdom and teach him the Book [the Quran]

LIFE

1.11 Truly, my Prayer [*Ṣalât*], my worship, my life, and my death are for Allah

1.41 O Allah, I seek refuge in You…from the trial of life and that of death

1.46 O Allah,…let me live as long as You know life to be good for me, and take my soul when You know death to be good for me

2.2 All praise is for Allah who has given us life after He has taken our souls

2.11 O Allah, I ask You for pardon and well-being in my religion, my life, my family, and my wealth

5.8 O Allah,…give life to this lifeless land of Yours

9.5 O Allah, I ask You for pardon and well-being in my religion, my life, my family, and my wealth

12.3 O Allah, I ask You for the best of requests…and the best of death.…I ask You to bless for me…my family, my life, my death, and my deeds

LIGHT

1.14 O Allah, put light in my heart, light in my sight, and light in my hearing

1.47 O Allah,…deliver us from darkness to light

3.12 O Allah,…make the Quran the springtime of my heart, the light within my chest

4.13 O Allah,…widen for him his grave and give him light in it

12.3 O Allah, I ask You to raise my renown, to alleviate my burden, to set aright my affairs, to purify my heart, and to guard my chastity. And illuminate my heart

12.5 Indeed, all praise is for Allah. We praise Him and we seek His help

LOVE

5.12 O Allah, bring it forth upon us with securi-

PARENTS

PEACE AND TRANQUILITY

PROPHET MUḤAMMAD ﷺ

6.15 In the name of Allah, O Allah, bless Muḥammad

6.16 Peace and blessings be upon the Messenger of Allah. O Allah, forgive us our sins

6.18 In the name of Allah, O Allah, bless Muḥammad

6.19 Peace and blessings be upon the Messenger of Allah. O Allah, forgive us our sins and open for us the gates of Your bounty

6.20 Peace and blessings be upon the Messenger of Allah. O Allah, distance me from Satan

PROTECTION

1.36 O Allah,...protect me from the evil of what You have decreed

2.11 O Allah, protect me from before me and from behind me, and from my right and from my left

2.22 O Allah, protect it [my soul] as You protect Your righteous servants

4.17 And protect him from the trial of the grave and its torment

4.18 O Allah,...enter him into the Garden and protect him from the torment of the grave

4.20 O Allah, indeed [name of deceased] is under Your protection. So save him from the trials of the grave

9.5 O Allah, cover my faults and soothe my fears. O Allah, protect me from before me and from behind me

PROVISION AND WEALTH

1.2 O Allah,...make spacious for me my residence, and bless me in my provision

1.25 O Allah, none can withhold that which You give, and none can give that which You withhold. And wealth will not avail the wealthy against You

1.34 O Allah,...replenish me, exalt me, provide for me

1.35 O Allah,...grant me well-being, and provide for me

1.59 O Allah, I ask You for...provision that is wholesome

3.15 O Allah, suffice me with what You have made lawful against what You have made unlawful. And enrich me with Your favor so that I need none but You

3.16 May Allah bless for you your family and your wealth

5.8 O Allah, provide water to Your servants and Your beasts

7.8 O Allah, bless for them what You have provided them

8.24 O Allah,...provide for me *(See also 10.15)*

10.20 O Allah, increase him in wealth

12.10 O Allah, bestow upon me the most bounteous of Your provision when I reach old age and near the end of my life

PRUDENCE IN JUDGMENT, AND DECISIONS

1.13 O Allah,...You judge between Your servants regarding that which they dispute. Guide me, by Your permission, to the truth of what is disputed

1.46 O Allah,...I ask You for prudence in poverty and wealth

3.17 O Allah, enable me through Your knowledge to choose what is best

PURIFICATION

1.3 O Allah, make me one of the purified

1.10 O Allah, purify me of sins as a white cloth is purified of dirt

1.30 O Allah, give my soul its Godfearingness and purify it. You are the best to purify it

1.52 O Allah, give my soul its Godfearingness and purify it. You are the best to purify it

4.4 No harm. It is, God willing, purification

4.18 O Allah,...cleanse him with water, snow, and coolness. And purify him of sins

12.3 O Allah,...I ask You to purify my heart

REFUGE

Refuge from Bad Character

11.5 O Allah, I seek refuge in You from abhorrent character, actions, and inclinations

11.8 O Allah, I seek refuge in You from schism, hypocrisy, and bad character

11.9 O Allah, I seek refuge in You from any desire that leads to vice and from any desire that leads to what is undesirable

Refuge from Debt and Poverty

1.42 O Allah, I seek refuge in You from sin and debt

2.23 O Allah,...release my debts

2.24 O Allah,...satisfy our debts for us and suffice us against poverty.

8.34 O Allah, I seek refuge in You from...ruthlessness, heedlessness, dependency, humiliation, and indigence. And I seek refuge in You from poverty, disbelief, unrighteousness, schism, hypocrisy, ignominy, and showing off

11.1 O Allah, I seek refuge in You from disbelief, from poverty, and from the torment of the grave

11.2 O Allah, I seek refuge in You from being overpowered by debt and being overpowered by an enemy and from the malice of enemies

11.3 O Allah, I seek refuge in You from hunger, for it is a miserable bedfellow. And I seek refuge in You from betrayal, for it is miserable company

11.4 O Allah, I seek refuge in You from ruin

11.13 O Allah, I seek refuge in You...from the evil of wealth and poverty

11.14 O Allah, I seek refuge in You from insufficiency, poverty, and humiliation

12.6 I seek refuge in You from any impoverishment that causes me to forget. And I seek refuge in You from wealth that causes me to transgress

Refuge from Evil

1.41 I seek refuge in You...from the evil of the trial of the False Messiah [al-Dajjâl]

1.45 I seek refuge in You from the evil of everything You know exists

1.57 *Say: I seek refuge in the Lord of the daybreak, from the evil of that which He created* (Sura 113) *(See also 8.29)*

1.57 *Say: I seek refuge in the Lord of all people... from the evil of the sneaking whisperer, who whispers in the chests of people, from the jinn and people* (Sura 114) *(See also 8.30)*

2.4 I seek refuge in You from my own wrongdoings, and the evil of Satan and his traps

Refuge from God's Displeasure, Punishment

Refuge from Going Astray

9.2 O Allah, I seek refuge in Your majesty—there is no God but You!—from letting me go astray

11.4 I seek refuge in You from dying while retreating from Your path

Refuge from Harm and Misdeeds

1.61 O Allah,…I seek refuge in You from the harm of whatever I may have done

2.4 O Allah,…I seek refuge in You from my own wrongdoings and…from any harm that I may commit against myself or that I may bring to a Muslim

2.16 I seek refuge in You from the harm of what is in this night and the harm of what comes after it

4.1 I seek refuge in Allah and His might from the harm of which I suffer and fear

5.2 We seek refuge in Allah from its harm and the harm of what is in it and the harm that was sent with it *(See also 5.3)*

6.3 O Allah, I seek refuge in You from…harm that may upset wealth and families

6.8 O land, my Lord and your Lord is Allah. I seek refuge in Allah from your harm and whatever harm is in you and the harm of what was created in you and from the harm of whatever treads upon you

6.9 O Allah,…we seek refuge in You from this town's harm and the harm of its people and the harm of whatever is in it

7.13 I ask You the good of this garment and the good it has been made for. And I seek refuge in You from its evil and the evil it has been made for

10.7 I seek refuge in You from the worst of her [*or* him] and the worst of what You have endowed her [*or* him] with

11.6 O Allah, I seek refuge in You from the harm of my hearing, the harm of my sight, the harm of my tongue, the harm of my heart, and the harm of my seed

11.10 O Allah, I seek refuge in You from the harm of what I have done and the harm of what I have not done

11.14 O Allah,…I seek refuge in You from doing wrong or being wronged

12.5 We seek refuge in Allah from the evils of our selves and from the harm of our actions

12.6 O Allah, I seek refuge in You from any deed that disgraces me

12.6 I seek refuge in You from wealth that causes me to transgress

Refuge from Satan

1.15 I seek refuge in Allah, the All-Hearing, the All-Knowing, from Satan, the accursed

1.16 I seek refuge in Allah from Satan, the accursed, from his inspirations, his promptings, and his incantations

1.57 *Say: I seek refuge in the Lord of all people… from the evil of the sneaking whisperer, who whispers in the chests of people, from the jinn and people* (114:1–6)

2.4 I seek refuge in You from the evil of Satan and his traps

2.9 I seek refuge in Allah, the All-Hearing, the All-Knowing, from Satan, the accursed

2.23 O Allah, forgive me my sins and impel away my devil

2.31 I seek refuge in the perfect words of Allah…from the promptings of satans and from them coming near me

3.13 I seek refuge in Allah from Satan, the accursed

6.11 In the name of Allah, I seek refuge in Allah from every demon and demoness

8.25 The *Adhân* said at anytime drives Satan away

8.26 O Allah, I seek refuge in You from Satan, the accursed, from his promptings, his inspirations, and his incantations

8.31 *My Lord, I seek refuge in You from the urgings of the satans. And I seek refuge in You, my Lord, from their presence* (23:97–98)

10.8 O Allah, keep us away from Satan and keep Satan away from whatever 'offspring' You grant us

11.4 I seek refuge in You from being battered by Satan at the moment of death

Refuge from Sickness and Weakness

1.52 O Allah, I seek refuge in You from feebleness, laziness, cowardliness, miserliness, senility

2.16 My Lord, I seek refuge in You from laziness and the ills of old age

4.15 O Allah, I seek refuge in You from leprosy, insanity, vitiligo, and from the worst of ailments

8.34 O Allah, I seek refuge in You from feebleness, laziness, cowardliness, miserliness, senility

8.34 O Allah,...I seek refuge in You from deafness, dumbness, insanity, vitiligo, leprosy, and the worst of ailments

11.4 I seek refuge in You from drowning and burning....I seek refuge in You from dying from a poisonous sting

11.7 O Allah, I seek refuge in You from the removal of Your bestowed well-being

Refuge from the Trials

1.41 O Allah, I seek refuge in You...from the trial of life and that of death, and from the evil of the trial of the False Messiah [al-Dajjâl]

11.11 O Allah, I seek refuge in You from the misfortunes of fate, the malice of enemies, the depths of misery, and the distress of trials

11.13 O Allah, I seek refuge in You...from the evil of wealth and poverty

Refuge from Other Forms of Harm

1.52 O Allah, I seek refuge in You from knowledge that does not benefit, from a heart that is not humble, from a soul that is never satisfied, and from any prayer that is not answered

2.11 O Allah,...I seek refuge in You from being seized from beneath me

6.2 O Allah, I seek refuge in You...from oppressing or being oppressed, from ignorance or from the ignorance of others against me

6.3 O Allah, I seek refuge in You from the rigors of travel, distressing sights

6.8 I seek refuge in Allah from lions and cobras and from serpents and scorpions, and from the dwellers of the area, and from whatever begets and whatever is begotten

8.9 *My Lord, I seek refuge in You from asking You of what I have no knowledge. And if You do not forgive me and have mercy upon me, I shall be of the losers* (11:47)

9.4 O Allah, I seek refuge in You from knowledge that does not benefit, from a heart

REMOVAL OF SINS AND INDECENCIES

REPENTANCE

RESOLVE

REVERENCE AND OBEDIENCE

SINCERITY

SOUNDNESS OF HEART

THANKFULNESS

TRUTHFULNESS

WELL-BEING AND HEALTH

Quranic Verse Index

Subject and Name Index

Acknowledgments

O Allah, endow me with Your love and the love of all whose love benefits me with You. O Allah, with whatever You have endowed me, of that which I love, let it strengthen me in what You love. O Allah, whatever You have kept from me of that which I love, let it strengthen me in what You love.

— Prophet Muḥammad ﷺ

THIS BOOK HAS been a unique experience for me from start to finish. In the course of years of primary work on the Quran (its interpretation, explication, and word elucidation), it has not been unusual for me to spend my days and nights absorbed more in the lives and circumstances of the prophets, the great believing men and women, and the angels than in the dramas closer to home. Yet from the moment the idea came to present to the English-speaking world the prayers of the Quran and the Prophet Muḥammad ﷺ, it was as if I had taken a flawless diamond and held it up to the sunlight. In its brilliance and play of prismatic colors, I saw instantly that the prayers inlaid in the Quran and in the words of its Messenger ﷺ could give people an indelible glimpse of the resplendent spirituality that indwells Islam. Virtually all the reviewers and readers of this book have been as instantly enamored of its concept as I was. I attribute this to the power with which God has vested prayer and to the great spirits of those who voiced them. It is to God, then, that I give all thanks for the completion of this work. And I express my gratitude to the enduring model of prayer, Prophet Muḥammad ﷺ. I would feel remiss were I not to mention my deep appreciation for all of those from whom I have learned Islam or who have refined my understanding of it, especially Shaykh Muḥammad al-Ghazâlî and Professor Muḥammad Quṭb.

Moreover, it would be inappropriate for the ink to dry on these pages without expressing gratitude for the invaluable, inspiring, and supportive friendship of Bashir al-Rashidi, Saad al-Barrak, and Ibrahim al-Khulaifi. Also, a dear friend, Mohammad Jaghlit, deserves special mention for his wise advice to me to focus on the message of the Quran and to help make it accessible in the English language. And a special prayer for John Pembroke for his wise counsel over the years.

For this effort, I express appreciation to the many involved in this work: To Amer Haleem and Ibrahim Abusharif, whose combined editorial skill and spiritual maturity form a special blend that evidences itself throughout these pages; to Linda Thayer, whose detailed reading of each line, and between the lines, enabled her to capture the essence of the work and to help push it toward its target; to Zeba Siddiqui, whose comments on a middle draft were both encouraging and determinative as to the direction of the final work; to Noah Keller, for his diligent reading of important portions of the manuscript which proved of fundamental benefit; to Ahmad Sakr, for his encouragement and for lending to it the insight that his vast experience brings; to A. R. Kidwai, whose genuine enthusiasm for sincere and scholarly presentations of the Sources of Islam and whose wealth of editorial experience continually proves invaluable; to Gaylord Toft, who read a good part of the work and whose ability to grasp the significance of things and cheer them on toward completion has been a priceless resource for me; to Betsy Blumenthal, who proofread both the pre-final and final manuscripts with her usual unusual precision; to Hatem and Bridget El-Gabri, for their reading, comments, and encouragement in this and other endeavors; to Ann Hutchinson, whose initial proofreading of an early draft made an important contribution; and to Alice Sawaf, Maryam Salah, Nadia Salem, Nur Nasr and her mother, Lucella, Elizabeth and Julia Martin, Amina Assami, Sayid Iftikharuddin, Elvira Kudia, Hamid Ali, Shirley Gazori, Abd al-Hakim and Heather Jackson, Seema Imam, Omar Fisher, and Mona Mobarek (of Australia), all of whom read the manuscript and made valuable comments; and to Martin Hertzel, who perused the book's design and offered important suggestions.

In addition, I have been blessed to have the services and companionship of Jamal Sawaf, my research assistant, whose methodical ways give much to admire. Also, Siamak Kargar, who has volunteered his diverse skills in this effort, deserves special thanks.

Special thanks go to Shaykh Osama ʿAbd al-ʿAẓîm Ḥamza for lending his remarkable expertise to proofread the Arabic texts of the *ḥadîths*. Heartfelt thanks, as well, to my truly unique mother-in-law, Al-Ḥajja Suʿâd, for too much to mention.

I reserve the mention of my daughter Salma and my son Osama until the end. This does not reflect less of a contribution on their behalf. Indeed, Salma's input in the text, having read it at every stage with her keen eye for detail and smart sense of clarity, has been material. And Osama's graphic arts proficiency testifies for itself in the floral pattern that covers this book. Finally, it is my joy to close with that which is most pleasing, for certainly no living person deserves more of my thanks than their mother, in whose soul prayer runs like a stream that revives whomever it touches.

ALSO BY THE AUTHOR

THE OPENING TO THE QURAN
Commentary & Vocabulary Reference of al-Fâtiḥa

"THE OPENING" CHAPTER (or sura) of the Quran—called al-Fâtiḥa—is undoubtedly the most often recited portion of revealed scripture in the world. Its impact on the psyche and soul of more than a fifth of the human family cannot be overstated. One who comes close to the meaning and import of its seven sacred verses draws near indeed to understanding the religion of Islam and the Muslim men and women who seek to follow its "straight way." In *The Opening to the Quran*, a leading scholar of the Quran (the Muslim scripture), Dr. Ahmad Zaki Hammad, introduces the English-speaking reader through the gateway of the Quran and to the treasure trove of vivid meanings and penetrating themes of this concise sura and the Book it opens.

"The format, substance, and writing are superb."

— *DR. ROBERT CRANE, Editorial Consultant, Washington, D.C.*

"I am deeply inspired by this new interpretation. The English reads well and is accurately close to its original Arabic. The Commentary is very prayerful. It helps the reader to come closer to the Word of God and enjoy its riches."

— *DR. MUZAMMIL SIDDIQI, Director, Islamic Center, Orange County, CA*

"The interpretation is clear and smooth. The Overview and Commentary . . . extract such deep religious experience. I think [the] discourse is most edifying."

— *DR. WILLIS GERTNER, Prof. of Religious Studies, Univ. of Wisconsin*

ISLAMIC LAW
Understanding Juristic Differences

WHILE INTEREST IN Islamic law is on the rise in the English-speaking world, there remains the need for greater accessibility and understanding of its issues and Sources. Of all its aspects, however, least has been written on the topic of *al-Khilâf al-Fiqhi*, the science exploring the world of juristic differences. In *Islamic Law: Understanding Juristic Differences*, Dr. Ahmad Zaki Hammad introduces the major principles governing juristic variance among established schools of law and well-known Muslim jurists, and their different methods of interpreting Texts from the Quran and the statements and deeds of the Prophet Muḥammad ﷺ. *Islamic Law* outlines the major categories of *khilâf*. It then surveys more than a dozen subcategories, delving into actual readings and interpretations of legal Texts from the Quran and statements of the Prophet ﷺ, from the point of view of several schools of Islamic jurisprudence. As Dr. Abd al-Hakim S. Jackson wrote in the preface to the work:

> *Islamic Law* makes a stunning contribution by laying bare the issue of juristic variance, explaining its causes and distinguishing those forms that are legitimate from those that are not. Dr. Hammad guides the reader to a fascinating rediscovery of the spirit of tolerance and mutual recognition in Islam.

REVIEWS ON LASTING PRAYERS

DR. AHMAD SAKR

(*President, Foundation for Islamic Knowledge*)

LASTING PRAYERS is an outstanding book for Muslims and non-Muslims; for the young and the old; for the Arabic- and the non-Arabic-speaking; for the individual and the group in society; for the highly educated and the less educated; for the Imam, the ʿ*Âlim* (the religious scholar), as well as the faithful member of the congregation. It is to be read collectively as well as privately.

When one begins its reading, one desires to read the whole of it. Yet it is not meant for a one-time reading, but for many occasions and diverse situations. The selected prayers make one feel happy in communicating with the Creator of the whole universe, namely, God, the Glorified and Exalted. These prayers enrich a person with spirituality and help him or her to live in peace and harmony at all times and in most occasions. The author has successfully brought into relief the prayers of fourteen prophets of God, eloquently presenting their supplications in summary from the Quran.

The writing style of the book is profound—highly literary in approach but easy to read and understand. I do recommend this book to all readers of English: the politician and the lawyer; the social service worker, the physician, the nurse, and the sick; the professor, the student, the librarian. Such individuals and many more do need this book to use in their daily lives. I, for one, will be very happy to add it to my personal library and to use it for my own day-to-day needs with God. A good work has been done by Dr. Ahmad Zaki Hammad. I do congratulate him for the wonderful job he has done in this field of scholarly and literary work on Islam. May Allah accept his work, and reward him for all that he is doing. *Âmîn.*

DR. LINDA THAYER
(*Editorial Consultant*)

LASTING PRAYERS of the Quran & the Prophet Muḥammad ﷺ discloses the height and depth, the length and breadth of Islamic spiritual energy. The all-inclusive introduction summons the hesitant to come close to God, to come boldly before his Lord, who stands ever ready to give and to forgive generously. By allowing oneself to become absorbed into the prayers recorded in the Quran and those spoken from the lips of the Prophet Muḥammad himself ﷺ the seeker establishes a dynamic relationship with the Creator. As he seeks refuge in Allah, the human being is brought into balance with the entire worshipping universe.

The second section begins by examining the opening prayer of the Quran (Sûrat al-Fâtiḥa), thereby setting the tone for the requests made by the various previous prophets in their dire circumstances. It ends, culminating the prophetic voices, with a profile of the remarkable inner life of Muḥammad ﷺ, whose status as exemplar can be truly appreciated only as he is seen at prayer and in remembrance of his Lord. Understanding these prayers helps the *muslim* to follow closely in the footsteps of Muḥammad ﷺ, cheered on by the support of angels, such that one is guided towards success in the Final Reckoning.

By means of the last section, contemporary believers, seeking the pleasure of their Lord, are likewise privileged to view the heart and soul of their role model as it is poured out to God across the multitude of human experience. Here, the ritual Prayer (*Ṣalât*) comes alive with awareness of the Master to whom it is addressed. The plethora of glorifications and supplications (*duʿâ'*) associated with the stages of the ritual prayer, or with various life situations, can be studied or learned in their original Arabic for rewarding personal development.

In summary, the compilation of prayers in this comprehensive book serves to teach the *muslim* to be ever sensitive to his intended purpose on earth, to his own standing before God, to his social interaction, and to the entire creation's incessant need for and welcome access to Allah. One learns how to ask God's blessing for this life and for the Next.

"O Allah, You change hearts, so change our hearts to be obedient to You."

QURANIC LITERACY INSTITUTE

THE PRESENTATION OF THE *Lasting Prayers of the Quran and the Prophet Muḥammad* ﷺ flows from the moral imperative that inspired the founding of the Quranic Literacy Institute (QLI):™ *To bridge the spiritual breach between Muslims in the English-speaking West and the Quran, and to close the widening information gap among non-Muslims regarding the Quran's universal message.* Symbolized by its motto "Advancing Islamic Literacy,"™ QLI's mission is to alleviate Islamic illiteracy among English-speaking Muslims and other faith communities and, in the words of the QLI Charter, "to aid men, women, and families of all creeds and from all walks of life to understand the seminal Sources of Islam and to help Muslims live Islam as a way of life."

ABOUT THE AUTHOR

DR. AHMAD ZAKI HAMMAD received his Islamic and Arabic training at the world's foremost center of Islamic learning, al-Azhar University, Cairo, and was awarded the graduate degree of ʿ*Âlamiyya* from the Faculty of Theology. He also holds a Ph.D. in Islamic Studies from the University of Chicago. Author of the well-received *Islamic Law: Understanding Juristic Differences* and the study and translation of al-Ghazâlî's quintessential work on Islamic jurisprudence, *al-Mustaṣfâ min ʿIlm al-Uṣûl*, Dr. Hammad has also written the widely acclaimed *The Opening to the Quran: Commentary & Vocabulary Reference of al-Fâtiḥa.* He is the Founder and President of the QURANIC LITERACY INSTITUTE and the Editor-in-Chief of THE QURAN PROJECT.